I TA L I A N
ARCHITECTURE
of the **16**TH CENTURY

~

ITALIAN
ARCHITECTURE
of the 16TH CENTURY
~

COLIN ROWE
&
LEON SATKOWSKI

PRINCETON ARCHITECTURAL PRESS
NEW YORK 2002

Princeton Architectural Press
37 East 7th Street
New York, NY 10003

For a free catalog of books published by
Princeton Architectural Press, call
1.800.722.6657 or visit www.papress.com

Printed in China

Editor: Jan Cigliano
Copy Editor: Kenya McCullum
Designer: David Konopka

Special thanks to
Nettie Aljian, Ann Alter, Nicola Bednarek, Janet Behning, Penny Chu,
Russell Fernandez, Clare Jacobson, Mark Lamster, Linda Lee, Nancy Eklund Later,
Jane Sheinman, Lottchen Shivers, Katharine Smalley, Scott Tennent, Jennifer
Thompson, and Deb Wood of Princeton Architectural Press
—Kevin Lippert, Publisher

ISBN 1-56898-331-X

Library of Congress Cataloging-in-Publication Data
Rowe, Colin.
    Italian architecture of the 16th century / Colin Rowe and
        Leon Satkowski. p. cm.
    Includes bibliographical references and index.
    ISBN 1-56898-331-X
        1. Architecture—Italy—16th century. 2. Architecture, Renaissance—
        Italy. 3. Architecture and society—Italy—History—16th century. I.
        Title: Italian architecture of the sixteenth century. II. Satkowski,
Leon George, 1947- III. Title.

    NA 1115 .R68 2002
    720'.945'09024-dc21   2002-022092
                                                  CIP

ACKNOWLEDGMENTS
~

I have always liked looking at 16th-century buildings in Italy, and I find them gratifying and refreshing as the spectacle of Modern Architecture becomes more depressing.

COLIN ROWE,
lecture at the University of Maryland, March 1998

Colin Rowe (1920–1999) is widely acknowledged as one of the twentieth century's most important historians of architecture and teachers of architectural design. His well-deserved reputation derives from a series of articles that linked modern architecture to the history of ideas; he was among the very first to recognize that the 1920s work of Le Corbusier was profoundly influenced by historical examples, and especially, by the villas of Palladio. Yet Rowe's interests extended beyond the modern era. He studied at the Warburg Institute of the University of London, where he encountered Rudolf Wittkower and E. H. Gombrich, two of the most important scholars of Italian Renaissance art and architecture. Rowe's M.A. thesis in 1947 examined the drawings of Inigo Jones, a subject that could easily be studied in London. But the architecture of cinquecento Italy had captured his heart and continually challenged his fertile mind. This book serves as a testament to the buildings and architects he deeply appreciated.

VII

During his twenty-eight-year tenure at Cornell University, Rowe frequently taught a course on Renaissance architecture. The lectures soon assumed legendary status, and notes prepared by some of his students began to circulate around the Cornell architectural community. The two characteristics that distinguished Rowe's courses from those taught by other historians were an emphasis on perspective and architectural representation in painting and sculpture and a prominence given to sixteenth-century architecture. To Rowe, the architectural analysis of the backgrounds in Ghiberti's *Gates of Paradise* and Piero della Francesca's paintings was deemed as important as the buildings of Brunelleschi and Alberti. Similarly, the frescoes of Raphael in the Vatican and the altarpieces of Giulio Romano assumed an importance equal to their completed buildings. Later in his career, Rowe continued to travel to Italy even though his own interests turned to other subjects. At various times, he taught for Cornell in Venice and in the school's recently established center in Rome, for the Notre Dame (also in Rome), as well as for Syracuse University in Florence. Excepting a brief trip to England to celebrate his brother's birthday, Rowe made his last visit to Europe in 1997. Typically eclectic, it concluded with visits to the Gonzaga towns in Lombardy after stops in Berlin, Potsdam, Dessau, and Trieste.

Initially we planned a publication that took on a larger view, one with additional chapters on Michelangelo, Palladio, garden design, and antiquarianism. Our work on these chapters was cut short by Colin's death in November 1999. After discussing the status of the project with colleagues, with Colin's family, and with his friends, I decided that any publication resulting from our collaboration would include only material we had discussed and begun during his lifetime. The project may be unfinished, but as a publication the book is not incomplete: its focus is on the personalities and topical issues central to the development of a new kind of architectural practitioner in the Cinquecento.

In its final, published form, our book comprises the text of essays written jointly by Colin Rowe and Leon Satkowski between 1994 and 1999. Although the essays proceed in more or less chronological order, readers will realize that the text focuses mainly on Rome and Venice. As a consequence the treatment of some centers is abbreviated: Florence is studied in terms of Medici patronage throughout Tuscany; there is little mention of Genoa, and none of Milan after the era of Leonardo and Bramante. Those written largely by Colin Rowe had been completed at the time of his death and were augmented by further information from his lecture notes for his course on Renaissance architecture at Cornell, and from a series of six lectures at the University of Maryland in spring 1998. The Maryland lectures were recorded and tapes of those lectures were kindly provided by Brian Kelly. Because much of this material was still in lecture form, I made difficult decisions as to how colloquialisms and personal mannerisms were to be preserved in the final publication. If something of Colin's unique voice may have been lost in completing this book, his ideas are still present.

Thus our book makes no claim to constituting a complete history of cinquecento architecture. It is addressed primarily to architects and architecture students (though we believed there would be much for architectural and art historians). There are no footnotes, and the bibliography discusses only the publications relevant to the questions discussed.

I am certain that Colin would wish to join me in thanking the following people who have contributed to the completion of this book: Matt and Sheryl Bell, Joel Bostick (for a memorable trip to the Gonzaga towns in Lombardy), Alexander Caragonne, Judy DiMaio, Tom Fisher, Steve Hurtt, Brian Kelly, Henry Millon (for insisting that this book should be completed), Larry Mitsch (for two days of travel in the Farnese lands of northern Lazio in 1999 and to Caprarola and Genazzano in 2001), Andrew Morrogh, Steve Peterson and Barbara Littenberg, David Rowe and Briony Soper, as well as Tom Schumacher and Pat Sachs. The College of Architecture and Landscape Architecture of the University of Minnesota granted me a single quarter leave in winter 1999 to complete the manuscript, and it also generously supported the cost of foreign travel. The Department of Architecture also provided a release from teaching in spring 2001 for final research and writing. The generosity of the Rowe family also contributed to the acquisition of photographs and photographic rights for the publication.

A special word of gratitude must be expressed for the assistance of the Visual Resources Center in the College of Architecture and Landscape Architecture at the University of Minnesota, and the assistance of its director, Jodie Walz. It is a pleasure to acknowledge again the collaboration of Dave Bowers, whose magic transformed many dubious images into compelling illustrations. Ralph Lieberman provided numerous images, many of which are published here for the first time, from his archive. Ralph also deserves special recognition for executing at the last minute new photographs for this project. And my editor, Jan Cigliano, has an author's heartfelt thanks for continuous support.

Finally, I wish to thank my wife, Jane, and my daughter, Christina, for their unstinting patience with my absences during many trips to Washington and to Italy. Their encouragement contributed in no small way to the completion of this book.

LEON SATKOWSKI
Minneapolis, Minnesota
Fall 2001

THE POPES, ROME
~

1492–1503	Alexander VI (Borgia)
1503	Pius III (Todeschini)
1503–1513	Julius II (Della Rovere)
1513–1521	Leo X (Medici)
1522–23	Hadrian VI (Dedal)
1523–1534	Clement VII (Medici)
1534–1549	Paul III (Farnese)
1550–1555	Julius III (Del Monte)
1555	Marcellus II (Cervini)
1555–1559	Paul IV (Carafa)
1559–1565	Pius IV (Medici)
1566–1572	Pius V (Ghislieri)
1572–1585	Gregory XIII (Boncompagni)
1585–1590	Sixtus V (Peretti)
1590	Urban VII (Castagna)
1590–1591	Gregory XIV (Sfondrati)
1591	Innocent IX (Fachinetti)
1592–1605	Clement VIII (Aldobrandini)

FLORENCE: ESTABLISHMENT OF A MEDICEAN STATE
~

1494–1512	The Republic Restored
1512–1527	The Return of the Medici and the Subjugation to Rome
1527–1532	The Republic Re-established
1532–	Ducal Florence Under the Medici

Duke Alessandro I de'Medici (1532–1537)
Duke Cosimo I de'Medici (1537–1574; after 1569 Grand Duke)
Grand Duke Francesco I de'Medici (1574–1587)
Grand Duke Ferdinando I de'Medici (1587–1609)

VENICE: SIXTEENTH—CENTURY DOGES
~

1486–1501	Agostino Barbarigo
1501–1521	Leonardo Loredan
1521–1523	Antonio Grimani
1523–1538	Andrea Gritti
1539–1545	Pietro Lando
1545–1553	Francesco Dona
1553–1554	Marcantonio Trevisan
1554–1556	Francesco Venier
1556–1559	Lorenzo Priuli
1559–1567	Girolamo Priuli
1567–1570	Pietro Loredan
1570–1577	Alvise Mocenigo
1577–1578	Sebastiano Venier
1578–1585	Nicolò da Ponte
1585–1595	Pasquale Cicogna
1595–1605	Marino Grimani

PROLOGUE
~

*In practice certain words, when they are abused by too common use, suffer in
their meaning . . . style is one of these. Its innumerable shades of meaning
seem to span all experience. At an extreme is the sense defined by Henri
Focillon, of style as the ligne des hauteurs, the Himalayan range composed
of the greatest monuments of all time, the touchstone and standard of artistic
value. At the other extreme is the commercial jungle of advertising copy,
where gasolines and toilet papers have "style," and . . . where annual
fashions in clothes are purveyed as "styles."*

GEORGE KUBLER,
The Shape of Time, 1962

The subject of this book is sixteenth-century Italian architecture. Its objective is to trace a *ligne des hauteurs* during the cinquecento (the Italian term for this period), and hence, its dominant strategy is to present a series of eminent personalities and something of the sociopolitical background which is the context for their achievement. Recognizing the richness and complexity of our subject, our *ligne* is rarely direct, and the topography of our *hauteurs* includes heights and valleys that are both familiar and unfamiliar.

XṼII

This book grew out of a profound dissatisfaction with much scholarship in cinquecento architecture. The primary cause of this dissatisfaction is the presence of an all-encompassing zeitgeist or other kinds of historical determinism. In our area of study, the best known example is Giorgio Vasari's teleology for the development of Italian art, a questionable construct despite our admiration for Vasari's sensible observations and his vast (and sometimes incorrect or incomplete) knowledge of his material. Each generation seems to find its own kind of determinism, and at the end of the twentieth century, new teleologies have replaced old ones. Those seeking guidance from various fashionable social and cultural theories must look elsewhere. By contrast, our approach evolves, whenever possible, out of the first-hand examination of concrete examples, which is central to the understanding and enjoyment of a work of architecture. To paraphrase an often-quoted remark on museums by Max J. Friedländer, we try not to come to buildings with pre-conceived notions, but to leave them with ideas.

We begin with Bramante and the work of his generation because it is generally recognized that about 1500 something very decisive happened in Rome, a new approach to volume and space, which persisted until at least the early nineteenth century—if not later. Our approach is inclusive but not comprehensive. For instance, we consider the architecture of Bramante and Raphael that is illustrated in prints and paint to be more important than the built work of their contemporaries in Sicily, Naples, Puglia, and the Piedmont. No doubt, in making this choice, we shall be heavily criticized in some quarters.

What we see as one contribution of our approach is redressing the balance between architecture and the other arts. If accounts of quattrocento architecture—such as that of Heydenreich—sought to display links with the sculpture of Donatello, Ghiberti, or Antonio Rosselino, the painted buildings of Raphael, Giulio Romano, or

Peruzzi are generally avoided by architectural historians. If this is, in part, the result of establishing architectural history as a distinct form of inquiry, it also creates a degree of division between the arts that cinquecento artists would have never recognized. Hence, the model of the architect as a professional explains the achievements of Sangallo the Younger or Palladio, but it cannot illustrate how Raphael's *Fire in the Borgo* is important as an architectural statement, or how Michelangelo displayed active forces in inert stone as he did in both *David* and his contributions to St. Peter's.

Architecture plays an important role in the larger theater of cultural and political history. This, of course, raises the question of *whose* cultural history and *which* political history. To be certain, our book consciously exhibits an old-fashioned prejudice for the macro-history of political entities and their rulers over the micro-histories of families, neighborhoods, or material culture that are currently fashionable. If preeminence is given to patrons such as Julius II and Grand Duke Cosimo I de'Medici, it is because they understood, either consciously or intuitively, the capacity of architecture to advance their goals. To claim that Bramante's plan for St. Peter's or Vasari's design for the Uffizi cannot be understood without the contributions of their patrons may sound commonplace, but it is also a fact of history.

Our wish is to demonstrate how and why this is true. For this reason, we have included thematic chapters such as "Domestic Typologies" or "Architecture at Court." Although we would like to think our chronological and geographical scope is sufficiently broad to do justice to our subject, it would be incorrect, we think, to conceive of this book as comprehensive survey. It is neither a *handbuch* of the kind propounded by Nikolaus Pevsner in the *Pelican History of Art* nor a survey of Renaissance architecture as generally understood by historians.

Characterizing the stylistic achievement of a building or an architect is another of our concerns. In fact, the premise of architectural style has been considered debatable. Its discussion was deemed reprehensible by protagonists of the former Modern Movement in architecture—the writings of Walter Gropius come immediately to mind. Nowadays, architectural style is considered as old news by historians. Even worse, is how style has become booty for plunder by many architects. We do not share these inhibitions and instead seek to apply the concept of style with considerable flexibility. Stylistic paradigms are never universally applicable. John Shearman's characterization of *maniera* as the "stylish style" is as inapplicable for Sangallo the Younger as Alfred North Whitehead's view of style as the highest example of professionalism is for Raphael, Giulio Romano, or Giorgio Vasari.

As the reader will see, we avoid using loaded terms such as Renaissance or Mannerism because they obscure the stylistic diversity of cinquecento architecture and the momentous achievements of its architects. Instead, we seek to introduce authority and subversion as representations of two types of artistic (and architectural) ambition that avoid insinuations of a dominant idealism. It is, in our minds, an extension of Sir Isaiah Berlin's famous distinction between the hedgehog, which knows one thing, and the fox, which knows many. As theoretical concepts, authority and subversion also provide a flexible means of categorization that does not deny the various factors behind the creation of any building and the intentions of its architect.

The reader will also see that we have been extremely sparing in the use of the terms authority and subversion in our text. What matters more is how authority and subversion take on many forms—contrasting backgrounds as a painter or practitioner, age and generational conflict, style and personality, precedent, and politics are among those easily detected in this book. But there are certainly others. We invite our readers to detect other examples of authority and subversion that have eluded us.

We dedicate this book to the memory of Sydney J. Freedberg (1914–1997), who, though primarily as a historian of cinquecento painting, offers much to the study of its architecture. We feel compelled to follow his example in detecting three major centers of dissemination—Rome, Venice, and to a lesser degree, Florence. In doing so, we also admire his balance between historical structure and geographical structure, just as much as we admire his balance between historical narrative, formal analysis, and connoisseurship. By contrast, we find what many architectural historians have to say is limited in the appreciation of works of architecture. It is unfortunate that we never informed Sydney about our pet project, which was conceived, initiated, and in large part, written only a couple of miles from his home in Washington, D.C.

Very important advantages, without doubt, resulted to architecture from the new methods of proceeding adopted by Filippo Brunelleschi, he having imitated, and, after the lapse of many ages restored to light, the most learned and excellent masters of antiquity. But no less useful to our own age is Bramante, for preserving the traces of Filippo and following in his footsteps, being also full of determination, power, genius, and knowledge, not theoretic only but extensively and thoroughly practical, he rendered the road to the acquirement of true science in architecture most secure and easy to all who followed him . . . But not even all these qualities were more than was demanded at that time, seeing that Julius II, a prince full of the boldest designs and earnestly desirous of leaving due memorials of himself to succeeding ages, was then Pope. And very fortunate, was it, both for him and for us, that Bramante did meet such a prince (for very rarely does such good fortune happen to men of great genius) one at whose cost he was furnished with the opportunities which rendered it possible for him to display all the resources with which he was endowed. . . .

GIORGIO VASARI,
Lives of the Artists, 1568

Bramante, the man who revived well-conceived architecture, was he not first a painter and highly skilled in perspective before he devoted himself to this art?

S. SERLIO,
Second Book, 1545

1

BRAMANTE & LEONARDO

1 G. da Sangallo: Prato, S. Maria delle Carceri, begun 1484
2 Prato, S. Maria delle Carceri
3 A. da Sangallo the Elder: Montepulciano, S. Biagio, begun 1518
4 Montepulciano, S. Biagio, interior

In cinquecento Italy, an architectural revolution took shape with the advocacy and active support of a remarkable pontiff. Julius II (1503–13) was unanimously elected Pope in a conclave lasting a single day—a conclave not without bribery—and the name he chose for himself is expressive of his ambition. Born Giuliano della Rovere (1443–1513), he was a contemporary of Bramante (circa 1444–1514) and nephew of Pope Sixtus IV (1471–1484). According to the Florentine historian Francesco Guicciardini, except for dress and title, there was nothing of the priest in Julius II. It was by war that he reestablished the temporal power of the Papal States (with the exception of Modena, Parma, and Piacenza) in the form which was to survive until 1859–60. And all of this stands apart from his patronage of Michelangelo, of the young Raphael, and of Donato Bramante.

3

So Bramante "entered the road to the acquisition of true science in architecture most secure and easy to all who followed him;" but, to continue with Vasari, he also "added unwonted graces and beauties to the art, which we receive ennobled and embellished by his efforts." And as late as the nineteeth century, this judgment still persisted. Brunelleschi and Leon Battista Alberti were thought to have recalled the ancient style of architecture to life, but Bramante was responsible for its firm establishment and adaptation to the requirements of modern life. This is the notion of Bramante as the inventor of a canon of form and meaning, and, to obtain an elementary conception of what must have been his immediate impact, it may be rewarding to compare two churches with a Greek-cross plan, one begun in 1484 and the other in 1518—though neither is completely finished. These are the works of the brothers Sangallo, the earlier one of Giuliano (1443–1516) and the later of Antonio the Elder (1453–1534). The churches are, of course, S. Maria delle Carceri at Prato (1–2) and S. Biagio at Montepulciano (3–4). And if their differences are as startling as their similarities are evident, perhaps it should be enough to suggest that though members of the same species, almost as soon as the new imagery from Rome has been received, the old quattrocento Florentine style was considered to be superseded—or at least in central Italy.

In its exterior, the Prato church is a matter of colored marbles in which a sheer and geometrically organized surface predominates; while, at Montepulciano, this veneer is dispensed with and everything becomes an affair of monochrome orders, entablatures, and moldings that behave in a more assertive fashion. But with the interiors, the differences become more acute. At Prato there is a rendition of thematic material from Brunelleschi—white walls and gray *pietra serena*, Corinthian pilasters, and an enriched and highly detailed entablature. But at Montepulciano, it is as though some explosion of the mind has swept this all away. The interior is as much without color as the outside, the pilasters become active as three-dimensional semi-columns (their bases raised slightly above the floor), and an engaging version of the Corinthian gives way to the Doric style at its most severe.

This is the new solemnity resulting from Bramante's Roman innovations. The old eloquence—of Brunelleschi, Piero della Francesca, Alberti—has been left behind and we have a new gravitas—as exemplified by Raphael and others—which has begun to exert itself. The new ideal is that of antique tragedy, and in this context, the columns begin to behave like personalities. They are no longer pilasters elegantly drawn upon the wall; they now have acquired an animation that extends beyond their limits. These columns have become expansive in a way that was not known before.

To transfer attention to the plans only reinforces these remarks. The walls at Prato are thin and reveal little more than the existence of untouched planes; even the niches, which were hidden by sixteenth-century altars but still seen in a plan from Giuliano's Sienese sketchbook, must have appeared timid when compared to the deeply excavated solids at Montepulciano. The fully three-dimensional concept of architectural mass in Montepulciano was the presentation of something which, until almost the twentieth century, no one was able to ignore.

Such is almost certainly the most easily available evidence of the influence of Bramante and his revolution in architectural form. The church at Montepulciano does not derive from Prato without the emanation and the existence of a number of buildings in Rome. Bramante's classic achievements—the Tempietto of San Pietro in Montorio, the Palazzo Caprini, and the apse of S. Maria del Popolo—are what lie behind the different conceptions of these two churches. Accordingly, it is to Bramante's origins, those of his earlier career, that attention must be turned.

It was the conviction of Federico da Montefeltro (1422–82), duke of Urbino, that architecture was an art of great learning and great intellect. As an ideal patron of everything connected with architecture, he made his small territory a major center of humanist culture. In fact, he is imagined to be as intimately involved with the general concepts and particular details of his residence, the Palazzo Ducale, as he was of the plans of battles he fought as a *condottiere* for Venice, Florence, and the papacy. Doors, windows, fireplaces, and entire rooms seem to have been executed under his very close control. Attracted by his liberality, those who came to his celebrated court included, in succession, the architects Luciano Laurana and Francesco di Giorgio, and among painters, most notably Piero della Francesca and Melozzo da Forli.

It must have been Bramante's first good fortune to have been born adjacent to Urbino at Monte Asdrualdo. It was into this humanistic situation at Urbino, where architecture and painting intersected, through which he must have quite early on made his way. Could this have been as early as the late 1450s? Before Laurana appeared on the scene in the later 1460s? It seems likely, but it is generally agreed that Bramante's first employment was as a painter of architectural backgrounds.

Just how Bramante may have been introduced to architecture when he approached the age of thirty can be seen in a series of panels depicting scenes from the life of S. Bernardino. The paintings are quite elaborate with figures perhaps supplied by Perugino and other Umbrian masters. The artworks' settings are variations on the Albertian tradition in perspective, and in each, architecture serves to define a stage-like space for their figures. In some, the backgrounds are conventional and appear to be related to the courtyard of the Palazzo Ducale. But the *Miracle of the Man Wounded by a Stake* is much more challenging and enigmatic than its cohorts, never revealing buildings, spaces, or natural environments in their entirety (5). With a closed atrium and, lying behind it, some sort of circular temple, there are obvious premonitions of Bramante's Tempietto in Rome of some three decades later.

Bramante's education as a painter and as an architect can be located within the general ethos of Urbino, within that style of the most elegant and sophisticated of Italian palaces. An example of how he must have absorbed this style, with its emphasis on mathematics and perspective, is illustrated by the well-known group of three perspective panels now in Urbino, Baltimore, and Berlin (6–8). As

Richard Krautheimer has reminded us, the panels were architectural manifestos that depicted humanist urban settings. If the construction of such grand panoramas was not yet feasible, it at least defined the potential for architectural ambition by the princely painters who commissioned the works. The meaning of this message was not lost on Bramante.

Nowadays, scholars are skeptical of common authorship for the panels and even of their approximation of date, and, as one examines them, it is easy to subscribe to the reason for their doubts. The Berlin panel is just that much different. It depicts a city by the sea, which is seen through a monumental portico. The Baltimore panel, on the other hand, is of great consistency in architectural style, distributing various categories of ancient buildings about a vast, multitiered space. But it is surely the one remaining in the Ducal Palace that must be the more significant one for Bramante. In all probability, the Urbino panel was, in fact, commissioned by Federico de Montefeltro for the palace, which he was building and decorating, and this greatly increases the likelihood that Bramante was familiar with its visionary content. The Urbino panel, then, is an indication of the *genus loci* to which he was exposed, and with its circular temple, it is again a premonition of Bramante's Tempietto. Like the relationship of the Prato to the Montepulciano church, it is very comparable to the Tempietto—from a reticent planarity to bold relief, from colored panels to travertine, from a Corinthian to a Doric order.

Sometime in the 1470s, after Francesco di Giorgio had entered the service of Duke Federico, Bramante left Urbino and, according to Vasari "made his way to Lombardy, where he went now to one city, and now to another, working as best he could but not on things of much cost or much credit." Bramante's first documented activity (all his Urbino activity is conjectural) is in Bergamo in 1477. There he was responsible for a painted facade with architectural backgrounds on the Palazzo del Podestà, now only known from a few fragments, which seemingly are rather remote from what may have been his earlier practice.

Far more important to Bramante's development was what he would have seen on his journey through Northern Italy. Bergamo was then a province of the Venetian Republic, and this might argue for Bramante's acquaintance with the art of Venice and the Veneto. And as for the way he got there, the most plausible answer is via

5

7

8

Padua. It must be obvious that, for a painter of architectural back-grounds, the achievements of Andrea Mantegna in Padua would pre-sent a first alluring subject of study. In its enthusiasm for antiquity, Padua presented a different theater of operations than Urbino. There was less of mathematics and more of an archaeological glamour, less of small-scale and meticulous precision and more of large-scale elo-quence. Photographs of Mantegna's frescoes from the church of the Eremitani (before their destruction by bombing in World War II) illustrate the nature of this cult. The architectural backgrounds are resonant with a greater implication of historical variety than that of Piero. They alternate episodes that quote the starkness of Roman engineering and the protracted details of Hellenistic precocity; they are even equipped with Venetian chimneys. The backgrounds exude a different rhetoric from Urbino. The point of view of the observer is extremely low; one looks *up* to them than *at* them. But Mantegna by this time was established in Mantua—he had been there for a decade or more—and Mantua must have been Bramante's other crucial destination point.

Mantua now offered a juxtaposition of the approaches of both Mantegna and Alberti who, along with Piero, had been such signifi-cant factors of the style of Urbino. Mantegna's own house may have been almost in its present form by this time; Alberti's S. Sebastiano was begun in 1460 and his S. Andrea in 1470. Although Bramante couldn't have seen much of S. Andrea as we know it today, he never-theless would have had intuitions of the enormous scale of its inte-rior, a scale to be without rival until the mid-sixteenth century. Bramante could barely have been aware of S. Andrea's quite devastat-ing presence as completed.

About 1480, Bramante arrived in Milan, which was something of a metropolis when compared to Urbino, a provincial town invigo-rated by the presence of a court. Here the scale of the Milanese undertaking was enormous. Already in the twelfth century the city had built a canal, the Naviglio Grande, that connected it with the waters of the Ticino River some 20 miles to the west, thereby equip-ping it with the facilities of a port. The vast, spreading bulk of the Castello Sforzesco loomed over the city as the primary symbol of Sforza domination. Conformity with the Gothic building traditions of Milan's gigantic Duomo determined the design of its *tiburio*, the tower situated over the church's crossing.

Bramante would have been immediately attracted to the work that challenged the prevalent late-Gothic idiom of Milan. Filarete's Ospedale Maggiore, dating in its design from the early 1460s, is, even by modern standards, an extremely big hospital, and to someone coming from Urbino, it must have given occasion for thought. Stylistically the building is something of a hybrid, on the one hand, a pure product of Lombardy, but on the other, filled with the spirit of Florentine *razionalità*. Perhaps this is not so true of those many projects for domed and centralized churches illustrated by Filarete in his treatise where he recounts the construction of the imaginary city of Sforzinda. In these examples, there is to be found a very specific local tradition—Roman with Byzantine overtones, as in the fourth-century church of S. Lorenzo—that continued to serve as a model for ecclesiastical buildings not only within the city but also within its sphere of influence.

And then there are two 1460s buildings by Michelozzo, favorite architect of the Medici, in which the architect from Florence appears to be conciliating Lombard stylistic conservatism. The building for the Medici Bank, as recorded by Filarete, is an impressive and similarly hybrid affair—an extended Albertian palazzo in which, on the *piano nobile*, an arcade of Gothic windows has intruded itself. The Portinari Chapel, built at the church of S. Eustorgio for the agent of the Medici Bank, is another attempt at what must be a deliberate compromise. The chapel is nothing less than Brunelleschi's Old Sacristy from S. Lorenzo with Lombard details as a concession to local interests.

This is but a rough overview of what Bramante found when he arrived in Milan. The first evidence of a reaction to this is his design of the bizarre architecture in an engraving by Bernardo Prevedari entitled *Ruined Temple*. The attribution is certain from the inscription *Bramante fecit*. It illustrates an interior of considerable complexity and overt eclecticism—there are cross vaults, barrel vaults, and what appears to be a polygonal, twelve-sided dome (9). To the rear, there is an apse in the form of a niche, a likely recollection of Piero della Francesca's *Brera Altarpiece* (32). A multiplicity of circular openings and plaques mostly serve as windows and are equipped with portrait busts looking outward or subdivided by balusters so as to look like curious wheels. Although the perspective is not exact—there are multiple vanishing points—the observer is

9   Bernardo Prevedari after Bramante: *Ruined Temple*, circa 1480
10 Bramante: Milan, S. Maria presso S. Satiro, begun 1478
11 Milan, S. Maria presso S. Satiro

guided to something like a candelabrum that supports a not very
assertive cross. All in all, with the compounding of piers and
pilasters, what one finds here is a very clear miniature composite of
the influences of Alberti and Mantegna, which is overlaid with a profusion of the detail like that Michelozzo also felt obliged to supply.
But as rightly observed by Constantino Baroni, in both the lighting
and the dignity of this ruin, there is the distinct survival for a Gothic
"atmosphere." In Bramante's contemporaneous S. Maria presso S.
Satiro, this is an element that has largely disappeared.

11

Conceptually, the plan of the pre-Romanesque church of S.
Satiro, a cruciform within a square, is much the same as that of the
Prevedari engraving (10–11). As early as 1478, it was decided to add
to this an oratory housing a miracle working image—thus, in fact,
reducing the old church to the status of a chapel. While work was
underway on the oratory's elongated, rectangular interior, it was
decided to further enlarge the project by constructing a nave for an
altogether new church. Because of a conflict between the conditions
of the site and the requirements of architectural iconography, the new
arrangement could not accommodate a Greek cross plan. With this
revision in orientation, the oratory now became the transept, posing
a problem to Bramante that was solved by applying the perspective
principles of architectural backgrounds to a built structure. The result
was the famous illusionistic choir, where in the depth of less than a
meter, he depicts a space as deep as the arms of the transept.

Bramante's arrangement of barrel vaults no doubt was prompted
by those planned for S. Andrea in Mantua, though the arrangement's
diminutive scale might prompt the question as to whether Bramante
had understood the greatness of Alberti's prototype. Still, for all of its
evocations of antiquity, its mood is closely related to the Prevedari
perspective in its lighting and most of its details. In the transepts,
there are circular windows looking like the many wheels and niches
that are versions of the more developed concavities that Brunelleschi
had surrounded within his church of S. Spirito in Florence. Also
worth emphasizing for its retrospective aspects is the baptistery now
used as the sacristy. Northern Italian baptisteries are usually eight
sided and tall spaces, as at Parma, and Bramante is very careful to follow this medieval tradition.

The church of S. Satiro is even more distinguished externally
than it is inside. In its redevelopment, Bramante builds up his exterior

as a succession of contrasting geometric shapes—the cylinder with its precisely articulated niches, the cruciform vestige of S. Satiro rising above it, and the octagonal tempietto at its vertical terminal, which has something of the look of an early fire extinguisher. The background architecture of the oratory itself is similarly sophisticated— the very serious facade on the Via del Falcone, the paired pilasters at the corner that give the facade weight and depth, and finally, the very suave cylindrical drum and the repetition of the vertical terminal. These are emphatically the statements of a very great master. But before all of this could have been completed, in late 1481 or early 1482, Leonardo da Vinci arrived in Milan.

The Cathedral of Pavia is evidence of the interaction between the man from Urbino and the man from Florence (12). The building has a long history, beginning in 1487, before any intervention by Bramante, and was not completed, even in its present form, until the early years of the twentieth century. As the principal church in the city, which had been the ancient capital of Lombardy, it must have been something of a showpiece for its builder, Cardinal Ascanio Sforza, the brother of Ludovico il Moro. In concept, the new cathedral was ambitious in size and aspired to be seen in the company of equally ambitious churches in Siena, Florence, Bologna, and Loreto, which combined a longitudinal church plan with a polygonal dome. In August 1488, Bramante was called to Pavia for consultation on the new cathedral, and in 1490, both Leonardo and Francesco di Giorgio were called for further consultation as well. But, whatever the original notion for the cathedral and its subsequent alterations might have been, construction lagged and there is still little more than an interior left today.

At first glance, the model constructed from 1488 onward provides few clues of Bramante's contribution to the cathedral's design. Its incorporation of earlier models contributes to a singular lack of stylistic unity. In contrast to the reticence of S. Maria presso S. Satiro, its exterior offers a spectacle of almost incredible Late Medieval profusion of apses, pinnacles, and buttresses—certainly distinctive but not at all extraordinary since equivalent excess is also to be observed at the Certosa of Pavia, which was being built nearby at the same time. However, this is not so with the interior, crude in detail perhaps, but a huge, solemn, and magnificent space, which may well be

the product of a debate between Leonardo, Bramante, and whomso-
ever might have been concerned.

The architectural consequences of this debate are best understood by analyzing its plan. Recently, scholars have suggested the
cathedral was initially conceived as a centrally planned structure that
in some ways anticipated Bramante's initial idea for S. Peter's nearly
two decades later. In the longitudinal plan that replaced it, the influence of Brunelleschi's S. Spirito is profound in its suggestion of the
profusion of apsidal chapels and geometric schemata. Its powerful
axial thrust counteracted by satellite chapels also suggests the impact
of the Early Christian architecture of Milan, and in particular,
sketches by Leonardo. But none of Leonardo's designs could be considered an exact prototype; the cathedral at Pavia has neither the
hierarchy of geometric shapes nor the organic relationship of spaces
on diagonal axes seen in a sketch by Leonardo for a church with a
composite plan. (In Paris, see Institute de France, ms. B, fol. 24.) Any
contribution by Francesco di Giorgio remains conjectural, although
the vaulting in the cathedral's crypt has been connected with
Francesco's sketches of Hadrian's Villa.

Is Pavia's cathedral, with its confused building history, in any
considerable part to be ascribed to Bramante? Plausibly, Bramante
was responsible for the severe and undecorated forms of the crypt
and the plan from which it rises. Yet the argument of who might
have been responsible fails to adequately characterize the importance of this experience. For Bramante, what he learned must have
mattered more than what he built. In the interaction with a determined patron with diverse architects and competing designs, Pavia
became some sort of a dry run for what he was to propose and what
he was to encounter in Rome at S. Peter's approximately fifteen
years later. However, for Bramante, it still must have seemed a compromised job to be revised in his next project, the reconstruction of
the crossing of S. Maria delle Grazie, with which he was concerned
from 1493 onward.

Completed only two decades earlier by Guiniforte Solari, S.
Maria delle Grazie was little more than a horribly *retardataire* example of a rather fatigued Gothic structure. Bramante's eastern addition, which he planned as a mausoleum for the ruling Sforza dynasty,
could be regarded as a spatial consummation of what this nave *ought*

to have been (13). And, since it was a centralized and domical affair which Bramante had planned, the conjunction of the nave and eastern addition became one of the most spectacular resolutions of what was to be a frequent conflict in fifteenth- and sixteenth-century architecture. This was the dialectic between basilica, with a horizontal axis, and a dome, where the necessary axial stress is vertical, perhaps most beautifully resolved some eighty years later by Palladio at the Redentore in Venice.

More than anything else by Bramante so far, the interior of S. Maria delle Grazie is an incredible refreshment to the spirit. It is no longer cramped and small in scale as in S. Maria presso S. Satiro; no longer—like Pavia—is it just a touch provincial. Without apparent effort, the longitudinal axis is carried through the space of the dome, completing itself in the choir, where umbrella vaults seem to recall the church's Gothic origins. To the left and right, the great dome receives the generous visual and structural contributions of buttressing tribunes and supporting pendentives. If the forms of the eastern addition reveal their origin in Brunelleschi's Old Sacristy, the enormity of its scale was unprecedented, comparable perhaps only to Alberti's S. Andrea in Mantua, whose nave by the 1490s had been vaulted and largely completed. It is all a great but delicate triumph because it is accompanied with the least modulation of its bounding surfaces. The wall is plane rather than mass, and its few details appear to be inscribed upon it. Seen in this context, the vertical surfaces of S. Maria delle Grazie are like the shell of an egg. The exterior is an altogether different matter. By comparison, is it not another specimen of patriotic Lombard regionalism, drawing on mostly Lombard precedent? And how much is Bramante involved here? The question is legitimate, and there even has been an attempt to attribute the project to another architect, Giovanni Antonio Amadeo.

But we must continue to think about the proximity of Bramante and Leonardo. While Bramante was working on this dome, Leonardo was painting his *Last Supper* (circa 1495–97) only a few meters away in the adjacent refectory of S. Maria delle Grazie's monastery (21). We can only assume that their meetings were frequent and productive. One can only imagine how, over a few years, both Leonardo and Bramante—foreigners and equally attracted by the theme of the centralized church—had much to question and discuss. Of course, Leonardo offered much more than a critique of Filarete's earlier

12 Pavia, Cathedral, view of model
13 Milan, S. Maria delle Grazie, interior of choir, begun 1493

12

13

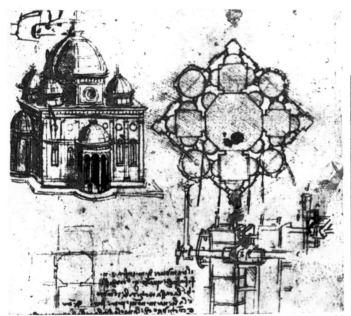

14

15

efforts. In numerous sketches that seem to be intended for an architectural treatise, Leonardo develops designs that follow two broad
themes—the church as a coalition of domes and the church as a compact form with four facades. All designs reflect an ideal of reconciling
the monumental mass of a building's exterior with interior spaces
that seem to have a life all their own. Leonardo's drawn spaces could
be inhabited by the same vital forces shown in his nature studies. In
one plan, he shades the interior while leaving solid walls blank, thus
anticipating the figure ground studies of the twentieth century (14).

~17

All in all, Leonardo created many of the formal characteristics of
cinquecento architecture without ever constructing a single building. This was accomplished largely through his impact on Bramante,
and the crossing of S. Maria delle Grazie was at the time the greatest
fulfillment of Leonardo's architectural legacy. But the fulfillment was
not complete. It seems that, like Alberti in Mantua, Bramante was
not yet able to combine bigness of conception with massiveness of
episode. This would occur at a later moment in Bramante's rapid
development as an architect—in the Rome of Julius II.

Quite by accident, Bramante's architecture became intertwined
with the creation of modern Milan. In Augustus Hare's *Cities of
Northern Italy* (1896), there are commentaries about vandalism in
post-risorgimento Milan, and among them are references to
Bramante. At one point, there arose a proposal to reconstruct the
entire exterior of S. Maria delle Grazie in stone, in which its brick
and terra-cotta had been admired for centuries. For example, Hare
claimed that the great cupola is a very rich and picturesque work of
Bramante. Yet, in Paris in 1881, the Milanese architect Angelo Colla
(1837–91) received a gold medal for his scheme for the reconstruction, apparently with the approval of Charles Garnier. Obviously, the
church did not come up to late nineteenth-century academic standards. Hare was rightly incensed. But may not this deplorable proposal (and also the gold medal) be a continuing tribute to the
hegemony of Bramante's Roman style?

During these years, Bramante was also concerned with the creation of arcaded buildings, mostly cloisters, enclosing open-air spaces.
The best known of these are the three cloisters at S. Ambrogio,
attached to the twelfth-century church dedicated to the bishop and
patron saint of Milan who converted St. Augustine in 386 A.D.
Significantly, the cloisters provided Bramante with a commission for

structures on a grand scale, which previously had eluded him. This was almost certainly the result of Bramante's first encounter with the remains of ancient Rome, which he presumably saw in the 1490s. In style and content, the cloisters are surely to be seen as indications, on Bramante's part, of a determination to rid his expression from the more traditional regional detail still so visible in S. Maria delle Grazie.

Each of the cloisters exploits a different architectural mood. In the unfinished courtyard to the north, that mood is both licentious and historicizing in equal measure. The order of the lower arcade is composite, its rhythm is broken at the center by a larger triumphal arch with Corinthian pilasters, and the columns adjacent to it evoke the column in its most primitive form—that of a tree. The Doric and Ionic cloisters to the south are, on the other hand, exercises in restraint (15). Indeed, for Milan, it must have been a surprising austerity. The area below the loggia obviously traces back to Brunelleschi's Loggia degli Innocenti—but developed with far greater severity. While up top, the highly abstracted presentation of pilasters and cornice now appears as a fairly complete divorce of Bramante's intentions from the Lombard taste which, hitherto, he had so skillfully adapted. In these cloisters, which are intrinsically part of an urban space, his future intention—to leave Milan for Rome—is almost overt.

Of all of Bramante's projects in Lombardy, the most extraordinary is the Piazza Ducale in Vigevano, which was constructed from 1492 onward. If the actual documentation for his authorship is scanty, the design presents a compelling example of Bramante's architectural thinking on the scale of a small city. The square is a very long rectangular space on a slope, with the cathedral at the lower end very subservient to it, and it has continuous arcades and brilliant illusionistic paintings of its upper wall surfaces (16). Vigevano was a minor residence of the Sforza Dukes of Milan, an otherwise unimportant town, and what one finds here is in some ways just a provincial performance. There are lapses of grammar with major arches, which are rather ineptly incorporated in the general sequence of the arcades. The frank demonstration of Sforza power called for the omission of the porticoes in front of the adjacent castle, creating a dominating prospect for its great tower. But in visual terms, it must be an incredible delight to all who come upon it.

What we have here is the first ideal plaza to be built, the first regular piazza of what used to be called "modern times." Deriving from Alberti's ideal of an ancient Roman forum, its continuous arcades of three sides create a *piazza salone* of the sort that would be proposed in Sansovino's reconstruction of Piazza San Marco in Venice. It is the bold and somewhat ruthless concept of the square — a forum where the powers of bishop and a princely ruler intersect— rather than its details that demonstrate Bramante's intervention. Above all, it is a space that a later generation of architects would associate with Bramante's much more monumental Cortile del Belvedere in the Vatican, as when Bishop Caramuel de Lobkowitz some two hundred years later provided the cathedral with its present facade—four doorways, one leading to a courtyard, two to the cathedral, and the fourth admitting to a street! But in any case, if the cathedral of Pavia may be interpreted as a dry run for what was to be proposed at St. Peter's, the Piazza Ducale is to be thought of as containing at least some crucial suggestions for the Belvedere. We shall return to the Piazza Ducale in chapter 11.

Bramante finally left Milan, after a residence of some eighteen years, probably in 1499. This was in no way too soon. The army of Louis XII of France was already approaching Milan, and with its arrival in September, the independence of the Sforza state was to be destroyed and Lombardy was to be subject to foreign rule, mostly Hapsburg, first Spanish, and then Austrian. Milan's subjugation would continue until 1859–60, when it was incorporated along with the Piedmont, Tuscany, and parts of the Papal States into the new kingdom of Italy.

So Donato Bramante left for Rome at the age of fifty or thereabouts as a refugee. It might be useful to ask what could have been his expectations. Surely not much from the reigning Pope, Alexander VI (1492–1503). And there could be no knowledge, waiting in the wings of this historical stage, that there was any such person as Julius II. But there was one situation that might have been expected—that if he found himself any work, the fifty-seven-year-old Giuliano da Sangallo would be his most serious competitor.

Though Bramante's credentials as a court architect were excellent, Sangallo's were equally so. He had designed a palace for the King of Naples. For Lorenzo de'Medici, he also built the previously mentioned church at Prato and the villa at Poggio a Caiano, equally elegant in its facades and plan. Even more to the point, after the expulsion of the Medici from Florence, Sangallo entered into the service of the future Julius II and built for him in the late 1490s a family palace, the Palazzo della Rovere at Savona. So, at the time that Julius was elected, Sangallo must have entertained very high hopes and Bramante correspondingly few. Nevertheless, when the Pope became determined to build the new St. Peter's, it was not to Sangallo he turned but Bramante.

Emphatically this could not have been because of what Bramante might have already built in Rome—there couldn't have been very much of it on which to base a judgment. Could it have been Bramante's experience in the design of domed and vaulted churches in Lombardy, most particularly S. Maria delle Grazie and the Cathedral of Pavia? Sangallo instead had distinguished himself as the planner of grand palaces and villas and the designer of impeccable detail. In any case, when Julius had made his decision, Sangallo went off to Florence in something like disgust, and, in Rome Bramante was left in undisputed control. Which, one might say, was not bad work for a time of little more than five years.

There was, for example, in the time of Pope Julius II a certain Bramante of Casteldurante in the Duchy of Urbino, a man of great gifts concerning architecture. With the help and authority given to him by the above named pope, he brought back to life the fine architecture which, from the ancients to that time, had lain buried.

S. SERLIO,
Third Book, 1540

Bramante was the first to bring to light the good and beautiful architecture which from the time of the ancients to his day had been forgotten.

A. PALLADIO,
Quattro libri, IV, 1570

Bramante, chronologically and artistically the mediator between Alberti and Palladio, represents at the same time the apex of this trio of great humanist architects.

RUDOLF WITTKOWER,
Architectural Principles in the Age of Humanism, 1949

2
~
BRAMANTE *and the* ROME *of* JULIUS II

17 Bramante: Genazzano, Ninfeo, after 1501
18 B Pontelli (attr.): Rome, Cancelleria, begun circa 1485

17

18

The small town of Genazzano, which is located some 40 kilometers to the southeast of Rome, was not always as accessible as it is today. It was a feudal holding of the Colonna, with the fortress at the head of the town. It was the birthplace of the pope who restored papal power after the Great Schism, Martin V Colonna (1417–31). In the 1540s, Palladio must have made a special attempt to visit Genazzano. As witness to this, there is the entrance motif of his Villa Poiana, being a memory of the garden loggia, or the Ninfeo, which must have been what he went to see and which is often attributed to Bramante (17).

The Ninfeo is situated alongside a small stream at the bottom of the town. Its date is problematic. According to Bruschi, it may have been built as early as 1501–02, as a compliment to Alexander VI, or, as Bruschi thinks more likely, in the years following 1507. In any case, it was commissioned by Cardinal Pompeo Colonna as something of a multipurpose building. On occasion, the stream could be dammed to create a lake for simulated naval battles and the audience might sit inside the building, or alternatively, the action might take place within the building and the audience sit on the other side of the lake. But in whatever usage, this is a building clearly affiliated with Bramante's Milanese practices, and at the same time, very much predictive of future buildings. The Belvedere courtyard of the Vatican was intended to serve the purposes of theatrical display, and a similar, three-bay loggia came to dominate the garden facade of the Villa Madama.

Although nowadays a ruin, the Ninfeo is once more a principal object of attraction because it leads us to compare with the internal elevations of S. Maria delle Grazie. This comparison is especially revealing for the sake of the stylistic continuities and divergence that the two disclose between Bramante's architectural language of the 1490s in Milan and that of some ten to fifteen years later in Rome. Of course, the Genazzano Ninfeo is a translation *alla Romana* of the eastern parts of S. Maria delle Grazie; but since one of these is a church and the other a specimen of garden architecture, for this reason one doesn't automatically connect the two.

In both cases, we are presented with different forms of a tripartite composition. At S. Maria delle Grazie, the three major arches leading to the drum of the dome enclose the minor arches leading to the choir and side apses. Below, all of these are articulated by Corinthian pilasters inscribed upon the wall, and above, the infill between the archivolts is equipped with circular plaques of the kind Bramante had used in his *Ruined Temple*. But at Genazzano, the latent becomes the overt, the Corinthian pilasters become Doric columns, and the circular plaques become oculi. In other words, the development of surface has given way to a development of volume, and through a miniaturization of the internal elevations at Milan, the typical bay at Genazzano is presented with monumental economy. Bramante, building on the achievements of the previous century, has taken the first steps toward an architecture emphasizing space over surface.

Now, before Bramante, the new architecture in Rome is certainly not much to be talked about, that is if one might use the same criteria when thinking about buildings in Florence or Urbino. Within the circuit of the Aurelian Walls, the city remained not much more than a shrunken nucleus—Hibbard describes it as "a desiccated nut within its shell." Even though its growth might have been accelerated beginning with the policies of Martin V and continued in the days of Sixtus IV, its future and imminent grandeur must have been still less than evident. By the most exacting standards, the quattrocento facades of S. Maria del Popolo (1472–77) and S. Agostino (1479–83) and their interiors are of little more than local importance and do not approach the inventiveness and eloquence of Alberti's solutions in Rimini, Florence, and Mantua. For all the richness of their subsequently added chapels and painting, they are far less than exceptional.

Indeed, before Bramante, there is only one building that might be described as dazzling, and this is the Cancelleria, a combined church and palace, built from 1485 onward for Cardinal Raffaello Riario, nephew of Sixtus IV (18). Breaking from the archaic and medieval forms of earlier quattrocento places in Rome, the Cancelleria is remarkable for its eloquent and diverse facades, its elegant courtyard, and its comfortable staircase, which was much admired by Vasari. Traditionally, of course, it had been attributed to Bramante. But this was when a knowledge of his Milanese achievements was still only fragmentary. It is difficult to conceive that he could have been simultaneously so active in Lombardy and have arrived at such an alternative, accomplished expression during brief trips to Rome. Thus, though the rhythm of narrow and wide bays may be an anticipation of what he was to do later at the Cortile del Belvedere, it is hardly possible to suggest he was responsible for a similar arrangement so much earlier. While Vasari does propose that there were some Bramante interventions at the Cancelleria, it may be accepted that, whatever these may have been, they must have come later in its long building campaign. So this very prominent building remains a problem in terms of assigning responsibility for its design. Vasari attributed at least its execution to the distinctly unknown Antonio Montecavallo, and recently, Christoph Frommel suggested the name of Baccio Pontelli as the Cancelleria's architect during its initial years of construction.

27

The first architectural work connected with Bramante in Rome, with which he is known to have been associated with as early as the summer of 1500, is the cloister of S. Maria della Pace (19). This was commissioned by Oliviero Carafa, Cardinal of Naples (who served as a representative of Spanish interests at the papal court), and, like the Ninfeo at Genazzano, it is another development on Milanese themes, in this case the Doric cloister at S. Ambrogio. For example, if one takes the upper level from S. Ambrogio, enlarges its scale and shifts it down below, one finds something very like the solution at S. Maria della Pace, wherein the more obtrusively Milanese elements having migrated upward. But, with a combination of delicacy and diffidence, Bramante is being very cautious, the work is very transitional, and Vasari evidently understood the dilemma of Bramante's reticence:

> It is true that the building was not one of distinguished beauty,
> but it obtained a great name for the architect, seeing that there
> were but few masters in Rome, who then devoted themselves
> to architecture with the zealous study and promptitude of exe-
> cution which distinguished Bramante.

Distinguished beauty or not, to a twentieth-century sensibility, perhaps the most interesting aspect of the cloister is that its composition is a square of four bays—four bays rather than three or five. As a consequence of this arrangement, there is a solid instead of a void at the center of each side of the cloister, creating a courtyard that is a prismatic space. Therefore, interest becomes transferred—but very quietly—from the space open to the sky to the ambulatory movement within the cloister itself. And may it not be this incipient spiral that contributes an intriguing vitality to the whole?

Bramante's Tempietto in the courtyard of S. Pietro in Montorio is one of those rare and elusive architectural masterpieces that characterize the aspirations of an epoch (20). Despite its familiarity, there is little concrete evidence regarding its date. According to one school of thought, it is typically dated 1502 (and according to some, even earlier!). Yet in the less than two years after the work at S. Maria della Pace had been begun, hesitation and diffidence have given way to confidence and complete control. In fact, one might insist that the designation of the Tempietto as one of Bramante's early Roman works seriously strains the capacities of belief. Until quite lately, the date 1502, to be discovered in the lower chapel or crypt of the Tempietto, was generally accepted without dispute. But most recent scholarship has been skeptical about this and suggests that this is no more than a date for the lower chapel. Thus, there is a division of opinion, with the later opinion leaning toward a later date—tending to bring the Tempietto in line with Bramante's work at St. Peter's, and perhaps, also to see it as a small-scale version of his proposal for its dome.

Just how far Bramante has grown beyond his roots in Urbino can be illustrated in the Tempietto's subtle and aggressive visual effects. When compared to the temple in the Urbino panel (6), which is a lively affair of colorful marble inlays surrounded by attached Corinthian columns, the Tempietto's *gravitas* derives from its Doric order and essentially monochromatic tone despite subtle variations in the colors of its travertine, granite, and warm, creamy stucco. Significantly, there is a difference in the lighting, which seems to have been a preoccupation of Bramante. At Urbino, it is the brilliant light of the quattrocento that isolates and clarifies detail, but at the Tempietto, in the interest of the whole, Bramante wishes to homogenize detail and light, which he imagines is, correspondingly, something more caressive and enveloped in *sfumato*. So the relationship of the Tempietto to the circular temple in the Urbino panel is very much the same relationship as the church at Prato to the church at Montepulciano, and it might be suggested that this is the difference between the Albertian and the Leonardesque.

According to taste, the process is one of gain or loss. But by transferring our attention to painting, there is a similar difference in attitudes toward form and space. This can be easily grasped by comparing Andrea del Castagno's *Last Supper* (1447) at S. Apollonia in Florence with Leonardo's famous version of the same theme at S. Maria delle Grazie in Milan (21). With Andrea del Castagno, we are firmly within the rational world of the scientific perspective grid, and with the familiar apparatus of marble paneling behind them, the

19 Bramante: Rome, S. Maria della Pace, cloister, 1500
20 Bramante: Rome, S. Pietro in Montorio, Tempietto, circa 1508–10

19

20

21   Leonardo da Vinci: *Last Supper*, 1495–97
22   Piero della Francesca, *Flagellation*, circa 1455–56
23   Leonardo da Vinci: *Adoration of the Magi*, begun 1481

21

22

23

apostles sit on a rather narrow and inconvenient shelf, looking, in the end, as if they were having dinner in the nicest of all possible Howard Johnson hotels. But with Leonardo, we have been transported to a less contracted and rigid world, where lighting is softer and more somber, and where gestures are, always, more ample and more magnificent.

Andrea del Castagno's spatial proposition is in the world of Alberti and Piero della Francesca, in which depth is the product of the perspective grid and in which columns occur as punctuations of, or caesuras within, that grid. This is, of course, the condition of the temple within the Urbino panel. There the floor of the piazza is a checkerboard—the field and the temple are a larger representation within it. But this is by no means the condition of the Tempietto, where the intention was to locate it within a circular courtyard, and where the rectilinear grid is unable to operate. Inevitably, a system of radial interrelationships becomes privileged—as a result, the column coming to enjoy a very different mode of being. In the new dispensation, the column becomes more highly charged, more positive, more animated, and more palpable.

The new status that the column was to acquire may, at the risk of slightly redundant analysis, be further emphasized by another comparison of two pictures that present an opposition between the systems of Piero and Leonardo and help us to understand an evolution. These are Piero's *Flagellation* (1455–56), painted for the court at Urbino, so it was probably familiar to Bramante, and Leonardo's unfinished *Adoration of the Magi* (1481) for S. Donato a Scopeto, a Florentine monastery that has long since disappeared (22-23). So, while Leonardo's basic composition, the group of the Virgin and Kings, signals a dissent from Piero, he is careful to provide indication that his deviation is self-conscious. In the upper left of the *Adoration*, he lays out abundant evidence that he knows what Piero had been (and still was) all about. There is the little episode of a building derived entirely from the directives of a perspective grid and almost disconnected from the rest of the picture. In this composition, action and space, while at center stage, are constructed according to a principle which had been unknown to Piero and which would render his practice no longer interesting to the immediate future. The vitality of the *Adoration* has been most eloquently characterized by Sydney

31

Freedberg in his monumental *Painting of the High Renaissance in Rome and Florence* and restated in *Painting in Italy 1500–1600*:

> The image that results is visibly distinct from normal expecta-
> tions, and aesthetically and ethically far superior to them.…
> Leonardo's space begins not as Alberti described it with a
> perspective grid, which is then populated with figures, but
> oppositely, with the figures: their volume gives shape to the
> surrounding space. A history of the evolution of the classical
> style that would be not only formal of its kind could be composed
> with the fulfillment of this beginning in the *Adoration* as a
> central thread.

It is with this picture that late in 1481 or early the following year, Leonardo left Florence for Milan, and it must have been about then that he began his long association with Bramante. The *Adoration* was, according to Freedberg, "an unfinished manifesto…left behind to bemuse the Florentines…and not comprehended until some two decades later, [when] the more ordinary processes of history caught up with it."

This is a pregnant and succinct suggestion, and it might lead to the further suggestion that, if Bramante might have been temporarily bemused by Leonardo, he too, after a comparable lapse of two decades, had become able to understand the message which the new figuration had for the column. The status of the figures in the *Flagellation* is roughly equivalent to that of the columns in Brunelleschi's churches. They are chess pieces with their moves on the board of perspective, and as already perhaps over asserted, this is very far from their behavior in the Tempietto.

But to return to specifics: the Tempietto was built under the auspices of the king and queen of Spain, Ferdinand and Isabella (patroness of Christopher Columbus), and since Cardinal Carafa was the Spanish representative in Rome, it is tempting to believe that he also might have been active in recommending Bramante on this further occasion. According to tradition, St. Peter was crucified on the Janiculum, and even if this theory was unfounded, it was still sufficiently compelling for its patrons to conceive of the Tempietto's site as a sacred spot under Spanish protection. In form and function, the

Tempietto is a Christian *martyrium* intended to memorialize the reputed site of St. Peter's crucifixion, and this was presumably the reason for Bramante's use of the Doric order. Vitruvius had claimed that the Doric temple was appropriate for heroic male deities, and in the cinquecento, Serlio extended this definition to include saints who had led an active and virile life in the service of Christ. St. Peter enjoyed the reputation of strength and masculinity, and consequently, Bramante's interest in the expression of the orders was in part conditioned by symbolic concerns.

Apart from its highly specific iconography, the Doric order (as at Genazzano) was just as much subject to Bramante's newly acquired tastes. It departed from traditional usage in antiquity where circular temples were apt to be Corinthian (as is the temple in the Urbino panel). But in other ways, and particularly in its plan, the Tempietto can be differentiated from the temples of ancient Rome, which, superficially, it so much resembles. When compared to the circular temples of Roman antiquity, the Tempietto appears absolutely heretical. Neither the balustrade above the circular portico nor the drum supporting the dome is sanctioned by ancient precedent. In its ancient counterparts, its ring of Corinthian columns stands apart from a simple cylinder, which fails to acknowledge their presence. By contrast, the force of the Tempietto's columns seems to invade the central cylinder and give it a plasticity quite unlike anything in Bramante's earlier work. Both outside and in, the cylinder of the Tempietto is animated and enriched by scooping out of it a whole apparatus of niches, which simultaneously contribute a Leonardesque chiaroscuro and establish an organic fusion of the cylinder and its intended surroundings.

So was this little building something more than an act of restitution? Or was it meant to present Bramante as more Roman than the ancient Romans themselves? It would fit the cultural politics of the time to assume both, and, in connection with proposals for buildings of this kind, perhaps his only serious competitor was Francesco di Giorgio Martini (1439–1501), who, maybe fortunately for Bramante, was already dead. But Francesco also had produced numerous studies for further specimens of the same species of round churches, and some of these are splendid and historically important novelties. However, are any of them to be regarded as the culmintion of a significant revolution in form? They may come close to it, but had any of them been built, it is hard to believe that they would have eclipsed the celebrity and influence of the Tempietto. Both as a conclusion and a new beginning, the Tempietto must remain a thing unto itself, an organic and living condition of spirit and Bramante's chief claim to fame.

In his *Architectural Principles in the Age of Humanism*, Rudolf Wittkower is elaborate in his discussion of the platonic ideality of which the Tempietto is a physical manifestation, and in making this point (which was not so obvious until Wittkower made it), the basic texts, needless to say, are Plato's *Timaeus* and a selection of quotes from Alberti. The basic tenet of this proposition is that the cosmos is a sphere and since divine creation is to be imitated, it follows that, in temples raised to the Divinity on earth, there should be some reflection of His creation. And hence, Bramante's circular building was to have been at the center of its own cosmos, in the circular courtyard that he proposed for it. And also, for St. Peter's, there is a Bramante-style drawing in Uffizi A 104 *verso* that seems to show it—a further enclosing courtyard which would extend the building's orbit of influence by responding to its perimeter. That there were ancient precedents for both—the Teatro Marittimo at Hadrian's Villa for the Tempietto and Imperial baths for St. Peter's—is undeniable, but for the selection of these arrangements, the philosophical underpinnings are also irrefutable.

So it is entertaining to bring these two courtyard projects to juxtaposition. For if, at S. Pietro in Montorio, the circular courtyard was a probable means of receiving the Tempietto, at St. Peter's, there was no comparable courtyard that was a possible solution. Quite obviously, the historically significant buildings of the Vatican impinged too closely upon the basilica itself. And there also was the problem of what to do with the grandiose remains of the choir begun by Rossellino a half-century earlier for Nicholas V. Ironically, the more Bramante built in the Vatican the more he diminished any hope of an ideal solution for the church. The problem could have been solved by what was apparently never considered—a radical detachment of the two.

It is in this conflict of interest that there is to be found the ultimate sources for embarrassment about what Bramante attempted to do in these two papal strongholds. And, if this is obvious to us, when we think about it, we are apt to wonder why it was not equally obvious some five hundred years ago. Just why did Bramante and the Pope simply charge ahead with what seems to be three incompatible building campaigns: St. Peter's and in the Vatican, the Cortile del Belvedere and the Cortile di San Damaso? The determination must have been led by the Pope.

The strict chronological order of these campaigns is as follows: the Belvedere courtyard became the subject of consideration in 1504–05; St. Peter's emerged into prominence in 1505–06, and the Cortile di San Damaso, a minor work but because of its situation, highly visible, followed as early as 1507–08. But in this discussion, it seems most opportune to begin with S. Peter's.

Bramante's first project is known from the foundation medal of 1506 and the so-called "Parchment" plan in the Uffizi (24). The foundation medal shows a church of generally Leonardesque configuration—dome, subsidiary domes and semi-domes, and corner towers. It looks like the sort of thing the Sforza might have been prepared to build in Milan had they remained in power and had the money for it. From the parchment plan one may receive the same impression, because both documents on a casual inspection appear to be related to a centralized church—a composite of memories particularly of the Cathedral of Pavia and of S. Maria delle Grazie. It is evidently a structure that is identical on all sides. But this need not be, without question, the solution that they predicate. For, just as S. Maria delle Grazie is a Leonardesque addendum to a longitudinal church and the Duomo at Pavia a combination of these same elements, so, for reasons political, the Pope and Bramante may have been offering ambiguous evidence. Should it be centralized or should it have a traditional longitudinal plan? With the information shown in the medal and parchment plan, the option remains available.

And if the Pope may have oscillated in his intentions, apparently, so did Bramante. Subsequent plans for St. Peter's were for various longitudinal schemes derived in some form from the parchment plan and the existing quattrocento choir. So Bramante hedged his bets, and he committed to neither solution but emphatically adhered to largeness and grandness, which he may have equated with *virtù* and magnificence.

At a slightly later date, but when very little had been built, Serlio found the whole undertaking to be hazardous. From this it can be

35

understood how, in this case, Bramante was more impetuous than thoughtful, because a work of such great size and weight would require exceptionally strong foundations to secure it, not to mention constructing it over four arches of such a magnificent height.

Significantly, Serlio fails to publish a plan by Bramante for the church (though he would publish those by others). However, Serlio does illustrate in the *Third Book* the elevation (25) of the dome, "I wanted to put this figure here because the invention is beautiful and ornate, and in order to give inspiration to the architect—" but with the proviso that "such a volume...ought to prompt every sensible architect to build it on the ground story, and not at such a height."

Now, the story has always been that it was Bramante's ambition to erect (his version of) the dome of the Pantheon on top of (his version of) the Basilica of Maxentius, which was known in his era as the Temple of Peace. It is to this that Serlio seems to take objection—to doubt the stability of such an undertaking. And there is no antique precedent for such a hybrid, the most likely being the dome of the Hagia Sophia in Constantinople. But externally, this is not obtrusive and is far from being the "beautiful and ornate" display which, as Serlio anticipated, would prove to be an inspiration to so many generations of architects. At the Hagia Sophia, there is no intervening drum between the dome and the arches which support it, and, in "ornate" form, this must have a peculiar contribution. There are, of course, the five domes with five drums as at St. Mark's in Venice, and these might suggest that in the evolution of late Byzantine style, the drum must have been something imminent. However, in Italian medieval churches, such as the Siena Cathedral, the dome rests directly upon the arches of the crossing, and the drum or tambour make no appearance. Nor is it to be found in depictions of the Florence Cathedral—as shown for instance in the Spanish Chapel at S. Maria Novella. It is not until Brunelleschi takes over that it emerges as something of a consummate and overwhelming importance. But the dome of the cathedral immediately, and out of necessity, dominated the city, and it seems that it must have been some time after his own involvement with the dome of Pavia Cathedral (on the whole, had it been built, a skimpy affair) that Bramante came to recognize this. Hence, what must have been his resolution to revise and to exceed Brunelleschi by eliminating all Gothic overtones and

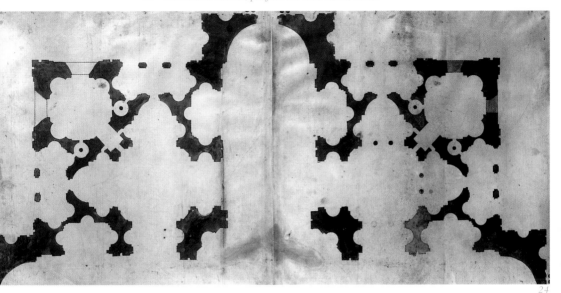

24

DELLE ANTICHITA

Questo è il diritto di dentro, e di fuori della pianta passata, dal qual si può comprendere la gran massa, & il gran peso che saria questo edificio sopra à quattro pilastri di tanta altezza: la qual massa(sì come io dissi avanti)dovería mettere pensiero ad ogni prudente Architetto à farla al piano di terra, non che in tanta altezza: & però io giudico, che l'Architetto dee esser più presto alquanto timido che troppo animoso: perche se sarà timido, egli farà le sue cose ben sicure, & anco non sdegnerà di volere il consiglio d'altri, e così facendo, rare volte perirà: ma se sarà troppo animoso, egli nò vorrà l'altrui consiglio: anzi si considerà so

lamente nel suo ingegno, onde spesse volte precipitaranno le cose da lui fatte, & però io concludo che la troppo animosità proceda dalla presuntione, & la presuntione dal poco sapere: ma che la timidità sia cosa virtuosa, dandosi sempre à credere di sapere è nulla, è poco. Le misure di questa opera si troveranno con i palmi piccioli che sono qui à dietro.

La pian-

25

38

26

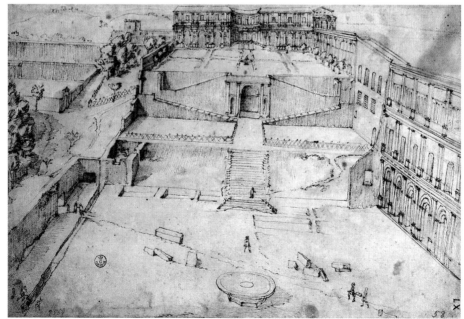

27

by providing Rome with the very latest of domes, complete with drum, circular rather than octagonal, and—just as important—*to decorate this drum with a colonnade.*

After all is said and done, one may agree with what Serlio seems to intimate but didn't exactly say—no doubt it was all slightly ridiculous. But, on the other hand, as Serlio obviously and reluctantly confessed, it was something imperial and triumphant, something both nostalgic and new, almost (though Serlio couldn't have said this) a thunderbolt from heaven. It was almost as a part of the divine revelation for what a monumental church ought to be that, when acquiring a Florentine profile as edited by Michelangelo, the dome with drum and colonnade (colonnaded omitted for Catholics and retained for Protestants and enlightenment *philosophes*) via St. Paul's in London, Ste. Geneviève in Paris, and Schinkel in Potsdam became one of the greatest of all possible paradigms—the symbol of a just and enlightened government in Washington, D.C., and ever so many places in the United States.

This strange destiny for the ambitions of Julius II is enough to permit a brief parenthesis. Serlio publishes his illustration of the dome of St. Peter's immediately before he publishes his illustration of the Tempietto. In his life of Bramante, this is also the order of which Vasari follows. Apparently, both of them saw the colonnades as related: a big cylinder and a little cylinder. And may this rather strange coincidence assist the argument in favor of a later dating of the Tempietto?

Bramante gives us a hint that he is conceiving of the interior elevations of St. Peter's as a species of a facade, with all the suggestions of projection, recession, and relief. This must compel us in yet another return to Alberti's S. Andrea in Mantua (26). Bramante's familiarity with S. Andrea, which he must have known certainly before the completion of its nave in the 1490s, is to be inferred from the nave of S. Maria presso S. Satiro (a miniature erected when Alberti's building could have scarcely risen very high) and from the eastern parts of S. Maria delle Grazie (when its great scale was surely apparent). Therefore it is only to be expected that the interiors of the new S. Peter's might prove some reflection of the Mantuan prototype. But preparatory drawings of St. Peter's interior space, which must have been made, have rather surprisingly not survived. Did Bramante assume, like so many others since his time, that the elevations were

39

already implicit in the plan? Or did he consider the elevation an independent element, as in medieval architectural practice? However this may have been, there is fragmentary evidence to be discovered about what the cornice and entablature looked like after construction has reached that height.

In its relationship to the height of the wall, the cornice projects more vigorously than the same elements at S. Andrea. This is shown in the vedute of Maerten van Heemskerck (circa 1534), and in the same context, the background of Raphael's *School of Athens* (1508), the architecture of which Vasari attributes to Bramante (37). It shows a corresponding enlargement, simplification, and projection. And also, the pilasters have become broader, less decorative, and more applied to the wall. This seems to be congruent with the greater ampleness and width of the piers, which now become animated in a behavior congruent to that of the columns at the Tempietto. The eighteenth-century historian and critic, Francesco Milizia (in a nineteenth-century translation), says of S. Andrea: "It is imposing, well united, and generally evinces a good style of building, except that the projections of the cornices are small, the members too trifling, and the taste petite." Though Milizia is rather patronizing, something like this could have been Bramante's critique of Alberti's church and the *School of Athens* an afterthought for the interior of St. Peter's.

But a little more might be said about the *School of Athens*. If we could think of S. Andrea as the architectural background for a fresco with figures, it is not too difficult to imagine their appearance. They would be slightly Mantegnesque, with a few heroic figures and some Frenchified young men displaying elegant legs in the Paduan style of Marco Zoppo. And they would seem to be emanations of the architecture. But, then, to transfer attention to Raphael's figures in *School of Athens*, they are not imaginable in an Albertian interior. Their clothes are voluminous, their legs are invisible; simultaneously they are both static and excited by a spiraling motion. And is this not the same stability, equipped with a mysterious internal rotation that distinguished the *School of Athens* from anything conceivable by Alberti? In this architecture, should we not, yet again presume the influence of Leonardo?

But, if most statements about Bramante's St. Peter's must be conjectural, his intention with regard to the Cortile del Belvedere is more obvious (27). Intended to connect the old nucleus of the Vatican with the small villa (1485–87) built by Innocent VII on a hill more than 300 meters high, the structure's purposes were entirely secular and pleasurable. Its attenuated courtyard on three levels was flanked on its long sides by logge and galleries and terminated at the upper end by an exedra that masked the imposing design's non-axial arrangement with the statuary court and villa beyond. The disposition of the building's symmetrical stairs immediately discloses that one of the primary sources of its inspiration was the Temple of Fortune at Palestrina, an arrangement that influenced two of the greatest Italian gardens, the Villa d'Este at Tivoli and the Villa Lante at Bagnaia, a half-century later. Other sources are not difficult to discover: the terraced courts and perhaps the semi-circular exedra similar to parts of Hadrian's Villa at Tivoli; the overall proportions of the space linked to the Circus Maximus and the sunken gardens on the Palatine; and the themes of the three-story portico related to the Golden House of Nero. As a collection of such memories, the Cortile del Belvedere was clearly meant to be regarded as the emblem of a new *imperium*.

Serlio tells us that the structure was built in the form of a grand theater. This has a double meaning: *teatro* commonly refers to any large undertaking, and the steps in Nicchione on the upper level were originally constructed as something of a theater in miniature. But one of the functions of the entire space was to serve as an enclosure for theatrical performance—pageants, tournaments, and, as at Genazzano, simulated naval battles. But it also had a function that was entirely new. The space was to provide a setting for newly excavated antiquities such as the *Laocoon*, which had been added to the papal collection. So the Belvedere was a museum of ancient sculpture open to the air—primarily on the upper level and in the statuary court—that provided a modern setting for statuary recalling their original settings in antiquity.

Completion of the Cortile del Belvedere was beyond the grasp of Julius II, and it evaded subsequent pontiffs as well. It should not be surprising that, in the climate of opinion sponsored by the Council of Trent, the hedonistic overtones of the Belvedere should become less than acceptable and the wreckage of Bramante's intentions should begin. The final blow was delivered during the papacy of

Sixtus V (1585–90) when Domenico Fontana constructed the Vatican library across the intermediate terrace. Even before this, the walling up and mutilation of the logge had begun leaving only fragments of the original scheme unchanged.

But, all the same, sufficient evidence in the form of drawings and engravings permits the understanding of a garden of unprecedented novelty and self-confidence which, for a very few years, was able to attract and absorb the attention of numerous architects and other visitors. The garden was perhaps at its best in 1565, when, on the occasion of the marriage of Giacomo Altemps, a nephew of Pope Pius IV (1559–65), it was the setting for a medieval tournament, and from the document of these festivities, it is possible to judge something of Bramante's resounding success (28). He had shown a great control of internal space in the church, and he demonstrated an even more prodigious control of external space in the garden.

Immensely influential among Bramante's later works is the Palazzo Caprini, often called the House of Raphael, purchased by Raphael in 1517 (29). Although the exact date of construction is uncertain (circa 1510), and the structure is completely destroyed, the building is known primarily from Lafrery's engraving of 1549—a representation so decisive that effectively one can believe that the building still exists, and which makes entirely comprehensible the almost obsessive attraction, which it exerted for so many generations of architects.

The essential contribution of the Palazzo Caprini to the design of palaces is the conception of its facade in plastic, three-dimensional terms. It is both elementary and highly assertive, while it has the simplest of thematic materials. There are two major floors—a *piano rustico* of shops with mezzanines, and a *piano nobile*, the owner's residence, where the counterpart to the Doric order in the Tempietto can be found. These two floors are sharply characterized and equipped. Upstairs the Doric order suggests the attributes of intellect while downstairs the rustication alludes to a personality of a more primitive dispensation. In no cinquecento palace is there such a distinct contrast between the supporting and supported, in Marxist terms between the structure and superstructure. Most surprisingly, in this most emphatic of facades, it was built with neither stone nor brick but with rubble masonry stuccoed over to achieve the desired textures and contrasts.

28 Vatican, Cortile del Belvedere, woodcut by Master H.C.B.,
    showing a tournament in the Cortile del Belvedere
29 Bramante: Rome, Palazzo Caprini, circa 1510
30 Bramante and Cola da Caprarola (?): Todi,
    S Maria della Consolazione, begun 1508

28

29

30

There is some commentary here on what might be called the willfulness of Bramante's late style. Ostensibly, the Palazzo Caprini is obedient to the properties of logic, but its minor elements are subject to the rhetorical exaggerations of which its architect dictated. Other evidence suggests that Bramante designed a more extravagant basement than Lafrery had chosen to illustrate. There are local idiosyncrasies. For example, the coupled keystones above the shops are suggestive of the more "licentious" dispositions of Giulio, just as their arrangement reveals no structural function. Bramante emerges as a master dialectician. Up above, it seems he is content to offer correctness, but down below, he is working to make it all so strange.

The Palazzo Caprini, for all its revolutionary content, was not later copied in Rome. It enjoyed a brief success—in the Jacopo da Brescia, Alberini, and Vidoni-Caffarelli palaces. But after Giulio's Palazzo Maccarani (begun circa 1520–21), in terms of Roman taste, the Caprini came to be eclipsed by the prototype of Antonio da Sangallo the Younger's much more modest and astylar Palazzo Baldassini—a model which prevailed in Rome until the late nineteenth century. In other words, the facade of the Palazzo Caprini became an export item, Roman culture for the provinces, and in this way, with regional variations, it was proliferated by Sanmicheli in Verona (Palazzo Pompei), Palladio in Vicenza (Palazzo Porto), and an unknown architect in Florence (Palazzo Uguccioni). Also, the building's style crossed over into the English speaking world where, because of a passion for columns, until the impact of modern architecture, it was to remain the very best idea for a highly respectable bank.

The impact of Bramante's architecture on his Roman contemporaries was immediate and profound. S. Maria della Consolazione in Todi (begun 1508), one of the numerous centrally planned churches constructed to house a miracle working image, evokes several aspects of Bramante's architecture (30). Typically understood as a simplification of his plan for St. Peter's, there is evidence for Bramante's participation in its design at some level. The design, after all, has much in common with the Leonardesque themes that Bramante brought with him from Milan. Above all, the Consolazione's pristine combination of cube, drum, dome, and apses shows its origins in the sketches by Leonardo that were central to his development as an architect. Placed as it is on a rough terrace below the town, the church nevertheless commands a sublime landscape and diffuses its influence throughout that landscape. It is a far more poignant evocation of Leonardesque themes than was possible in Lombardy during Bramante's middle age, and in its three-dimensional solids and monumental voids, the church embodies those ideals that differentiated the cinquecento from the quattrocento. On the other hand, S. Maria della Consolazione evinces many unsolved questions: its authorship is not clear; its construction and subsequent modifications continued into the next century; and only the apse containing the image is semicircular. Though in most respects the ideas of Bramante are undeniably present, the flaccid orders on the exterior of this otherwise impressive church suggests that he may not have participated directly in its execution.

$\widetilde{45}$

It logically follows that Bramante worked out ideas for St. Peter's in his own commissions. The church of SS. Celso e Giuliano in Banchi (begun 1509), whose plan was a reduced, more abstract version of St. Peter's, was never completed and later demolished. More significant in this respect is the choir of S. Maria del Popolo (1508–09), which was also a mortuary chapel containing tombs of two cardinals from the Sforza and delle Rovere families (31). In this design, Bramante transformed the original cross-vaulted choir into a telescoping sequence of rectangular spaces covered by barrel vaults, a domical vault, and an apsidal semi-dome.

The choir has become an extension of the nave, and the effect of the ensemble is undeniably similar to Piero della Francesca's *Madonna and Child with Saints and Donor* (the "Brera Altarpiece"), which Bramante would have seen in its original setting in Francesco di Giorgio's church of S. Bernardino just outside Urbino (32). It shows figures within an intimate yet monumental interior, dominated by an important shell from which an egg is suspended. Though a jewel case in its dimensions, it may be suggestive about what Alberti had begun at S. Andrea in Mantua. But in the apse and preceding choir of S. Maria del Popolo, the picture's quattrocento detail has disappeared and everything has been heroically enlarged in scale and brutally abstracted into weighty masses, as if cut by some gigantic chisel. If the tendency in architectural backgrounds (like those of Piero) was to emphasize the episodic, the monochromatic effect of the choir delineates the unity of its diverse parts. Bramante, then, has seen Piero with new eyes conditioned by the choir in his early schemes for St. Peter's, whose plan Bramante's executed choir resembles.

31   Bramante: Rome, S. Maria del Popolo, choir, 1508–09
32   Piero della Francesca: *Madonna and Child with Saints and Donor,*
      after 1472. Also known as "Brera Altarpiece".

31

32

Of Bramante's Roman projects, the choir of S. Maria del Popolo is the only church interior that was completed and survives intact. The events that led Bramante to this dramatic solution can be traced to his work as a painter of architectural backgrounds, and there were three essential sources—Piero della Francesca in Urbino; to some extent Andrea Mantegna in Padua; and to a very great extent, Leonardo da Vinci in Milan. Then, as an architect, Bramante progressively emancipated himself from these controls, though his Milanese buildings illustrate his continuing ties with Leonardo. Finally, he is called into prominence by the political and religious ambitions of Julius, assuming the independence still visible in the Tempietto and the choir of S. Maria del Popolo.

Having already identified three painters who influenced his architecture, might not we add a fourth? All we need to do is look at Raphael's figures with their intense spiraling motion and see in them the anticipation of the more amplified solids of Bramante's buildings. In the end, Bramante had begun to take hints from his junior by more than forty years, the painter who became his chosen successor at St. Peter's.

47

"Let us enjoy the papacy since God has given it to us."

ATTRIBUTED TO LEO X BY MARINO GIORGI

3
ARCHITECTURE *and the*
PAPACY *of* LEO X

In the next decade, Bramante's preeminence in S. Maria del Popolo was challenged by a project that represented a remarkably different approach toward antiquity than that of his choir. The funerary chapel for the immensely wealthy Sienese banker Agostino Chigi, designed by Raphael in 1513, the year of the election of Pope Leo X (1513–21), is located on the north aisle of the church (33). From the outset, Raphael had intended the plan to be a reduction of the crossing of St. Peter's as begun by Bramante. Like its model, it is composed primarily of a dome and its drum, which are supported by pendentives and crossing piers. To Raphael, however, it was insufficient to merely repeat a structural and spatial conceit invented by the architect whom he would succeed as the architect of St. Peter's. Raphael was intimately familiar with the Pantheon, as indicated by his often illustrated drawing of its interior, and it was the arrangement of pier pilasters in the vestibule of the ancient monument that Raphael was to repeat in the chapel. Alternative proposals employed attached columns as enframement for its proscenium-like entry, but their omission in the executed design dramatically changed the observer's relationship to the intimate space. By placing the pilasters squarely on the chapel's floor, as in the Pantheon, and not on tall bases, as at St. Peter's, the chapel's tombs, statuary, and image of the Creator were immediately accessible to the observer. In doing so, Raphael heightened the distinction between the interior of the chapel and that of the church. Unlike Bramante's choir, which still retains an external viewpoint derived from quattrocento perspective painting, Raphael's chapel is understandable only to an individual who stood inside.

The contrast could not be greater in the effect of their materials. The choir, though constructed of brick and stucco, gives the effect of great scale and the implacable density of mass that was the lesson learned from antiquity by Bramante. Raphael's chapel, on the other hand, employs a rich arrangement of shapes and material to give the effect of an intimate interior revealed by light and color. No doubt the sumptuous materials—Carrara marble for the piers, red Portrasanta and dark Africano marbles for the cladding and the tombs, Oriental granite for the threshold, bronze reliefs for the tombs, and mosaic for the dome—were as emblematic of the banker's wealth as they were of Raphael's desire to fabricate a modern chapel as it might have been done in antiquity. If the architecture in Bramante's choir was meant to culminate a grand vista commencing far back in the church's nave, the Chigi Chapel's architecture serves as the frame for a personal vision culminating in an image of the Creator in a fictive oculus.

To call Raphael's architecture "classical," as is customarily done, is just as insufficient as it would be to characterize his achievement as a painter's approach to architecture. Although both Bramante and Raphael were originally trained as painters, it cannot be denied that Raphael was introduced to architecture through painting and apprehended architecture in a fundamentally pictorial way. To understand this, we must we must first gain knowledge of the role of architecture in the cultural priorities of Leo X.

Leo X was the heir to two distinct forms of artistic patronage. As Giovanni de'Medici (born 1475), the second son of Lorenzo the Magnificent, the future Leo X was a spectator to the last great period of Florentine cultural hegemony. As the successor to Julius II, he was fully aware of how the bold scale of Bramante's architecture could embody the imperial ambitions of the papacy. Yet, he was even more fully aware of his Florentine heritage and family responsibilities. Although his teachers included the poet Angelo Poliziano, and the philosophers Pico della Mirandola and Marsilio Ficino, the young Giovanni was destined at an early age for a career in the church. It had been made clear to him that the purpose of his career was to advance the reputation of his family in the theater of European politics. In this, Giovanni did not fail.

Thus, Medicean ambition led to his appointment by Pope Innocent VIII (1484–92) as a cardinal. After a period of travel in Germany, Netherlands, and France during the exile of his brother Piero (1499), the first Medici cardinal settled in the family residence near the Piazza Navona in Rome. His success in leading the Florentine partisans of the exiled Medici led to further positions of responsibility under Julius II, after whose death he was elected Pope. The election of Leo X was universally acclaimed, and there were great expectations of the youthful Pope. Most of all, Leo X's temperament was taken as a welcome change from the unpredictable, bellicose Julius II. The sentiments were best expressed by the ambassador of Emperor Maximilian, Alberto Pio di Carpi: "The

Pope … will act as a gentle lamb rather than as a fierce lion, and he will be a promoter of peace rather than of war. He will fulfill his duties consciously."

That Leo X enjoyed the papacy cannot be doubted, even if the veracity of the famous quotation attributed to the Venetian Ambassador Marino Giorgi has been called into question. No other Pope surrounded himself with musicians, poets, orators, and men of letters to the degree that he did. That Leo X genuinely loved learning is shown by the presence of the humanist Pietro Bembo and the playwright Cardinal Bibbiena as among his confidantes at the papal court. Music was a particular passion of the Pope, who had been trained in composition by the composer Heinrich Issac, and skilled musicians were even awarded religious benefices. Every October, he went hunting with members of the papal court at La Magliana, the papal hunting lodge, and during the remainder of the year, sumptuous banquets highlighted by buffoonery were given in the Vatican.

As a patron of the visual arts, Leo X preferred to follow patterns established by Julius II. In large part, this was determined by those projects left incomplete by Julius II, which then took on different directions reflecting the new Pope's own character. It is not surprising that a leisure-loving and sybaritic pontiff continued the decoration of the papal apartments in which he and his humanist cronies would spend much time. The primary beneficiary of Leo's cultural generosity was Raphael, whose frescoes in the Stanza d'Eliodoro and the Stanza dell'Incendio were the greatest artistic achievements of a papacy immersed in all of the arts. Responding to a request by the Pope in 1515, Raphael continued the redecoration of the Sistine Chapel with his designs for ten tapestries for the lower walls of the chapel that were woven in Brussels and in place by 1519. Similarly, Raphael also completed the logge overlooking the Cortile di San Damaso, which he and his assistants decorated with scenes from the Bible. Yet, Leo's reputation for extravagance masks a streak of common sense; he displayed no interest in completing most schemes hatched by Julius II and Bramante. Instead, Leo chose to focus his architectural patronage at the Vatican on St. Peter's, a task rendered necessary by Bramante's reckless destruction of the old basilica and subsequent difficulties in celebrating Mass, especially on festival days such as Christmas and Easter.

53

URBANISM
~

Leo X inherited from his predecessor a desire to execute grand urban designs. Under Bramante's supervision, two new straight streets already had been laid out: the Via Giulia, a thoroughfare running from the Banchi to the Ponte Sisto; and the Via della Lungara, on the opposite side of the Tiber, followed a course from the Vatican's Porta Santo Spirito to the Porta Settimiana in Trastevere and the harbor beyond (171). By virtue of their locations, the projects were appendages to Rome rather than transformations of her urban structure. They also bore the same arbitrary and impetuous patronage that can bee seen in other schemes initiated by Julius II and Bramante, and neither was completed during the lifetime of the patron or architect.

Leo X, however, sought to restructure the city by focusing on the central portion of the Campo Marzio, the area between the Pantheon and the Piazza Navona. Prior to his election, Leo lived in the Medici's Roman palace, which stood on the site of the present-day Palazzo Madama one block east of the Piazza Navona. But as Pope, one of Leo's first architectural commissions was Giuliano da Sangallo's grandiose project for a new Medicean residence employing the Piazza Navona as an extension of its design (34). With the combination of a palace and a circus, the proposal exuded an aura of ancient authority in its recollection of the imperial residences on the Palatine and in Constantinople. The Piazza Navona was to have been reshaped into a symmetrical design with hemicyles at each end by usurping the public space of the square and transforming it into the appendage of a private residence. The palace's axial arrangement suggested the classical atrium, peristyle courtyard, and garden of a large Roman house of the sort reconstructed by Fra Giocondo in his 1511 edition of Vitruvius. In form and content, it was a palace fit for the family of a Christian emperor.

Yet the idea of a new center around the Roman palace of Florence's most celebrated family was not forgotten by Leo X. Giuliano's project was also taken up by his nephew, Antonio da Sangallo the Younger, who prepared rough sketches for a structure designed around twin courtyards. Around this core other Leonine or Medicean commissions began to establish a visible and definable Medici district that encompassed almost the entire area between the Pantheon and the Piazza Navona at the southern end of the Via di

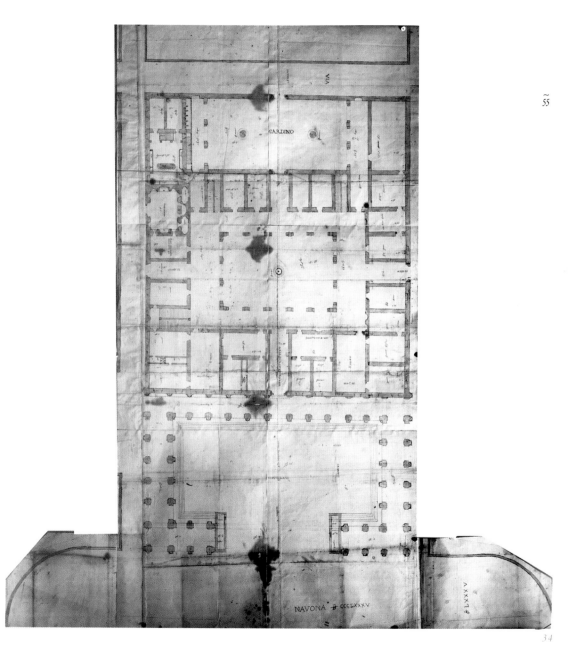

Ripetta. Just to the south, was the the Roman university, to which the Pope gave important privileges to accommodate its greatly expanded faculty. The university's eastern elevation was meant to look out on a new square, the Piazza della Dogana. On this square, the area's Medicean identity was advanced by the construction of a second palace, the Palazzo Medici-Lante, which was commissioned by Alfonsina Orsini, the mother of the Pope's nephew, Lorenzo. Other nearby buildings with Medicean connections included the hospital S. Giacomo in Augusta (which was remodeled by the Pope in 1516) and the French national church, S. Luigi di Francesi. By extending the Via di Ripetta (which was initially begun by Julius II) and the Via della Scrofa, this zone was directly accessible to diplomatic visitors who would normally enter the city through the Porta del Popolo. Similar motivations also led to Leonardo da Vinci's proposal for the reorganization of the Medici quarter in Florence (circa 1515), accommodating on a single square Michelozzo's quattrocento palace, a new palatial residence opposite it, and the church of S. Lorenzo with its new facade. Yet this scheme to memorialize the Medicean return to power, like that of the villa, required financial resources that would have outstripped those of Leo X, and when the presumed occupant of the Roman palace (the Pope's brother Giuliano) died in 1516, all of the reasons to create the Medici quarter disappeared as well.

ARCHITECTURAL PAINTING

Architectural historians of the Roman High Renaissance are curiously ambivalent about the relationship of architecture to the other arts. Architectural documentation in the form of buildings, drawings, or writings are discussed as independent phenomena, and their relationship to painting and how the imaginary architectural constructions of paintings and frescoes may have influenced the designs for real buildings is rarely considered. Such distinctions between the arts would have mattered little to Bramante, Michelangelo, or Raphael, all of whom had considerable experience as painters or sculptors before taking up careers in architecture. In fact, the most compelling architectural spaces created with the patronage of Leo X were painted rather than built.

The union of architecture and perspective painting originates in Urbino, where Raphael was born at around Easter in 1483. To be certain, the greatest achievements of quattrocento Urbino were to prove central in Raphael's training as a painter, and later, as an architect of distinction. But times had changed. Federico da Montefeltro had died in 1482, and Duke Guidobaldo, Federico's son and successor, had to fend off the ambitions of Cesare Borgia, who annexed the city in 1502, and removed some of its artistic patrimony.

Raphael's first experiences with architecture came through the absorption of painted architectural backgrounds and actual buildings. If the earliest years of Raphael's career are still unclear, the lessons learned from the works of Perugino (1446–1524) are manifest. In the paintings executed prior to Raphael's arrival in Rome around 1508, gentle landscapes contain buildings of a decidedly Gothic appearance, as if the buildings of the Rhineland had been transported to Umbria. Although this type of building was to occupy the canvases of contemporary Venetian painters such as Giovanni Bellini, they are also found in the background landscapes of Perugino's altarpieces. Nor did Raphael fail to be impressed by the buildings he saw around Urbino. For example, Francesco di Giorgio's mausoleum church for Federico da Montefeltro, S. Bernardino, appears in the background of the *Small Cowper Madonna* in Washington. Similarly, the austere architecture of the *Ansidei Madonna* in London's National Gallery appears as if the Cappella del Perdono in the Ducal Palace was shorn of its ornamentation.

What differentiates Perugino's painted architecture from that of Raphael is the essentially static quality of its forms. In the *Christ Giving the Keys to Saint Peter* (1481) in the Sistine Chapel (35), Perugino creates a vast perspective space with a frieze-like grouping of main figures in the foreground, clusters of figures in the receding middle ground, and three structures—two triumphant arches and an octagonal temple with four porticoes—at the rear. A similar compositional structure was employed in *Marriage of the Virgin* (1499–1504) where a similar structure with an octagonal plan and four small porticoes dominates its vertical altarpiece format. Here, the incredibly austere architecture of the temple avoids the polychromy of its predecessor, maintains an organic link with its figures, and dominates the altarpiece by exaggerating its vertical dimension as demanded by the tall format of the altarpiece. Yet in both pictures architecture is remote, as if the building did little more than to mark a predetermined mathematical recession.

In contrast, Raphael's architecture actively engages the spectator. Attention to the visual apprehension of a building is demonstrated by the justifiably famous sixteen-sided temple in his *Marriage of the Virgin* (1504). Unlike his mentor, Raphael has created a convincing vision of a building that separates it from the realm of background architecture (36). Its exterior is not a planar surface but a complex assemblage of architectural membering fully developed in light and shade. For instance, the angular piers on the lower level respond to the radial transverse ribs of the loggia's vaulting, while, on the upper level, pilasters fold around the angles of the polygon. In concept and detail, Raphael's temple is architecturally credible and has the same fully three-dimensional presence that appears in his Madonna figures of the same moment. But what truly puts this temple apart from other painted buildings is how the observer's glance is drawn into the picture by the concave arrangement of its main figures, emphatically continued by their gestures, and led to the vanishing point far in the distance through an open door. By accommodating the panel's original position some six feet off the ground, the viewer thus looks not at the architecture but sequentially up, into, and through the structure as it were. Raphael's pictorial system thus simulates the viewer's presence within an actual space, just as he was to structure the viewer's perception of the Chigi Chapel a few years later.

When Raphael arrived in Rome around 1508, he had already acquired a sensitivity to architecture. What he lacked in built works was compensated by artistic and intellectual skills. Raphael's inquiring mind was capable of both appreciating Bramante and offering an alternative to the aggressive classicism of his buildings. At the same time, Raphael would acquire a knowledge of ancient architecture in its entirety, a knowledge so detailed and penetrating that he would attempt to re-create in the Villa Madama an entire ancient environment—architecture, decoration, landscape, and building use.

This time, the groundwork was laid in an ongoing decorative project, the Vatican Stanze. The commission to decorate the square—squat official chambers forming the papal apartments—proved to be an architectural laboratory of sorts. The immediate impact of Roman

35 Perugino: *Christ Giving the Keys to St. Peter*, 1481
36 Raphael: *Marriage of the Virgin*, 1504

35

36

37   Raphael: *School of Athens*, 1510–12
38   Raphael: *Fire in the Borgo*, circa 1516–17

37

38

architecture and landscape can be seen in the *Disputa* (1509–10), a religious allegory of the concept of transubstantiation. Although architecture is not visibly present, it has structured the entire scene, which resembles a monumental apse with its architecture removed. The countryside beyond this imaginary apse also shows a typically Roman landscape, now filled with vernacular buildings of the kind found around Rome. To the right, behind the figures of Sixtus IV and Dante, Raphael shows us the fragment of a great pedestal of the kind Bramante was building in the nave in St. Peter's. Raphael's figures had now acquired a monumentality and grace; they simply needed an architecture to match.

61

Raphael's responses to this challenge followed in succession. In the *School of Athens* (1510–12), he turned to classical architecture of the past and present and to modify it to suit his own pictorial needs (37). When the cartoon for this masterpiece was prepared, the background architecture had not been fixed. As such, the imaginary architectural interior was designed as the perfect foil for the central figures of Plato, Aristotle, and the other Greek philosophers. For all the familiarity of its grand sequence of two barrel-vaulted "naves" broken by a dome supported by pediments, the plan and design of this imaginary space cannot be determined with any exactitude. For instance, do similar barrel vaults intersect with the dome, and what is the extent of architectural enclosure surrounding the figures in the foreground? Vasari has suggested that the design was prepared with the assistance of Bramante, whose centralized plan for St. Peter's it vaguely resembles. Yet when compared to this presumed source, Raphael's design is smaller in size, employs a different order set on higher bases that are more widely spaced, and makes greater use of ancient sculpture by placing it in every visible niche. There are also similarities in the pattern of its coffering to the Basilica of Maxentius, and in a more general way, to ancient baths in its suggestion of scale and grandeur. The incongruity of placing Greek philosophers in a setting so visibly inspired by ancient Rome perfectly fulfilled the myth of modern Rome as the Athens of the new era.

In the last years of the papacy of Julius II, Raphael began to decorate the Stanza of Heliodorus, the chamber that evidently served as audience chamber. The decorations in this room were full of movement and illustrated scenes that were inherently dramatic in content.

The architecture of the decoration that gives its name to the room, the *Expulsion of Heliodorus* (1512–13), is more evocative and less distinct than the *School of Athens*.

For a second time, Raphael turned to a rhythmic alternation of domes and barrel vaults as his main architectural concept, but now he achieved completely different results with it. Emphasis is now given to three domed units whose arrangement recalls Fra Giocondo's Venetianizing plan for St. Peter's. The sources of its color-drenched light are hidden and numerous, and a mysterious radiance seems to emanate from the barrel vaults. Thematically, there was no need to include ancient statuary in niches, and consequently, the piers and their attached columns are boldly three dimensional. If the fresco is dramatic and somewhat incoherent, its architecture is structurally implausible, as indicated by the use of columns rather than pendentives to support a circular dome placed over a square bay. This curious detail was suggested by the corner columns in the crossing of S. Bernardino in Urbino, which play an emphatic structural role by supporting a shallow domical vault. Raphael, on the other hand, deliberately committed an architectural solecism to enhance the pictorial logic of a dramatic composition.

By the time Raphael prepared the design for the *Fire in the Borgo* (1516–17), the primary fresco in the Stanza dell'Incendio (38), he had become an architect in the commonly accepted sense of the term. The work subject matter demanded the depiction of an actual location, and even though this led to the inclusion of fragments from ancient, Early Christian, and contemporary buildings, the design was never merely archaeological in content. The somber yet dramatic arrangement of architectural forms gives the fresco a sense of drama, suggesting that Raphael sought to emulate the Tragic Scene as described by Vitruvius in his treatise. The palace from which Leo IV (who is given the appearance of Leo X) gives a benediction is modeled on the Palazzo Caprini, which Raphael purchased in October 1517, as his own residence. Yet in the fresco, Bramante's design was transformed into a structure with overt papal associations by its position in front of Old St. Peter's, the omission of shops, and the inclusion of a loggia inspired by the window of the Sala Regia in the Vatican Palace. By including the horizontal rustication and the aedicular window on the palace's side facade from his design for the Palazzo Jacopo da Brescia, Raphael attests to the significance of the palaces he designed for sites in the Borgo. In many ways, the *Fire in the Borgo* is Raphael's most sublime architectural creation, freed as it was from the constraints imposed on architects. It was in paint, rather than in the ill-fated schemes for St. Peter's, that Raphael made his greatest impact on the architecture of the Vatican area.

SAINT PETER'S
~

Under Leo X, the design for St. Peter's proceeded by trial and compromise. For liturgical reasons, the new Pope was committed to the adoption of a longitudinal plan and willing to triple the funds allotted to its construction. During his reign, a bewildering variety of variants on this theme was produced by Bramante, Raphael, Giuliano da Sangallo, and Antonio da Sangallo the Younger, to name only four of the most significant architects employed by the Fabbrica di S. Pietro. Yet unlike other artistic endeavors, where Raphael was firmly in control, its architects had to consider the immense scale of St. Peter's, the inheritance of Bramante's designs, dissension in the workshop, and the Pope's own indecision. Lacking funding and clear direction, the project became a ship without a defined course and lacked a captain at the helm.

Bramante still had a year to live when Leo X was elected Pope, and his impact was substantial. With Bramante's age and incapacitated body in mind, Leo X appointed Fra Giocondo to a position of virtual equality at the head of the workshop. There were other reasons for the Pope's selection. Fra Giocondo was regarded as a specialist in building techniques who could solve problems in vaulting the church, and the experienced Giuliano was a trustworthy Florentine. In 1513, Bramante prepared a longitudinal design for Leo X, which in turn was modeled on a similar layout that he had proposed in 1506. What was noteworthy about the new project was the placement of ambulatories around the arms of the transepts, the elimination of the tomb for Julius II, and a portico of giant columns three bays deep that was inspired by the temples of antiquity.

At the time of Bramante's death in April 1514, Raphael was regarded as Bramante's hand-picked successor, having gained recognition as a professional architect without having completed a major project. Although Raphael was to accept most of the ideas found in Bramante's final design, it is surprising in the degree that he departed from it in a search for a more harmonious and balanced composition. Bramante's plans were always hierarchical in the repetition of elements that built up diagonally to the crossing. Raphael's project of 1514, known only from an illustration by Serlio in the *Third Book*, folio 37, is rigidly axial in the organization of its spaces. In this scheme, Bramante's choir is replaced by a third arm of the crossing, and with the exception of the projecting ambulatories, all elements of the plan fit neatly into a rectangular enclosure.

Raphael's second thoughts on St. Peter's, which date from 1516–18, show a greater engagement with the architecture of both Roman and Christian eras. By now, Raphael had acquired a deep, even scholarly knowledge of antiquity, and among the wealth of historical references two stand out (39). First-hand knowledge of mural structures such as the Pantheon or the ancient baths suggested a new emphasis on the bulk and mass of the enclosing wall. Second, the great scale of this enclosure is complemented by the columns of Old St. Peter's reutilized in the ambulatories and vestibule's lower orders on the facade. Yet for all its devotion to antiquity, the scheme retains a curiously Gothic effect with its long, dark nave and the fortress-like projections of its twin bell towers and sacristies.

For these very reasons, Raphael's second scheme did not appeal to Antonio da Sangallo the Younger, who in many ways was his collaborator in the St. Peter's workshop. Sometime around 1520, he prepared a brief memorandum summarizing Raphael's final project, which gained approval shortly before his death. To criticize Raphael was a bold if not foolish act, and no doubt Sangallo must have hoped that the Pope would change his mind in favor of one of his schemes. But he also had valid architectural reasons to proceed in this way. In Sangallo's eyes, the nave was like an alleyway—tall, narrow, and grotesque. Furthermore, the chapels were not sufficiently large and there were questions about the ability of the piers to carry the heavy dome.

Raphael's failure to achieve his goals of unity and harmony was in part a failure of his working method. In a letter addressed to Leo X (1519), Raphael describes a wide range of his activities, including his idea of creating a topographical map of ancient Rome. One section of the letter specifically addresses the graphic concerns of professional architects, and here he argues for the use of orthogonal plans, sections, and elevation in the description of buildings. While this document is arguably among the most important in the history

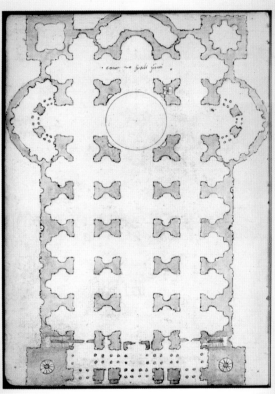

40 Raphael and others: Rome, Villa Madama, begun circa 1516,
    mid-eighteenth-century view by J-B. Lallemand
41 Rome, Villa Madama, plan drawn by A. da Sangallo the Younger
    after Raphael

40

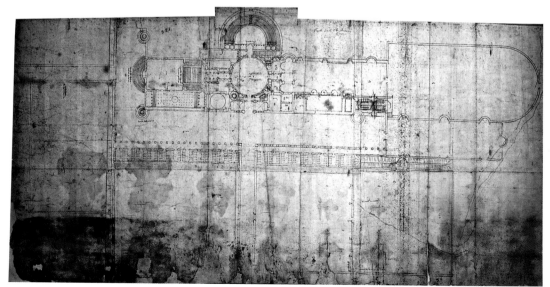

41

of building representation, it also presents limitations to designers. As Raphael describes it, this system of representation is based on parallel vertical and horizontal lines drawn on common bases to denote congruent dimensions. In plans, the system tends to promote modular elements, while in orthogonal sections and elevations, it invites corresponding (or nearly corresponding) dimensions through the use of horizontal lines parallel to the ground plane and the addition of multiple stories. With the accretion of horizontal zones or layers, as Raphael does especially in his elevation for the 1518 project, size is achieved only at the loss of a diminution of its scale. This same problem was also to plague Sangallo the Younger's wooden model of his project for St. Peter's and to precipitate Michelangelo's criticism of it.

THE VILLA MADAMA

Leo X's goal of creating a refined antiquarian culture is expressed best in the Villa Madama. Despite its fame and influence, its history is still blurred and unsettled. It was the most ambitious secular project begun during an uncommonly secular papacy. Its origins are read through tantalizingly few original sources—a handful of architectural drawings, its fragmentary remains, and a long letter written by Raphael that gives a guided tour of the villa as if it were complete. Nominally, its patron was Cardinal Giulio de'Medici, the Pope's cousin. However, in a larger sense it was a papal and even a Medicean project, as indicated by its design, the funds from the papal treasury that paid for it, and the continuing interest of Leo X in its development. Raphael's authority as the Villa Madama's architect has always remained unquestioned, yet throughout its brief but intense development, he was aided by members of the Sangallo clan, his collaborators on St. Peter's. In actuality, the villa defies conventional terms of artistic authorship, evolving as it did into a kind of *gesamtkunstwerk* that was continued by Antonio da Sangallo the Younger, Giulio Romano, and Giovanni da Udine after Raphael's death. Taken as a whole, the Villa Madama was intended to merge architecture, decorative arts, garden design, and performing arts into a single environment where living *all'antica* could be experienced to the fullest.

To fully understand the designs for the Villa Madama one must also understand its setting in the Roman landscape (40). Raphael's unfinished architectural masterpiece was begun circa 1516 on a site on the southeast slope of the Monte Mario, almost 3 kilometers due north of the Vatican across the open fields, or Prati. The location was a splendid one, with magnificent views across the Tiber Valley and back in the direction of Rome. In his letter, Raphael notes that the villa's orientation was also especially salubrious, with a loggia sheltered from the sun and separate suites of rooms for use in summer and winter. In spite of the precipitous slope, the Villa Madama was easily accessible from three directions—by a road leading directly up the hill from the Ponte Molle (the ancient Pons Milvius) and the Tiber, by another road from the Vatican, and by a third road from the direction of Viterbo over the hill to the northwest. Any extension along the remaining direction was contracted by a ravine that cut into Monte Mario. To Raphael and his collaborators, the topography of the immediate area around Monte Mario suggested the Villa Madama's hallmark arrangement—a cross-axial, asymmetrical grouping of spaces that is found in the various plans for the villa.

Raphael made three differing proposals for the Villa Madama, two of which are recorded in plans drawn by his collaborators and the third described in the letter. Common to each of the schemes is an axial arrangement of open and closed volumes set in a rectangular enclosure raised on a substructure set along the contours of Monte Mario. In spite of the difficulties posed by its hillside site, the villa was surprisingly accessible. Each of its three approaches offered visitors a different experience of the complex. Those arriving from the Viterbo road would descend into the villa's main courtyard through a Roman theater, seeing across the villa's roof a series of landscaped terraces set in a vast setting. From this direction, the villa proper was nearly invisible, without any architectural facade or indication of the complex's full size or design. By contrast, the principal approach from the Vatican was more stately, gently rising to a Doric portal flanked by impressive circular towers. The spaces beyond would have been a spectacular arrangement of open and closed volumes: an open rectangular court followed by a three-aisle vestibule; a narrow vaulted atrium; a second open court; another atrium, the impressive garden loggia; and finally, a garden terrace overlooking the fishpond and the Tiber Valley in the distance.

The approach from the Ponte Molle was meant to be truly impressive. From a distance, the visitor would see the villa's facade, a composition almost 200 meters long built up out of towers, closed blocks, and open spaces arranged on a manmade terrace. Parallel to the dominant axis formed by the roadway leading up the Monte Mario to the villa, a series of three differently shaped garden terraces would have established a meaningful relationship between the villa and the surrounding landscape. After passing stables for four hundred horses, the visitor would then come to the hippodrome, a grassed area in front of the villa for equestrian exercise. However, a differ-ence of 9 meters in the villa's levels created a planning challenge in achieving a coherent sequence of spaces on two floors. In addition to the kitchen and other rooms for servants, the lower level contained facilities for bathing with two pools—a smaller one with warm water and second large enough for swimming in cold water. The experi-ence formed by the contrast of these relatively smaller and darker chambers below with the open court above could not have been greater and more emphatic. Thus, by the simple device of contrasting shape and scale, the majesty of the Villa Madama was revealed.

The change from a rectangular to circular courtyard is what dif-ferentiates the initial scheme drawn by Giovanfrancesco da Sangallo for Raphael from the plan drawn by Antonio da Sangallo the Younger and from the villas described in Raphael's letter (41). Numerous reasons have been given for this, all of which are plausi-ble. Raphael's letter describes the Villa Madama in terms similar to Pliny the Younger's Laurentine villa, and it has been suggested that the circular court resulted from an error in identifying as an O a courtyard that was actually in the shape of the letter D. Circular courtyards could also be found in theoretical drawings by Francesco di Giorgio, Mantegna's house in Mantua, Bramante's unbuilt enclo-sure for the Tempietto, and the so-called Maritime Theater at Hadrian's Villa, which Raphael was among the very first to study. But the most compelling reason for the courtyard's distinctive shape was a purely architectural one. It formally resolves the intersection of four axes different in length and design, and its compelling centrality is appropriate to its function in the villa's plan.

Although it is never stated in the letter and other written sources, Raphael likely conceived of the Villa Madama as a critique of Bramante's architecture. Individual elements such as the villa's loggias were inspired by Bramante's Nympheum at Genazzano but now incorporated into a structured composition. Quite unlike Bramante's view of nature, which in the Cortile del Belvedere was limited to the area enclosed by its lateral corridors, the Villa Madama invites views to the surrounding environment and embraces vistas all the way to the Apennines beyond. And if the Cortile del Belvedere evoked the power of a single perspective in its view from the papal apartments, the spatial experience of the Villa Madama was established by individual units that never fully revealed the totality of the design. For this reason, the visual impact of its plan is closer to ancient Roman examples where spaces are understood by successively moving on, off, and around an axis never totally traversed *along* its length. To Bramante, antiquity was only a means of surpassing the achievements of the Caesars; to Leo X and Raphael, the evocation of ancient Rome through its architecture was an end unto itself.

Only a small fragment of the Villa Madama was built before Raphael's death. The completion of the garden loggia's decoration fell to Giulio Romano and Giovanni da Udine, whose frescoes and stuccowork harmonize with the antiquarian spirit of the building. After Cardinal Giulio's election to the papacy as Clement VII (1523–34), the completion of the Villa Madama was abandoned in favor of projects in Florence. Much to the distress of the second Medici Pope, what remained of the Villa Madama was set afire by allies of Charles V during the Sack of Rome in 1527. Subsequently, the villa passed on to the Medici, and it was in honor of Margarita of Austria, the widow of Duke Alessandro de'Medici, that the villa was given the name Villa Madama. The villa remained in Medici hands until 1555 when Catherine de'Medici, Queen of France, ceded ownership to Cardinal Alessandro Farnese.

If the Villa Madama had been completed, daily life within it would have alternated between private enjoyment and ostentatious public display. Although our knowledge of the villa's use remains incomplete, it was likely designed as a *hospitium*, a place where important visitors and their entourages would prepare for their ceremonial entry into Rome. What matters most is that this purpose was made manifest in its cross-axial plans. Access to two of the major roadways approaching Rome from the north was incorporated into its plan, and its vast stables could accommodate the large retinue that traveled with kings, dukes, or their ambassadors. After refreshing themselves in the baths, the most important members of the traveling court would enjoy a few days of papal hospitality and take in the villa's many delights before departing for Rome in the late afternoon. By sunset, they would enter the private world of the Vatican, to the amazement and wonder of all present.

In spite of its obvious debts to antiquity, the Villa Madama was never really a Roman villa in the modern meaning of the term. It bore no resemblance whatsoever to structures with porticoes flanked by towers, the ubiquitous villa form that had been employed in the Villa Belvedere and the Villa Farnesina. Nor could it accommodate the functions found in most Roman villas. Clearly lacking any agricultural facilities, the Villa Madama was too large to be a bucolic refuge for a member of the clerical aristocracy, such as the Casino of Cardinal Bessarion. It also lacked the extensive grounds of a hunting retreat such as La Magliana, which was greatly expanded during the reign of Julius II and regularly visited by Leo X. In formal terms, Raphael's design closely resembled Florentine examples such as Michelozzo's Villa Medici at Fiesole, which probably inspired its hillside site, garden loggia and terraces, and location of services in its substructure.

In many respects, Raphael's initial design for the Villa Madama evokes in particular one exurban building type, the *casale*. In Lazio and other regions of Italy, a *casale* was an enclosed structure where the residences of a landowner and his agricultural laborers were grouped around an open court. Essentially a fortified farm, it often employed crenellation or towers on its exteriors. In his letter, Raphael echoes the medievalizing exterior of this building type, stating that the most striking feature of the villa's approach from the Vatican was its round towers, which contribute to both its beauty and defense. Leo X, Cardinal Giulio, and Raphael would have known of the building type from one of its derivatives, the hunting lodge at La Magliana, which is similarly organized around a single rectangular courtyard (42). Evidently, the Pope wanted something both familiar and ancient in the Villa Madama, and its similarities to the *casale* type is, in fact, some of the most compelling evidence for his participation in its planning. Consequently, the challenges that Raphael faced were clear and numerous—reversing the inward orientation of the *casale*, outfitting it with the conveniences of a magnificent residence *all'antica*, and adapting facilities built to accommodate extravagant hunting parties to a completely different use. The villa's similarities to *casali* were visibly diminished but never completely eradicated in the schemes with a circular court that followed.

71

The Villa Madama can be considered a utopian structure because its design suggested a way of life that never existed. Apart from its presumed function as a *hospitium*, the villa was designed as an environment where a way of life *all'antica* could be lived within the extent of its confines. Here, the ancient ideal of *otium*, or the pursuit of activities free of urban distractions, could be re-created through study, bathing, theatrical and musical performance, and even gastronomy. In this context, fidelity to ancient drama or music mattered little; what counted was the setting offered by the villa for the kinds of activities that could have been found in Pliny's villas, the Golden House of Nero, or Hadrian's Villa.

With its origins in literature and archaeology, the Villa Madama seems to anticipate the eighteenth-century revival of styles based on historical sentiment. In effect, the villa was a folly on the grandest of scales worthy of comparison with "sham" structures such as Strawberry Hill or Fonthill. Had Leo X and Raphael lived long enough to bring their project to completion, it would have been easy to visualize them dressed in togas, walking through the gardens, and discussing Vitruvius and the topography of ancient Rome. Eventually, the naive optimism in the classical ideal of living as the ancients did dissipated as the result of the deaths of Raphael in 1520 and Leo X in 1521 and the Sack of Rome in 1527. The preoccupation with ancient architecture still remained but was shorn of its utopian ideology. For the remainder of the century, practical and functional considerations would define the architect's view of antiquity. The two greatest achievements of this fundamental shift in architectural thinking are Palladio's ingenious applications of classical architectural grammar to new purposes and Vignola's reduction of the architectural orders to simple and non-speculative rules in his *Regola delli cinque ordini d'architettura*.

THE END OF A GOLDEN AGE

The Golden Age of artistic patronage under Leo X disappeared even more quickly than it was created. Plagued by debts at the end of his papacy, Leo died in December 1521, twenty months after the death of Raphael. Having lost its friend and supporter, the Roman artistic community was in turmoil. The dour but earnest Dutch Pope Hadrian VI (1522–23) neither had an interest in art nor did he rule long enough to initiate or continue papal building projects. The election of his successor, Cardinal Giulio de'Medici, sparked hope for a renewal of the artistic vitality that he had existed in the Villa Madama. Yet as Clement VII (1523–34), his indecisiveness contributed to the Sack of Rome, and his most important artistic initiatives were either in Florence (The New Sacristy in S. Lorenzo) or late in his reign (Michelangelo's *Last Judgment* in the Sistine Chapel).

The legacy of Raphael's architecture is fragmentary; individual architects pursued separate aspects of the multiple dimensions of his architectural career. The antiquarian spirit of the Villa Madama was to reappear at the Villa Giulia, although it was never to be found to the same degree in other buildings by Vignola, Ammannati, or Vasari—its primary architects. The decorative style of the Chigi Chapel and the systematic study of Roman antiquities were reflected in Palazzo Spada, the garden facade of the Villa Medici, and Pirro Ligorio's archaeological studies and its impact on the Casino of Pius IV. Neither groundbreaking nor wholly original, these examples are instead a rear-guard revival of an era that had passed.

73

Pedant: "Let us proceed. Oh what fine structure is that palace which has issued from the architecture of (Giulio Romano's) exquisite model: he has imitated Vitruvius, the ancient perspectivist."

P. ARETINO,
Il Marescalco, IV

Third Gentleman: "No. The Princess hearing of her mother's statue, which is in the keeping of Paulina—a piece many years in doing, and now perform'd by that rare Italian master, Julio Romano..."

W. SHAKESPEARE,
The Winter's Tale, V

4

AUTHORITY & SUBVERSION:
GIULIO IN ROME AND MANTUA

43 Raphael, Giulio Romano and assistants:
    Decoration of the Sala di Constantino, 1520
44 Michelangelo: Florence, San Lorenzo, New Sacristy, detail, begun 1519
45 Giulio Romano: *Stoning of S. Stephen*, circa 1521

43

44

45

After the deaths of Julius II in 1513, and Bramante in 1514, artistic production in Rome was taken over by a generation of which the members were prone to behave as heirs rather than originators. From Julius and Bramante, they received an outstanding inheritance which it was, now, theirs to manipulate. As we have seen, the relationship of Bramante to Julius was curiously reproduced by the relationship of Raphael to Leo X. But there was a significant difference in attitude; the display of strength gave way to conscious refinement. And with the death of Raphael in 1520, this architectural development now became two separate paths: one was classical if not narrowly archaeological, as exemplified by Sangallo the Younger and Palladio, and the other more flexible and versatile as shown by Serlio, Sanmicheli, and Vasari. Admittedly, the two paths sometimes intersected and were tied into knots of Gordian complexity. Nowhere was this more evident than in the architecture of Giulio Romano (1492 or 1499–1546).

Already in Giulio's time, his painting and architecture were understood in dialectical terms. To Vasari, Giulio was, among the many disciples of Raphael, the proudest and the surest while, at the same time, the most capricious. In our own era, critics have stressed the bipolarity of his works, as Gombrich has so cleverly described it. To the late Manfredo Tafuri, surely the most perceptive critic of recent times, Giulio's art avoided easy classification by embodying both *sprezzatura* (studied naturalness) and human *ratio*. The range of Giulio's work was so vast, encompassing both altarpieces and pornographic illustrations, that the erotic and the spiritual came to be understood as the outer limits of his career. His buildings were capable of exhibiting both high seriousness and wit, sometimes employing contrasting scales in the same structure. Giulio's paintings follow a related stylistic strategy, simultaneously extending classical principles and denying them, to use the characterization of S. J. Freedberg.

Yet for an artist as well known as Giulio, his early biography is surprisingly incomplete. Giulio Pippi, who wished to be known as Giulio Romano, was the only important artistic personality of the sixteenth century to be born in Rome. There is major disagreement on the date of his birth. Vasari, who knew Giulio personally, cites the year 1492, therefore placing him where he seems to belong as an architect—a later member of the generation born in the 1480s, which includes Peruzzi, Raphael, Sangallo the Younger, and Sanmicheli. Other documentation suggests 1499; this date is more congenial to Giulio's career as a painter because he now becomes a highly precocious member of Raphael's circle who was barely a decade older than Vignola, Palladio, or Vasari.

PAINTED ARCHITECTURE
~

Not unexpectedly, Giulio executed the painted architecture in the last of Raphael's decorative endeavors in the Vatican, the Sala di Constantino (1520). Prior to his death, Raphael had created the major divisions of the pictorial scheme, which was completed by Giulio Romano and other assistants from his workshop (43). The decorations consist of battle scenes flanked by an apparatus of deep niches, wide pilasters, and enthroned popes flanked by allegorical virtues, all of which beg comparison with the frescoes in the Stanza della Segnatura. In the earlier room, there is no articulation of the corner, and, as a result, the viewer is confronted with the juxtaposition of two deep space pictures, without framing and rather embarrassingly disposed at right angles to each other. The strategy of arranging both figures and enframing architecture seems to have been drawn from the Sistine ceiling, which now has spilled down onto the walls of the chamber.

It is significant to note that Michelangelo arrived at a similar arrangement for the New Sacristy in Florence. The comparison is obvious enough. Just as the pictorial set pieces in the Sala di Constantino are separated by a build-up of corner emphasis, so does Michelangelo isolate his tombs by a highly developed corner accumulation of door, aedicules, and windows, employing niches to excavate the wall, and in the tombs, figures to project from it (44). Although it is uncertain if Michelangelo knew of Raphael's design—Michelangelo was in Florence occupied with Medicean projects and would not return to Rome until 1534—the difference is instructive. As executed by Giulio Romano and Giovanfrancesco Penni, the popes and the architecture that surrounds them, are deprived of energy and vitality as a consequence of their role in an essentially planar composition of dominant forms. Michelangelo, by contrast, always demonstrated in his architecture a sculptor's ability to infuse life into inert matter. This was the central idea in all of Michelangelo's architecture, in both Florence and Rome.

What distinguishes Giulio from his contemporaries—of either generation—is his deep understanding of antiquity and ancient architecture. All the ruins of Rome lay at his doorstep. He was born and grew up near the Capitoline, and so his earliest experiences were of the ruins of the Forum and the vast open areas beyond—the *dis-abitato*—on one side and the built up city—the *abitato*—on the other. Unlike other artists who studied Roman ruins, Giulio assimilated them into a resource of architectural experiences. As an apprentice of Raphael, he came into contact with the modern re-embodiment of those ruins. What he saw were the remains of a civilization that were in the process of decay and rebirth, an experience made vivid and palpable in the drawings of Giuliano da Sangallo's Barberini sketchbook. At the same time, Giulio was also an erudite and systematic student of antiquity, collecting ancient coins and amassing a collection of ground plans of ancient buildings in Rome and Campagna. Unlike most architects of his time, Giulio presumably had a knowledge of the Latin language, as suggested by his ownership of a copy of Alberti's *De re aedificatoria*. His broadly based *romanità* was a resource throughout his entire career, a source of ideas that he could transform to the point of subversion without ever denying its lasting authority.

The essential ingredient in Giulio's architectural painting was his tragic vision of Rome's ruins. His backgrounds are not the harmonious landscapes of Raphael; they are vivid personal reactions to the decaying condition of buildings with which he was intimately familiar. In two monumental altarpieces executed not long after Raphael's death, Giulio imparts the same vitality to his fictional architecture that he does to human figures in his paintings. For example, the dramatic lighting and rugged forms of the ruined Column of Trajan and large hall of Trajan's Markets, the Ponte Molle, the Temple of Vesta in Tivoli, and the Theater of Marcellus in the background of the *Stoning of St. Stephen* provide graphic contrast to the ballet-like martyrdom depicted in front of it (45). Down below, the saint is surrounded by a crowd of villains, which is hurling stones at him, as if to make antiquity the instrument of his death. There is an infatuation with broken arches and erratic lighting, and in the upper level, maniacal figures vandalize the dependencies of the large hall to provide further ammunition.

The *Holy Family with S. Mark and S. James* is an even more brilliant resolution of the accessibility of the holy figures and the remoteness of the hemicycle in the rear. The shallow space and planar composition of the former painting have now given way to a spiral motion of dramatic lighting and dark shadow. The figures and the architectural background seem to inhabit the same space, which is revealed to us by the angels in the picture's upper right-hand corner. The hemicycle has been identified as a part of Trajan's Markets, and even if the octagonal coffering of its annular vault originates in a different structure (the Basilica of Maxentius), this fragmentary vista demonstrates Giulio's masterful understanding of vaulted architecture. Giulio seems to have been especially attracted to the buildings of the architectural revolution that took place in the first and second centuries A.D., and from these buildings he would devise his own extraordinary architectural grammar.

Like the architectural backgrounds of Raphael, the imaginary constructions in these paintings are both believable and idealized. But now fragmentary in form and self-consciously sophisticated, they are seen in a peculiar kind of space and light that draws an emotional response from the viewer. Creating a harmony of experiences out of dissonant effects, Giulio shows how the spectacle of broken buildings can have a formative power on his own architecture. Both paintings contain the seeds of the extraordinary challenges to architectural convention that Giulio would make at the Palazzo del Te, challenges as profound as those made by Michelangelo in the Laurentian Library and St. Peter's.

ROMAN BUILDINGS
~

No less important than Giulio's painted backgrounds, of course, were his early experiences as a designer of actual structures. Precisely what he accomplished as an assistant to Raphael on architectural projects is uncertain, although evidence suggests that it was considerable. According to Vasari, Giulio was responsible for the development of Raphael's ideas into finished drawings with elements in correct scale. More recently, there have been claims made for Giulio's contribution to the design of the Palazzo Branconio dell'Aquilia and that

Raphael's architectural projects were designed with Giulio's assistance. Nevertheless, if the Villa Madama characterizes the relationship between these two important figures, it appears that Raphael exerted a taut control over his younger assistant, whose personality can be detected in decorations executed after the master's death.

A comparison of Giulio's Villa of Baldassare Turini of Pescia, commonly known as the Villa Lante on the Janiculum (begun circa 1518), with the Villa Madama shows his increasing freedom from Raphael (46). Both structures enjoyed splendid sites. The Villa Lante, which was built upon the ruins of the ancient villa of Julius Martialis, opened out onto an immense panorama that included the Ponte Molle, the seven hills of Rome, and the distant Alban Hills. Yet it was conceived as neither villa in the typical sense nor as a reconstruction of an ancient structure. Lacking a courtyard and extensive garden terraces, it was instead a small, nearly cubic casino originally decorated inside and outside with simulation of ancient marbles and other costly materials. If both structures sought to demonstrate the ancient unity of architecture and decoration, the Villa Lante did so at a lilliputian rather than gargantuan scale. The total effect has a miniature quality, as if it were an intimate cameo seen in the shadow of the Farnese Hercules.

Despite damaging effects of successive alterations and restorations, the expressive range of the villa's exterior is still remarkable. The viewer's experience of the villa begins with what seems to be a conventional architectural statement—Doric half-columns supporting a segmental pediment. Yet, upon further observation, what appears to be a conventional division of the block into two stories by paired orders is, in fact, much more. The abrupt contrast between the swaggering assertiveness of the Doric pilasters on the ground floor and the spectral apparition of Ionic pilasters on the *piano nobile* reveals the nervous tension that is one of Giulio's architectural hallmarks. The narrower dimensions of the side bays create a further tension between the pilasters and windows, which are read as a single vertical unit overlapping the upper floors. Ambiguity is one of the hallmarks of Giulio's architectural systems, as is the irony created by widening pilasters in the outer bays. The overall design is fascinatingly complex, but the architectural language is strikingly economical.

The villa's facade overlooking the city is no less masterful. Perched upon the edge of the slope, its singular feature is a loggia

46 Giulio Romano: Rome, Villa Lante, begun circa 1518
47 Le Corbusier: Drawing of Villa Lante, 1911

46

47

composed of three linked *serliane* opening out to the city below (a *serliana* is a motif composed of three bays, the central bay being arched and wider than the others). Perforated only by the attic windows and the loggia's arches, its planar and uniformly delicate surfaces stand in sharp contrast to the bold contrasts of the entrance facade. Its excessively attenuated Doric columns contribute to the effect of an open structure, wholly unlike the squat Doric pilasters on the entrance. As in most of Giulio's buildings, each facade is an autonomous surface with its own structural divisions and rhythms determined by the particular circumstances of existing construction of the location of internal divisions. The precocious originality characteristic of Giulio's Roman work is borne out by the reappearance of many of these ideas—most particularly that of the loggia—in the Palazzo del Te at Mantua.

83

More recently the Villa Lante also left its mark on the work of Le Corbusier. When the youthful Charles-Edouard Jeanneret visited Rome in October 1911, toward the end of his Voyage d'Orient, he seems to have been unaffected by Renaissance architecture. The Villa Lante, however, was singled out in a handsome drawing for its cubic form picturesquely set on a series of terraces at the edge of the Janiculum (47). The impact was immediate, and in some ways, more profound than other buildings he had seen on his trip. As seen from the northwest, its elevation anticipates some features of his early Villa Jeanneret-Perret in La Chaux-de-Fonds (1912–13) and the more famous Maison Domino (1914). It also appears to be a predecessor of buildings such as the Maison Cook or the Villa Savoye; the Villa Lante's loggia and side elevation playing the roles that *piloti* would assume in Le Corbusier's projects of the 1920s. After this period, the impact of Renaissance buildings becomes a small but still important part of the extremely wide range of Le Corbusier's architectural experiences.

MANTUA AND THE PALAZZO DEL TE

The losses of his teacher Raphael in 1520, his patron Leo X in 1521, and the controversy surrounding *I Modi* (the engravings by Marcantonio Raimondi of various sexual positions after drawings by Giulio) must have caused Giulio to reconsider his career in Rome.

Shortly after the pontiff's death, the protracted negotiations which brought Giulio to Mantua were begun under the supervision of Baldassare Castiglione, author of *The Courtier* and general agent for Gonzaga cultural interests in Rome. Giulio finally left Rome in October 1524, and arrived in Mantua in the company of Castiglione, who presented the youthful painter and architect to the Marquis, Federico II Gonzaga (1500–40). According to Vasari, Giulio was amicably received by his new patron, given a dwelling, a liberal stipend, and—having no horse of his own—one of Federico's favorite studs, which was immediately presented to his new master. As the story goes, Giulio rode mounted on his new gift with the Marquis to the site of the Gonzaga breeding stables. Here, the Marquis observed that, without destroying the old walls, he would be glad to have a little space arranged to which he could occasionally resort for amusement and for a meal. Such was the presumably modest origin of Giulio's Palazzo del Te.

By the time of Giulio's arrival, the Gonzaga had ruled Mantua for nearly two centuries. Lacking resources of their own, the Gonzaga flourished largely through taxation, strategic marriages, and their cunning military skill as *condottieri*. The fertility of the neighboring terrain and the financial and political policy of the Gonzaga led to considerable prosperity. Mantua's unique topography was a significant asset—the three swampy lakes formed by the Mincio River provided protection for the city in much the same way the lagoon did for Venice. Thus Mantua's physical setting was both secure and unhealthy, for endemic malaria was the price for its protection. Petrarch demonstrated no kinship for this famous city when he described it as foggy and full of frogs.

Mantua's political and artistic importance outweighed other cities of its size (a population of 25,000 in 1500, as compared to the 55,000 inhabitants of Rome or 70,000 of Florence). The Gonzaga were a family distinguished by their material acquisitiveness—a mania for building and collecting works of art, armor, antiques, and jewels. The center of courtly life was the Palazzo Ducale, a sprawling complex of buildings which—as a palatial residence—is exceeded in size only by the Vatican. To satisfy the urge for splendor and magnificence, they tended to import artists—Pisanello, Alberti, Mantegna, and (much later) Rubens—rather than develop local talent. As a consequence of the absence of a local school, the Gonzaga contributed to the creation of artistic dictatorships—or to use a more favorable term—princely artists. Giulio, as principal artist of the Gonzaga court, its prefect of buildings, and overseer of streets, enjoyed an absolute authority rarely challenged by Federico or his associates.

The Palazzo del Te is Giulio's greatest architectural achievement and one of the most original buildings of any era. Few facts are needed to outline its history. It was begun in 1526, on an insular meadow beyond the southern walls of Mantua. Its square plan was in large part determined by the existing colt stables that were incorporated into Giulio's building. According to Vasari, the project was meant to provide Federico II with "a small place where one might sometimes go and to which one might resort for supper or recreation." Almost certainly, this included the walls of the Sala di Psiche and the Sala dei Cavalli in the northeast corner, where a symmetrical arrangement of openings on the interior is cloaked on the exterior with syncopations, local symmetries, and asymmetries of its Doric pilasters, fenestration, and loggia arcades. It is still uncertain whether the design was proceeded by successive stages or was planned from the outset as a single-story pleasure establishment around its courtyard.

Vasari's statement that the Palazzo del Te was designed "in the *guise* of a great palace" is particularly clever because the building's sometimes brutal and truculent rustication is executed in brick and plaster, a result of the scarcity of stone in Gonzaga territories. The overall impression is that of a heavily rusticated building which, in reality, is slight and insubstantial. Such effects of wit and perception surely would have impressed visitors such as Emperor Charles V who was entertained at the Palazzo del Te in 1530 and 1532. Yet this pleasure villa remained unfinished, leaving only three of its exterior facades completed and the southwest quadrant of rooms undecorated. In the eighteenth century, Giulio's design was drastically modified by Paolo Pozzo who gave the garden facade an incongruous, neo-Palladian appearance with its blank surfaces and dominant pediment.

Giulio reconciled in the Palazzo del Te a singular exterior with a plan derived from the study of both antiquity and vernacular structures of his own age (48). It has been often pointed out that the Palazzo del Te's layout repeats the essential features of a Roman house as illustrated in Fra Giocondo's 1511 edition of Vitruvius. No doubt, Giulio was familiar with this reconstruction, as were the

85

48 Giulio Romano: Mantua, Palazzo del Te, begun 1525
49 Palazzo del Te, drawings of north (A), west (B), and east (C)
    facades by Ippolito Andreasi

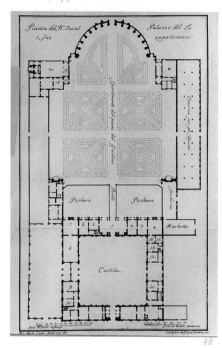

48

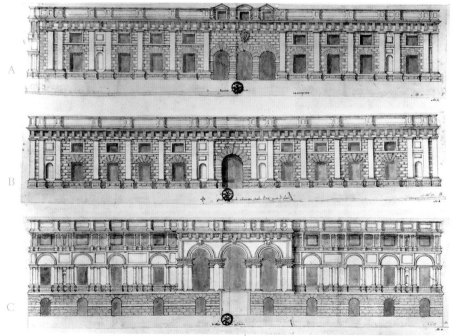

49

Sangallo family and other architects of an archaeological temperament who had studied it in detail. But in terms of building typology,
Giulio's pleasure villa has only one precedent—the Villa Madama.
But this is not to say that the two structures are similar. During the
period of his assistance to Raphael on the Villa Madama, Giulio
would have learned about the luxurious villas and palaces of antiquity, but it is not at all surprising that such structures had little impact
on the Palazzo del Te. What differentiates these two examples of a
cinquecento folly are their respective moods: the Villa Madama being
tragic in its evocation of ancient life and the Palazzo del Te suitably
comic with its witty paraphrases. A more appropriate source for its
layout are the *corti*, the agricultural structures organized around
quadrangular courts commonly found in the Lombard plains around
Mantua. To a great degree, the Palazzo del Te became a Mantuan
farm clothed in the decorous disorder of early cinquecento Rome.

87

Giulio's interest in asymmetries and irregular rhythms, for the
purposes of analysis, is best shown in the north facade (49A). At
once, the expressive potential of an exterior surface is disclosed; it
also makes one aware, yet again, that Giulio's metrical division of the
facade is neither regular nor proportionally fixed. It is an important
and highly dramatic introduction to the Palazzo del Te that contains
important thematic and compositional ideas found elsewhere in this
extraordinary structure.

The architectural elements of the north facade are manipulated
at will. The notion of a single, colossal order embracing the exterior
facades derives from Raphael at the Villa Madama. But the width of
Giulio's pilasters is an exaggeration of Raphael, and they are now
imposed on a rusticated background where the bays which they
define display a behavior far less than regular. Rhythmic regularity
gives way to the expansion and contraction of individual units set
against a highly textured, rusticated background. Tension is sustained
by conflicting central and peripheral accents. For instance, does the
triple loggia (where the pilasters no longer prevail) tear the facade in
two at the center or is the wall structure on either side centered
around it? And, at either extremity of the facade, do the half-bays
(very Bramantesque) composed of paired pilasters separated by a
niche serve as elements of disengagement accenting the corners as
pavilions or are they centers unto themselves? Giulio's architectural
syntax raises provocative questions but rarely provides answers.

Ambiguities of this sort were not unique to Giulio's architecture. Syncopated rhythms and irregular divisions of structural units had been employed by Alberti and Bramante, but none of their solutions were endowed with the architectural ingenuity or visual intensity as those of Giulio. It must be noted that, as Giulio left it, this facade was not visible from any great distance. It simply commanded a very small garden.

Then as we turn the corner and face the center of the west facade (the original place of entrance) we discover a more Bramantesque proposition than any of which Bramante himself could have conceived (49B). This second facade, in complete contrast, emphasizes symmetry, regularity, and repose in spite of visible differences of dimension. It is the uppermost level of the Cortile del Belvedere handled with sparkling contrast and vivacity, and it may permit the notice that every element of the Palazzo del Te's exterior is derived from a very limited tradition—that of Alberti, Bramante, and Raphael. Like Giulio's painted ruins in the *Stoning of S. Stephen* or the Fugger altarpiece, it is a tradition represented with a feeling for intricate conflict, flexible articulation, and dramatic vigor.

After this classicizing interlude of the west facade, the *androne*, or vestibule, lying behind its only arched opening is then something of a pseudo-primitive shock (50). In addition to Fra Giocondo's Roman house, Giulio undoubtedly knew of Antonio da Sangallo the Younger's vestibule to the Palazzo Farnese and Raphael's even more similar (in plan) vestibule anticipated for the Villa Madama. It is exceptionally assertive, and this may be his commentary upon these sources. The columns are rough and half-formed and the coffering of the vault is deliberately crude. And the almost primeval qualities of this vestibule become all that more apparent when its cross view is compared with the same view at the Palazzo Farnese. Sangallo's parade of columns now becomes impoverished, their intercolumniations become almost agonizingly wide, and this tradition becomes interrupted by the appearance of an abrupt and inexplicable keystone.

Proceeding to the courtyard, the mood of discomfort found in the androne is intensified rather than dispelled (51). The central part of each facade contains a loggia, all of which are different in plan. We see large and small columns sitting on the same base, and the pediment of the doorway leading to the loggia carefully and carelessly

51

50

52

jammed against the entablature above. Pediments over windows are supported by exaggeratedly crude consoles, and then, are further invaded by voussoirs with exaggeratedly rustic keystones. The columns and the entablature from the *piano nobile* of the Palazzo Caprini are beautifully reproduced as a stark accompaniment to the oscillation of the rustication. The effect created by the simulated stonework is at once suave and melodious, at other times, harsh and rectilinear. Serlio was wildly excited by Giulio's rustication and about it he said:

> ...the columns banded with rustic blocks, and even the archi-
> trave and the frieze interrupted by the blocks, show the work of
> nature, and the cornice with the pediment represent the work
> of the hand, which mixture in my opinion is very pleasing to
> the eye and represents in itself great strength.... This particular
> mixture was enjoyed more by Giulio Romano than any one
> else, as witness Rome in many places and Mantua with the most
> beautiful palace called the Te—truly an example to the architec-
> ture and painting for the times.

Serlio also said that his own designs were sometimes licentious. Frequently breaking an architrave, frieze, or cornice, he was sensitive to criticism that would portray his actions as mistakes contrary to the precepts of Vitruvius. This might encourage a little tour of Giulio's deliberate mistakes, such as the dropped triglyph, which served to act as some kind of keystone. One may look at the triglyph in all its splendid isolation, and one may notice how implacably its appearance is stretched. There is the ever so carefully conceived entablature, and then there is the lapse, this abrupt and witty descent into archi-tectural sin. If you are susceptible to the provocations of Giulio, the results—of course—are indescribably poetic.

The loggia behind the central bays of the garden facade creates a second classical interlude (52). It may be usefully compared with the loggia of the Villa Madama and what an extreme transformation is presented here. Raphael's cross vaults, domes, apses, and exedrae are replaced by a relentless barrel vault, curves now give way to right angles, and architectural orders sit squarely on the floor level. A com-parison to the rest of the Palazzo del Te is even more instructive—mural architecture is now trabeated, and the primary elements or ornament are no longer rustication but a rich variety of classical motifs. Columns appear in groups of four, and there is the carefully built-up duality of real and false entrance doors. The enclosure has become more ostensibly antique and monumental, and in doing so, the archaeological underpinnings of Giulio's architecture have emerged as preeminent.

On the garden facade, Giulio employed his favorite devices to achieve an exterior architecture fundamentally different from the rest of this building (49C). By contrast, it lacks rustication or stonework of any sort, and thus its design conveys a sense of open structure and the suggestion of refinement found nowhere else on the exterior. At first glance, the composition is simple; four *serliane* are disposed about the central axis marked by the great loggia. But within this symmetrical arrangement there is no pretense to a steady rhythm. Cinquecento architects typically employed a *serliana* either as an isolated element or as linked motifs in a syncopated rhythm; only rarely are these two strategies found in the same design. In the side wings, Giulio departed from this practice by overlapping the second and third bays and by widening the spacing between the third and fourth bays. This atypical solution was in part determined by fireplaces within the villa that altered the facade's regular sequence of arched and trabeated openings, but Giulio obviously relished the compositional challenge that was posed to him. The resulting design is fascinating and complex, with regular rhythms established more by suggestion than by actual presence.

A facade, of course, differs from an elevation in being a vertical surface endowed with a metaphorical or allegorical presence. Uniquely, all of the exteriors of the Palazzo del Te are a species of facade, typically concealing more than disclosing anything about the building's actual content. They are to be admired as demonstrations of Giulio's peculiar architectural bravura, which, on the garden facade, remains undiminished despite its radical transformation during Mantua's period of Austrian rule (53). The viewer's experience is nothing less than transcendental; the garden facade is mirrored in the fishpond, only to be dissolved into fragments of light and color suspended on the water's surface. These dazzling effects are a rare example of the influence of Venice and its buildings on Giulio's architecture.

It was in these circumstances that Giulio created the two L-shaped apartments that constitute the most important decorated parts of the Palazzo del Te. They are the result of two campaigns of decoration, one dating from 1527–29, and characterized by the pagan eroticism of its subjects, and the other from 1530–35, which celebrated Federico's fame and power. Because of the speed of their execution and the need to employ numerous assistants, the apartments exhibit notable discrepancies between quality of painting and brilliance of invention. But their succession of spaces demands our attention.

Probably the northeast apartment was thought to be the more important, as indicated by its grander rooms and two modes of access. For certain ceremonial occasions, as in the reception of Emperor Charles V in 1530, there was the Atrio delle Muse that led to the Sala dei Cavalli, the single space large enough for banquets and balls. But on more intimate occasions, one may assume an entrance via the big loggia, a traversal of three vaulted rooms, each increasingly greater in size and decorative effect. The sequence commences with the Camera delle Aquile, an intimate, square chamber, whose vault culminates in a depiction of the Fall of Phaeton in its central octagonal panel. The next room, the rectangular Sala dei Venti, is entered at its corner, exaggerating the size of the space and giving prominence to the intricacy of the vaulted ceiling's web of lozenges and rectangles. The unity between architecture and scenic decor is further reinforced by the paving pattern that almost mirrors the design of the ceiling.

In any case, it is an extraordinary room and a fitting approach to the Sala di Psiche, where the one-eyed giant, as a voyeur, looks out at the festivities of Psyche's marriage to Cupid. The room is once again a square in plan that now occupies the full width of the intersecting wings. From its walls, twelve consoles support clusters of acanthus leaves that, in turn, carry an intricate arrangement of eight octagonal coffers clustered about a square central panel. The illusionism of the individual scenes is as bold as their colors are dazzling, and the scenic decor is now a fundamental part of the architectural experience. The integration of planning and experience in Giulio's rooms, with their interconnected floors and ceilings, was scarcely before imagined in three dimensions. In spatial terms, the effect of the room is that of an explosion in contrast to the contraction of the preceding chambers. As an example of courtly art, the ensemble became a gift to the later eighteenth century, to Robert Adam, to the Czarina Catherine, to her architect Charles

53 Palazzo del Te, garden façade; present condition
54 Palazzo del Te, Sala dei Giganti
55 Palazzo Ducale, La Rustica, 1538–39: detail showing southern wing by
Giulio Romano and later addition in foreground

53

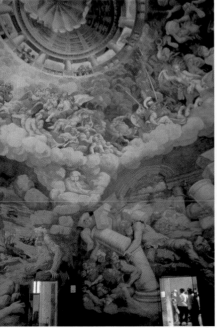

54

55

Cameron, and to everything which that age desired. In fact, they predicate palace style as it was received from about 1770–1830.

The Sala dei Cavalli can be understood as either an anteroom to the Sala di Psiche or a grandiose retrocamera to a linear suite of rooms. It is the most architectural of Giulio's decorations, and it derives its peculiar combination of beauty and outrageous display from the contrast of two systems of illusion—classicism in its architecture and hyper-realism in the horse portraits. Within the calm and introspective arrangement of Corinthian piers, there are visual jokes. The statues of gods and goddesses are depicted in oversized niches while there is insufficient space and support for the horses as they spill out into the observer's space. In the wooden ceiling, what are beams at first sight appears to be a kind of weaving and plaiting of structural elements. A great deal of color invigorates the architecture—simulated white marble in the piers, polychrome veined panels, bronze plaques with golden highlights, and jewel tones in the frieze, all of which are placed above a dado of red and gold leather wainscoting. The dissolution of the wall into a pattern of color and texture—so important to the evocation of antiquity in Raphael's Chigi Chapel, for instance—has now been pilloried by the satirist rather than defined by the scholar.

Inevitably, any tour of the Palazzo del Te leads to the Sala dei Giganti, which has achieved a fame bordering on notoriety (54). The room has been characterized by Hartt as "the most fantastic and frightening creation of the entire Italian Renaissance in any medium," and rightly so, for in this room, Giulio has demonstrated the power of emotional response in architecture. The room was designed as a demonstration of illusionism rather than regular habitation; from the summit of its domed vault, Jupiter (so much like the brutes throwing stones at St. Stephen) hurls thunderbolts at the brutish giants, whose world is shattered about them in ruin. The walls and the columns of the of earthly temples collapse before the avenging gods. The room is in the process of destruction, and even the floor resonates, as it seems to absorb the movement of the participants in this universal apocalypse. As the complement to the fairy-tale world of the Sala di Psiche at the other end of the eastern wing's sequence of rooms, the Sala dei Giganti is an artificial catastrophe.

The Sala dei Giganti is, in effect, a carefully arranged cyclorama in which the Palazzo del Te appears to crush the observer. This conceit, powerful as it is, would have been even more frightening with the rusticated doorway and illusionistic fireplace that Vasari claimed to have seen during his only visit to Mantua. Yet this fearsome and grotesque mutilation of actual architecture is an extension of Giulio's Roman background. In his own experience, the city was realistically defined by the ruins as he saw them and not by idealistic reconstructions of their original condition. Giulio does not, like Antonio da Sangallo the Younger and Palladio, attempt to derive his designs from specific ancient buildings or building types. His range of sources and allusions is too broad to permit narrow classifications. As recorded in Giuliano da Sangallo's drawings and vividly recalled in his *Stoning of St. Stephen*, Giulio's capture of the form and the effect of ruins in actual state are what made his own architecture "antiquely modern and modernly antique."

$\tilde{95}$

The Cavallerizza or La Rustica (1538–39) in the Palazzo Ducale is, in many ways, the fulfillment of the aggression displayed in the Sala dei Giganti (55). Built originally as an apartment intended to face a lakefront garden, La Rustica now sits on the southern side of the courtyard where the Gonzaga horses were once paraded at court, the result of three additional sides constructed shortly after Giulio's death. In actual size, it is a small structure, two stories tall, seven bays wide, and with a three-bay loggia inserted on the lower level. But its visual and emotional effect is another matter altogether.

La Rustica is closely related to Giulio's earlier scenes of destruction and death. It is a Bramantesque palazzo type, as if the Casa Caprini had been beaten up by one of Giulio's painted villains. But the parallel does not carry far because La Rustica's effects are seemingly irrational. The buildings arches are shaped, spaced, and irregularly filled. Windows are pushed upward so that their arches are roughly flattened between the lintel and the entablature, and their frames are dissolved into a pattern of rustication. Floor lines are uncertain. And the blocks forming the intermediate piers are pulled about so as to give the impression that the whole building is loosely piled, unstable, quivering, and teetering on the edge of collapse. Proportions oscillate. Spiral columns twisting first left and then right rest upon unstable podia, which in turn, are cantilevered on consoles dovetailed into the spandrels below. In its loggia, a world in collapse is increasingly more visible, rendering the Sala dei Giganti's architecture as fully three-dimensional.

Yet while there is no improvisation, there is a consistency of mood throughout. The customary allusions to Rome are numerous: in addition to La Rustica's filiations with Bramante's Palazzo Caprini, there are spiral columns modeled on those in Raphael's tapestry cartoon for the *Healing of the Lame Man*, the rusticated facade derived from the rear wall of the Forum of Augustus, and a window type drawn from Giulio's own house in Rome. Giulio's approach to ancient ruins has been called "romantic," but the term does not adequately describe his achievements. The mood that he creates is tragic and comic in equal measure—tragic in terms of its aspiration and comic in the way it challenges our senses. Giulio can tantalize us with the collapse and dissolution of architectural orders and other details because, in the end, they are just another form of ornament. The actual bearing wall exists behind a rough brick and plaster exterior.

LATER WORKS
~

For all intents and purposes, Giulio's authority over building in Mantua was absolute. In the two decades in which Giulio worked in Mantua, he dominated ducal projects. They included the Palazzo del Te and La Rustica, the Gonzaga villa at Marmirolo (destroyed without a trace of visual evidence remaining), the impressive rustication of the Porta della Cittadella (1530), and the temporary architecture for the second entry of Charles V into Mantua (1532). These mentioned projects were among numerous commissions for Federico II and his court. There were also major architectural enterprises that altered the face of the city. Street levels in areas prone to flooding were raised, and new structures were constructed for the fish and meat markets. Vasari sums it up by saying that Giulio made for Mantua "so many designs for chapels, gardens, and facades and took such delight in embellishing and adorning (the city) that he transformed it in such a way that where it was formerly in the grip of mud and full of foul water at certain times and almost uninhabitable, it is today, through his industry, dry healthy, and altogether beautiful and pleasing." There is a whiff of overstatement to these words, but their essential truth cannot be denied.

With the death of Federico in 1540, all this came to an end—almost. The style of patronage was about to be correspondingly changed by Cardinal Ercole Gonzaga, Federico's younger brother who became Giulio's patron. (Federico was succeeded by Francesco III, age seven.) When the Cardinal told Vasari that Giulio was more the proprietor of the state than he was himself, he was speaking in ironical terms.

The appearance of Giulio's city accorded with ducal interests. For this, Giulio was handsomely rewarded, and among the rewards for faithful service was his own house (1540–44), which was a major renovation to an earlier cinquecento house built on medieval foundations. Nowadays, the house is characterized by the crisp and extremely delicate relief on its facade. But the present exterior is not original, for it is actually the result of a reconstruction around 1800, when the final two bays on the right were added and the main entry moved from the third to the fifth bay. From the evidence provided by an original architectural drawing (56), Giulio intended the two-story facade to have bolder relief and greater contrast between the heavily rusticated arcades and the decorative use of brick masonry surrounding the windows. As a foil to the sobriety of the scheme, the pediment over the main entry changes function and becomes a string course. In this building, Giulio obviously aspired to create a house equivalent in status to those inhabited or projected by his teacher, Raphael, but now fully imbued with his own artistic convictions.

The commission to rebuild the Benedictine monastic church of S. Benedetto al Po (begun 1539) came not from the Gonzaga, with whom the abbey was closely affiliated, but from its abbot (57). Only a decade earlier, an ambitious new church was approved, but little was done before work was suspended after a flood in 1527. When work was resumed, a new scheme permitted the old structure and the new modifications to coexist within the newly reconstructed church. The primary challenge that Giulio faced was to harmonize the irregular bays of the older structure with newer elements. As at the Palazzo del Te, he had to create the appearance of regularity when it did not exist in reality.

As a strategy for dealing with an existing structure, Giulio's solution was clever and economical. The plan that he faced was that of a late Romanesque monastic church similar to Cluny III with transepts, an ambulatory with radiating chapels, and a prominent octagonal lantern. The response is fantastic. The nature of the project demanded as few structural alterations as possible. Some spaces and columns were shifted and others added, but the disposition of piers,

56 Giulio Romano: Mantua, own house, façade project, circa 1540
57 Giulio Romano: Polirone, San Benedetto al Po, abbey church,
   begun 1539
58 San Benedetto al Po, abbey church

56

57

58

outer walls, and vaulting remained unchanged. In the first three bays, *serliane* were placed between the nave piers, cleverly disguising the nave's irregular dimensions. For reasons of economy more than style, the columns supporting the arches of the *serliane* were those initially fabricated in 1494, for the monastery's library but were never set in place.

What makes S. Benedetto al Po so different from other cinque-cento churches is how a sense of visual unity and transparency is combined with an extreme multiplicity of spatial shapes (58). By inserting the *serliana* into the position occupied by two arched open-ings, linear divisions in the nave were now replaced by an ordered spaciousness. The new chapels built to either side of the old church were clearly visible from the nave, but they remained independent cells of space higher than aisle vaults to which they were attached. In fact, no dominant motif holds together the multiplicity of spaces—the nave and aisles are covered by species of cross vaults, the transepts are barrel vaulted, and the dome retains its octagonal ribbed Gothic vault above an octagonal drum supported on squinches.

On the side elevation of S. Benedetto al Po, delicate ambiguities contribute to its vitality. This flank of the church—the only exterior part that is wholly Giulio's—is composed by placing the same ele-ment in changing contexts, avoiding symmetry, and a rhythmic or other kind of emphasis. There is a play on the triumphal arch motif as employed by Alberti in S. Andrea in Mantua, only twelve miles away, and by Bramante in the Cortile del Belvedere. The sequence begins with two elements linked in the conventional way, but in the third, the bay on the right is expanded as a consequence of the nar-row space interrupting the rhythm of the chapels. Thus, the enlarged bay reads as a center and the facade's rhythm is reversed, only to be altered again by the omission of remaining side bays. For all of its various conditions on the side flank, the emphasis on the arches (which are all of the same dimension) contributes to an asymmetri-cal harmony not unlike that found in the Palazzo del Te.

Wolfgang Lotz, one of the most influential historians of Renaissance architecture in the twentieth century, said that S. Benedetto al Po is the sum of a number of studied effects of surprise and contrast that look petty on the church's side flank, because "the eye requires clarity balance, and proportion." This opinion, more appropriate to the works of Raphael than Giulio, evidently was not shared by Giulio's contemporaries. In 1543, Paul III visited this church, admired it, and it was perhaps this visit which caused him to remember Giulio in 1546, when Antonio da Sangallo the Younger died. Giulio was invited to return to Rome, the city of his birth, in order to complete St. Peter's but died before he could go. If Giulio rather than Michelangelo would have become the architect of the project begun by Bramante and Julius II, the entire course of western architecture would have been different.

To the end, Giulio continued to draw from a narrow range of sources—Alberti, Bramante, and Raphael—for his ideas. His reconstruction of the Cathedral of Mantua after a fire in 1545, is an exception to this development because his new patron, Cardinal Ercole, may have desired to demonstrate the religious renewal of his diocese by sponsoring the creation of an Early Christian basilica in cinquecento Mantua. The earlier structure was a church with a nave, two side aisles, deep chapels, and a crypt with a raised choir above it. Giulio's radical transformation exploited the arrangement by placing within the outline of its walls a five-aisle basilica flanked by an outer row of chapels. The architectural image that he sought to create was, quite obviously, that of Old St. Peter's, whose interior he depicted in the *Donation of Constantine* in the Sala di Constantino in the Vatican.

The spatial image was altogether different. From the portions of the nave still standing in Giulio's era, he would have seen precious furnishings and bright colors in its columns and mosaic decoration within an interior that was divided into a series of separate spatial units. Giulio's interior, on the other hand, is aggressively monochromatic in its whiteness and sought to stress spatial continuity by providing visibility for the high altar. Quite unlike the typical Christian basilica, Giulio decided to exploit lateral views by making the inner aisles roofed with barrel vaults, outer aisles beamed and covered, and chapels alternatively domed and barrel vaulted. The lateral views are stunning and are nearly as impressive as those found in Borromini's seventeenth-century renovation of the nave of the Lateran. But its religiosity seems cold, calculating, and conceived upon an intimate scale that makes the observer's experience fundamentally hollow and empty.

We can now summarize a few architectural principles employed by Giulio. Rarely is there a sense of a predetermined or all-encompassing order to his buildings. This is not to say that the Palazzo del Te, for instance is not systematic or is lacking in discipline. Almost all projects involved the creative incorporation of existing structures whose inconsistencies fed Giulio's voracious appetite for expressing syncopated and irregular rhythms based on those very unique circumstances. The subjective impression of regularity is further strengthened by a contrary element, by what the École des Beaux Arts used to call a *hors d'échelle*, or a calculated intrusion of an out-of-scale element—like the rusticated voussoirs in the Palazzo Maccarani or the slipping triglyph of the Palazzo del Te—to cite two very prominent examples. Rustication, which by definition is suggestive and poetic, emancipated Giulio's work from mere primitivism. It represented a state from which the more perfect would subsequently emerge.

Giulio's genius lay in the way his architecture and painting, both independently and together, actively engaged the observer's perception of a succession of architectural incidents or decorated spaces. He was readily willing to overthrow the *absolute* authority of Vitruvius and antiquity, so venerated by purists such as Sangallo the Younger or Palladio, and to subvert it with a kind of *relative* order that addressed personal experience. Buildings such as the Palazzo del Te were neither a joke nor an act of derision but a kind of self-conscious folly that was wisely expressed. Neither classical nor anti-classical, as they were characterized by critics such as Pevsner, Giulio's architecture creates the paradoxical but effective result of being licentious in its own disciplined way.

To sum up, Giulio as an architect left no heirs. His ideas were taken up by others, and his influence was most deeply felt in Northern Italy by Serlio, who was overwhelmed by Giulio's use of rustication, and by Palladio, who met Giulio when the Mantuan came to Vicenza to consult on the reconstruction of the Palazzo del Ragione. The impact on Palladio was most strongly felt early in his career, understandably because the Palazzo Thiene in Vicenza was based on a design drawn up by Giulio. Elsewhere, the influence is diffuse though present. Vasari's role as the court artist and architect for Duke Cosimo I de'Medici in Tuscany and some of the buildings he designed in this capacity were clearly influenced by Giulio's activities for the Gonzaga in Mantua.

The Palaces of Rome are generally built with rough stone, which is afterwards plastered over, though some few of them there be of brick, and also of square stones....I remember not any front to be adorned with pilasters etc. except the Library at the Vatican, and some few villa houses only. As to the Cancelleria it is old and ill-built and not worth taking notice of.

SIR ROGER PRATT,
notebook, 1644–45

Just imagine a people of whom one quarter are priests, one quarter are statues, one quarter do hardly anything, and one quarter do nothing at all.

CHARLES DE BROSSES,
Lettres d'Italie, 1799

5

DOMESTIC TYPOLOGIES:
PALAZETTO & PALAZZO IN ROME

59 Raphael: Rome, Palace of Jacopo da Brescia, circa 1515
60 Raphael: Rome, Palazzo Branconio dell' Aquila, circa 1515–20,
sixteenth-century drawing by unidentified Italian draughtsman

59

60

The memorable characterization of late eighteenth-century Rome by Charles de Brosses is, in many ways, equally descriptive of the Eternal City in the cinquecento. Apart from the church and religious tourism, there was scarcely any economy to speak of. At the apex of its hierarchical society were the pope and the cardinals of the great families, who were separated by a great gulf from the cardinals of modest means. The social and economic distance between this ecclesiastical nobility and that of the noble Roman families was even greater. Apart from the massive enterprise of St. Peter's, the popes constructed few churches during the first half of the century, and even fewer were actually completed. Instead, domestic buildings of varying degrees of size and scale constitute the most conspicuous constructions to be found in the inhabited quarters of the city.

Quite understandably, there is little to show in terms of papal initiatives in domestic architecture. From the Late Middle Ages onward, the pope and his retainers lived in labyrinthine apartments deep within the Vatican's core. Such an arrangement of cramped and dark chambers could not have afforded their occupants much comfort, let alone provided sufficient space for courtly ceremonies. In the quattrocento, numerous popes made modest renovations or additions to the Vatican. Although many projects involved the decoration of the existing structure, the most important new constructions were the Sistine Chapel and the Belvedere Villa. Under Julius II, however, an ambitious transformation of the Vatican was begun but never completed. St. Peter's and the Cortile del Belvedere were to be parts of a larger transformation of the Vatican palace into a structure that would rival the palace of the Roman emperors on the Palatine. The scale of the proposed undertaking was truly imperial. In addition to the Belvedere, Bramante planned a conclave hall modeled on the frigidarium of a Roman bath. Adjacent to it, there was to have been a conclave chapel in the form of a grandiose tempietto placed on top of the quattrocento tower built by Nicholas V. But the construction of a hall and chapel, whose only purpose was the election of a new pope—an infrequent event even in the cinquecento—was yet another project beyond Julius's grasp. Leo X's plan for a new Medici palace on the Piazza Navona was similarly improbable.

PALAZZETTI
~

What made Rome truly distinctive, however, was the presence of a class of lawyers, bankers, and doctors who formed the core of the Curia, the administrative arm of the church. The *palazzetto*, or small palace, emerged in response to the need for residences that were ambitious in terms of status but small in size. The *palazzetto's* archetype was Bramante's Palazzo Caprini, a structure that demonstrated how to achieve the scale and grandeur of antiquity for only a modest cost. Typically, these palaces were two stories in height and their facades were five or seven bays in breadth. Their courtyards were characteristically modest, but the planning of the residences was often ingenious. Although structures of this type can be found throughout Rome, the greatest concentration of *palazzetti* was in the Borgo, the area between St. Peter's and the Castel S. Angelo, which was traditionally home to members of the Curia.

The *palazzetti* designed by Raphael most fully express the ambitions of the Leonine era. Indeed, his designs for three palaces—two of which were built in the Borgo for papal associates—played a major role in creating an architectural career that was compressed into seven short years. Each of these palaces was to be as different from each other as they were from the Palazzo Caprini, which made its greatest mark on palaces outside Rome. With their construction leadership in architectural patronage passed from Leo X to members of the papal court (who elevated themselves in social status above the populace and nobility through the visibility of their residences), they now became the most avant-garde patrons in Rome. Taken as a whole, their palaces illustrate the wide range of sources, styles, and solutions that were embodied in Raphael's architecture. Although some of these palaces were already in disrepair in the seventeenth century, Pratt's appreciation of palatial architecture in Rome was distinctly limited.

The Palazzo Jacopo da Brescia, the earliest of Raphael's palaces, was designed around 1515, for the personal physician of Leo X (59). The palace occupied a somewhat triangular plot on the Via Alessandrina, the street laid out in 1499, by Alexander VI in anticipation of the forthcoming Holy Year in 1500. If the site's irregular geometry permitted little construction at its rear, it allowed the creation of a symmetrical suite of rooms along the facade. At every level of detail, it departs from the Bramantesque prototype, emphasizing both the independence of its three floors and the interrelationship of its architectural membering by superimposing pilasters on the *piano nobile*. Most of all, its unique arrangement allowed for simultaneous views of its main and side facades from the direction of the Vatican. This oblique "papal" viewpoint took into account the papal coat of arms on the highly visible corner and the diminishing size of the five bays of the facade proper, which increased the building's apparent size. The palace was dismembered during the creation of Mussolini's Via della Concilazione, the modern thoroughfare leading to the Vatican, and it was clumsily reassembled on an adjacent block to the north.

Further up the Via Alessandrina, the *palazzetto* Raphael built for Giovanni Battista Branconio dell'Aquilia (circa 1515–20) could not be more different. Avoiding the structural logic that characterized the Palazzo da Brescia, Raphael employed pictorial devices to bind architectural and decorative elements into a coherent design. Because this palace was destroyed during the creation of Bernini's Piazza di S. Pietro, its design must be reconstructed with the assistance of drawings (60).

A comparison of Raphael's Palazzo Branconio and Bramante's Palazzo Caprini (29) illustrates the deep chasm that came to separate their respective architectural styles. In Raphael's five-bay structure, anything attributable to Bramante is either rejected or radically transformed. Bramante's characteristic severity has given way to a festive air in Raphael's abundant display of antique bric-a-brac. Doric columns are now transposed down to the ground floor, whereby they ennoble shop exteriors rather than the main residence on the *piano nobile*. The suggestive structural role of attached columns has now become a form of ornament, because columns appear to support voids created by niches that in turn are surmounted by decorative panels. The vertical emphasis of individual bays now gives way to the horizontal development of each individual story. To further emphasize the facade's pictorial logic, the niches and panels above the columns increase in size, as if to reverse the expected order of things.

In the Palazzo Branconio dell'Aquilia, Raphael must have sought to create a modern palace whose exterior was ancient to the last detail. Its two upper floors are Raphael's most festive exteriors in their recollection of temporary architecture of the sort built for a papal *possesso* or other ceremonial events. At the same time, it is the most antiquarian of Raphael's palace exteriors, with its rhythmic pattern of windows inspired by the hemicycle of Trajan's Markets, and the decorative vocabulary of swags and other elements recalling ancient stuccowork. But what made the facade truly pictorial was its location at the point where the Via Alessandrina opened into the Piazza di S. Pietro. This made the palace, which was constructed for Leo X's Chamberlain and Keeper of the Pope's Elephant, a visible extension of the antiquarian concerns of the pontiff. One can easily picture Raphael and Leo X together on the Vatican loggia admiring from a distance the palace that embodied their shared interests in Rome both old and new.

PALAZZI
~

The palaces of most Romans—both aristocratic and otherwise—inhabited a world very different from that of the Curia. Their residences were built largely in the Campo Marzio, the densely populated district that had been the center of Rome from the Middle Ages onward. The structures were usually to be found on irregular, narrow streets that afforded little visibility to residences of social and architectural pretension. As a consequence, they often had no opportunity for the visible display of architectural orders characteristic of Raphael's *palazzetti*.

Greater size is not the only feature that distinguishes a *palazzo* from a *palazzetto*. While this is normally a function of a patron's wealth, it is particularly an index of his ambitions. A powerful motive in building palaces is the celebration of the status of families who are part of the old nobility as well as those with a pretense to dynasty. If one imagines a characteristic palace of the era, it would be a new structure with an imposing exterior, a grand courtyard, and a regular and symmetrical plan evoking the houses of Roman antiquity. Such a palace is, however, the exception and not the rule. New buildings in Rome regularly were modernizations of older structures, and in some instances, they actively incorporated ancient ruins. In fact, cinquecento Rome is remarkable for the number of buildings that depart from the plan of an ancient house than for those derived from it. The most original thing about a Roman palace is its discovery and exploration of pre-existing architectural circumstances.

Antonio da Sangallo the Younger's first independent commission, the Palazzo Baldassini (1513–19), is the first and perhaps the most sophisticated solution to the problem of designing a palatial residence in cinquecento Rome (61). Located just to the north of the Piazza Navona, the building occupies a mid-block site that offered scarcely any visibility for an imposing facade. But the short length of street was widened to increase visibility of the palace and give greater prominence to its *bugnato* corner. Architectural emphasis is given to the ground story, which is nearly half the height of the facade's three-story elevation. Similarly, it lacks both ground-floor shops and a display of rustication and architectural orders, making its elegantly austere exterior the antithesis of the Palazzo Caprini and its descendants. Yet Sangallo was sufficiently aware of the expressive potential of contrasting the palace's facade with its courtyard, which is composed of an elevation two stories equal in height (62). By employing Doric pilasters as the main form of the architectural membering, the courtyard's facade easily adapted to the varying conditions posed by elevations as different as an open two-story loggia on one side and closed blocks of varying height on the other three. In fact, the pilaster motif plays a major role in emphasizing circulation from the vaulted entry hall, up through the commodious stairs, and into the main hall of the *piano nobile*.

What we have witnessed thus far is the emergence of two approaches to facade design that were shared by both *palazzi* and *palazzetti*. An example of this weaving of ideas is the Palazzo Alberini (begun 1514–15) in the heart of Banchi, the district opposite the Castel S. Angelo where banker's offices were regularly found on the ground floor of palatial residences. Long considered a design by Giulio Romano but now convincingly attributed to Raphael, this palace also further demonstrates Raphael's independence from Bramante's legacy (63). An alternative solution indicates that a three-story design was modeled on the Palazzo Caprini and was considered but then rejected in favor of a four-story solution similar to the executed structure. In this case, frontal or distant views were not possible, and consequently, greater emphasis than normal is given to the ground floor and its rhythmic sequence of rustication derived from

109

Florentine examples such as the Palazzo Gondi. The result was a sequential diminution of the height of each story, an idea Raphael employed with considerable success in the Palazzo Jacopo da Brescia. Similarly, there was no need for elaborate plastic development of the exterior as in other palaces. Instead, Raphael conceives of the facade's *piano nobile* as a superimposition of a layer of architectural membering followed by several layers of finely laid brick cut back to reveal the actual bearing wall from which the rectangular windows are cut. On the third story, architectural membering is eliminated altogether. It is not surprising to learn that Giulio continued to oversee work on the palace after Raphael's death, deriving from it both the strategy and devices employed in his exterior of the Palazzo Maccarani. For more than three centuries, the Palazzo Alberini remained unfinished, and the three bays to the right of the main entry were completed only in the 1860s.

Only a handful of Tuscan palazzi showed the influence of Bramante or Raphael. The most Roman of these structures was Antonio da Sangallo the Elder's Palazzo del Monte in Monte San Savino (begun 1515–17), which was conceived as the residence for the hereditary rulers of this small city in southern Tuscany (64). The aspirations of the del Monte may have been ambitious—the siting of the palace adjacent to a newly created square may have been suggested by a desire to remodel the center of the city along the lines of nearby Pienza. Only the palace and the loggia opposite it were executed, and in stylistic terms, Sangallo's two-story design is schizophrenic—up top, orders from Raphael's palace for Jacopo da Brescia, and down below, a closed, rusticated ground floor from the Cancelleria. This Roman orphan remained exceptional in Tuscany because its distance from Florence and the lack of a local tradition made it impervious to the conservative architectural cultures of its region. Today, the Palazzo del Monte is the only palace from the era of Bramante and Raphael to retain its original appearance.

As expected, Florentines showed a patrician's disdain for Roman innovations in palace design. For example, Baccio d'Agnolo's Palazzo Bartolini in Florence (1517–20) was censured for its lapses in architectural grammar. The Palazzo Pandolfini (begun circa 1515–16), the only structure in Florence begun from Raphael's designs, was the only palace of the period on a par with Roman examples. Its patron, Giannozzo Pandolfini, was the Bishop of Troia

61 A. da Sangallo the Younger: Rome, Palazzo Baldassini, 1513–19
62 Rome, Palazzo Baldassini, courtyard
63 Raphael: Rome, Palazzo Alberini, begun 1514–15
64 A. da Sangallo the Elder: Monte San Savino, Palazzo del Monte,
    begun 1515–17

61   62   63

64

65 Raphael: Florence: Palazzo Pandolfini, begun circa 1515–16
66 Giulio Romano: Palazzo Maccarani, 1522–23

65

66

in Apulia and one of the intimate friends of Leo X. The initial designs were probably prepared when the Pope called Raphael to Florence to prepare a design for the facade of S. Lorenzo. Pandolfini had previously acquired a garden residence on the Via S. Gallo far north of the center of Florence, and it was on this suburban site where the palace was begun. Raphael's solution was, in effect, a suburban palace with a grand exterior nine bays long but only two stories high (65). While the facade had usually been understood as a reflection of the Florentine aversion to the use of orders on a palatial exterior, they were irrelevant on account of its setting. Nevertheless, it retains a specifically Roman air in its aedicular windows derived from the Palazzo Branconio dell'Aquilia, and in its rusticated corner and portal, a rare Florentine reflection of the Palazzo Farnese. Precisely what Raphael had envisaged for this palace is unknown. By the mid 1520s, members of the Sangallo family built a small villa in the tradition of the Villa Farnesina behind the imposing exterior, a bitterly ironic conclusion to the history of Florence's most ambitious palace of the early cinquecento.

Of all of the Roman palaces begun before the Sack of Rome, Giulio Romano's Palazzo Maccarani (1522–23) stands in a category of its own (66). The commission involved the restructuring of several houses into a palatial residence for a patrician family, and inevitably, the executed building reused foundations and walls from the original structures. Giulio evidently realized the expressive potential of the palace's trapezoidal site, and it has been suggested that he originally conceived of the palace as three facades of five bays each. In spite of the difficulties he had to face in the site's irregularities and the acquisition of surrounding structures, he managed to create the structure that still dominates the heterogeneous group of buildings on the Piazza S. Eustachio.

An analysis of this enigmatic palace reveals the germ of much else that Giulio was to build later in Mantua. An initial reading of its five-bay facade reveals three stories, the first two nearly equal in height, and the last, about two-thirds as high. The ground floor is rusticated, and the other two are plain. The *piano rustico* is divided equally by a Doric portal with a pediment; the *piano nobile* is articulated by a coupled order of flat pilasters.

So far, there is nothing to indicate a sharp break with the system laid down by Bramante in the Palazzo Caprini. Yet an essential change has taken place. In the Palazzo Maccarani, rustication does not cover the whole surface of the basement floor, but instead, it is divided into vertical strips intersected by a beam of massive voussoirs and keystones. The windows of the basement mezzanine are balanced on the beam, just as those on the *piano nobile* sit precariously on a string course. The upward thrust of the vertical strips is continued into the pilasters of the *piano nobile*, which, in their turn, fuse in an ambiguous fashion with a distinctly abbreviated cornice. Then, in the top story, there are more insidious moves. What appear to be pilasters turn out not to be so. Ultimately, they disclose themselves to be framing strips that are part of a system of gridding or paneling that has invaded the entire facade. It is from this grid that the entry portal erupts, only to be re-absorbed by the surrounding rustication. To all intents and purposes what appears to be structural is only ornament, a screen or scrim of architectural elements wrapped around the structure's true bearing wall.

It is as though there were two principles at work—there is elegance and there is savagery. There is the rational, intellectual order of the structural grid and there is the explosive, primitive order of the rustication. The primitive building, which is presented, is constrained in a sophisticated corset. In terms of creative constraint, it can be compared to one of Michelangelo's slaves for the tomb of Julius II. The building palpitates (one can only use sexual imagery for what is going on here), but in the end, it concedes to a cerebral order of things.

By a curious, freakish event, the destruction of the city during the Sack of Rome in 1527, brought about the construction of one of the city's greatest architectural masterpieces. The original Massimo family palace was largely destroyed in fire during the sack, and after the death of the paterfamilias the three heirs decided to construct new residences for themselves. Pietro Massimo, the eldest, selected Baldassare Peruzzi to design his new palace on the site of the destroyed structure, while his brothers commissioned designs from Giovanni Mangone and Antonio da Sangallo the Younger for sites adjacent to and across from the original house. By building individual and eminent palaces, a recognizable "Massimo district" was created along the Via Papalis, even if there were no other architectural boundaries to the zone than the residences themselves.

As in many of his commissions, Peruzzi prepared at least two alternative designs for the Palazzo Massimo (begun 1532). One proposal maintained the structure of what remained from the destroyed palace. While few changes were proposed for its oddly shaped rooms, trapezoidal courtyard, and discontinuous property lines, the single most important feature was a medieval loggia that survived Sixtus IV's order to close external porticoes in Roman houses. Although the loggia was symmetrically placed with respect to the axis of the Via del Paradisio opposite it, the loggia was asymmetrical when seen in the context of the facade as a whole. It continued two bays further to the right, masking part of the loggia, the remains of a tower, and part of an adjacent residence. The opening behind the loggia's Doric columns would have appeared awkward when seen from any other view other than the axial approach along an unimportant street.

The executed design was more ambitious and involved rebuilding most of the palace (67–68). It is designed around the preexisting axial approach, which now extends unbroken throughout the entire length of the palace. Although this axis diverges from that of the alignment of the palace's main portal, the discrepancies between the two are minimal and without any consequence for the overall design. The alignment of a three-room suite also conforms to the axis, as does the courtyard with its twin logge at opposite ends. More important to the apparently regular effect of the plan is the reconfiguration of property lines and the acquisition of space from the adjacent palace of Angelo Massimo to create a seven-bay facade that is now fully symmetrical. In this scheme, the facade also acquires its famous curve that contributes significantly to the palace's imposing appearance. In one sense, this was unintentional because the Palazzo Massimo sits on the site of the ancient Odeon of Domitian, whose semicircular exterior accounts for the prominent curve of the Via Papalis in this area.

The facade of the Palazzo Massimo, often portrayed as an example of artistic willfulness or Mannerist excess, is Peruzzi's response to specific architectural considerations. Even since Alberti, an axial approach to the main entrance of a noble palace had been considered desirable, and Peruzzi used this feature to stunning effect in the alignment of the palace's entrance and armature of circulation with the street opposite it. Although Raphael employed architectural orders on the ground floor of the Palazzo Branconio, Peruzzi did so because this was the only location where they could be used in any meaningful way. Prior to its radical nineteenth-century transformation into

67 Palazzo Massimo, plan
68 Palazzo Massimo
69 Peruzzi: Rome, project for Palazzo Orsini

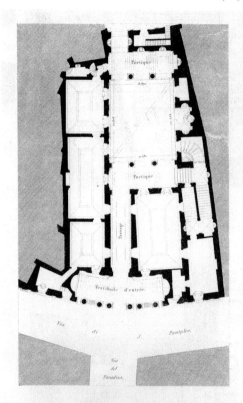

67

68

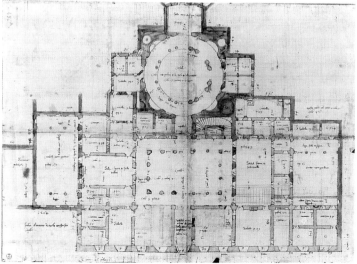

69

the Corso Vittorio Emanuele, the Via Papalis was only 4.5 meters wide, and the use of architectural orders on the upper floors of a grand palace would appear uncomfortably top-heavy. To Peruzzi, then, the drafted rustication was less a boldly expressive element than a form of ornament that defined the extent of the facade and contributed as much to its nobility as did the orders themselves. Specific grammatical elements, such as the windows on the first of the two mezzanines, owe their inspiration to similar examples in the courtyard of Giulio's Palazzo Maccarani. However, in Peruzzi's design the ornamental, strapwork quality of the first mezzanine is meaningful as a form of distinction from the floor above because it corresponds to the decorative frieze in the main hall of the *piano nobile*.

It came naturally for Peruzzi to utilize Roman remains in the design of two other palaces. The only project of this group to be built, the Palazzo Savelli, is less a palace than a fortified residence in the tradition of those built by the baronial families of medieval Rome. Contained within and perched atop the Theater of Marcellus, the Savelli's chief innovation was the subtle reconciliation of the radial arrangement of the chambers in the theater's *cavea* with the rectilinear geometry of its nucleus. Even more revealing is how Peruzzi employed the remains of the Baths of Agrippa, located just to the south of the Pantheon, as the framework for an elaborate double palace for the Orsini (69). The irregular outlines of the property impeded a strictly symmetrical solution, but Peruzzi nonetheless was able to create an axial scheme characterized by two successive courtyards, one rectangular and the other circular, which utilized the remains of the baths' central rotunda. The terminology of Peruzzi's annotations to his plan combines both contemporary and ancient architectural terms, as if here were the double origins of this unique solution.

THE ARTIST'S HOUSE

One of the consequences of the new status accorded to artists in the Renaissance was the accumulation of wealth. Not all artists, of course, enjoyed the kind of success that placed elegant (and even palatial) residences within their grasp. The artists who did typically worked for a court, and in the quattrocento, actual figures such as Andrea Mantegna in Mantua and imaginary ones such as Filarete's architect in his treatise constructed distinctive residences for themselves. As a representative building type in the cinquecento, the artist's house is emblematic of the owner's status and profession.

Sadly, Raphael's inventive design for his own palace remains on paper. In October 1517, he purchased Bramante's Palazzo Caprini from the heirs of its original builder. Not long afterward Raphael began to acquire property on the Via Giulia near S. Giovanni dei Fiorentini where he planned to construct a palace befitting his status as the primary artist of the papal court (70). The site of the projected residence was an irregular trapezoid surrounded by streets on all four sides, and into this block, Raphael planned to insert two independent residences with their own courtyards, a larger one for himself facing the Via Giulia and a smaller one at the rear for one of his assistants or for rental income. The building's position at the edge of the artisan's district near Banchi demanded the inclusion of shops on all sides, yet the prominent location and Raphael's own self-importance suggested encasing the structure in a colossal, two-story order similar to that planned for the facade of St. Peter's.

What distinguishes Raphael's Via Giulia residence from all other palaces, including his own, is the sophistication and ingenuity of its planning. On the upper floor two enfilade suites comprising the palace's main apartments were set parallel to the longest sides; an oblique fifth side similar to the one on the Palazzo da Brescia cut across the acute angle formed by the intersection of the Via Giulia and a side street. At the center of the block, irregularities were disguised through the use of devices such as niches, curved exedrae, and irregularly shaped staircases. The asymmetrical spaces that remained were appropriately given over to comforts such as lavatories and a private bath. According to Vasari, Leo X was considering nominating Raphael to a cardinalate, making the prince of artists also a prince of the church. But this design was conceived as an artist's palace, with his studio on the north side of the main floor and private stairs connecting him to his assistants in the shops below.

Raphael's death in April 1520, brought work on the Via Giulia palace to a halt, and a subsequent design by Antonio da Sangallo the Younger to turn the site into an apartment block was never built. Yet Raphael's creative use of irregularities in planning was carried on by Baldassare Peruzzi, most notably in the Palazzo Massimo. At the same time, this sector of the Via Giulia continued to attract artists.

70　Raphael: Rome, project for a palace on Via Giulia, 1517, drawing
　　attributed to B. della Volpaia
71　Giulio Romano, own house in Rome, drawing by Dosio, 1524
72　A. da Sangallo the Younger: Rome, Palazzo Farnese,
　　begun circa 1516–17, upper portion of facade completed by
　　Michelangelo after 1546

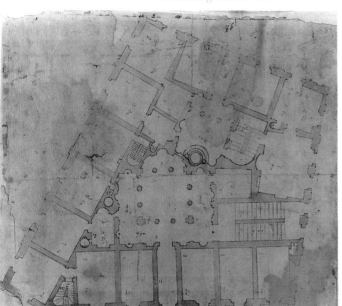

70

71

72

Raphael's ambition to celebrate an artist's status in his residence was achieved by Sangallo who built a handsome small palace for himself and his family opposite Raphael's site (circa 1534–40), and a second larger residence, the Palazzo Sachetti (1543–46), a few doors down the same street.

In contrast to these palatial residences, the main elevation of Giulio Romano's Roman house was only two bays wide and two stories tall (71). In 1524, Giulio acquired the title to his family residence in Macel de'Corvi and immediately began to modernize its exterior. What he created did not resemble any other structure in Rome. As if to demonstrate the variety of details offered by the use of rustication, each story was treated in a contrasting manner. On the ground floor, the blocks have bulk and volume, they extend across the entire facade, and an emphatic keystone appears to divide the arched entry rather than hold it in place. The Doric pilasters flanking the entry have been consumed by rustication, which affords only a glimpse of their refined capitals. But up above, the wall is treated as drafted masonry. Even the visual tension created by contrasting forms is exploited in single details. The principal feature of the facade is its main window, in which a weighty voussoir and cubic *bugnati* suggest an imaginary block out of which a refined Ionic aedicule is emerging. The tension is further reinforced by the inclusion of Roman spoils such as a sarcophagus and an ancient relief.

This small, intense facade contains several influential ideas. Giulio himself was to rework the relationship between rustication and architectural orders in the Palazzo del Te. Andrea Palladio was more selective, preferring instead to reinterpret Giulio's *bugnati*-encased window frames on the exterior of the Palazzo Thiene and purging the voussoirs of their eccentricities on the Palazzo Porto's facade. What were once considered unorthodox and even eccentric details from Giulio's private architectural language would become commonplace a generation later.

THE PALAZZO FARNESE
~

The Palazzo Farnese was the largest, the most conspicuous, and the most luxurious palace in cinquecento Rome (72). Its origins date back to 1495, when the young and ambitious Cardinal Alessandro Farnese acquired a palatial residence of a Spanish cardinal on the site of the present building. Although the extensive complex contained a courtyard, stables, and a considerable garden, the existing structure must have been insufficiently impressive in either social or visual terms. The site's shape was irregular, and the layout of the Via Giulia obliterated the garden at the rear. Apparently, the Cardinal was unwilling to orient his new residence toward this adjacent grand thoroughfare, and either for reasons of economy or tradition, the Palazzo Farnese turned its back on the nearby Via Giulia. By the second decade of the cinquecento, Cardinal Farnese began to acquire material for the new palace, and the streets flanking it were leveled and made parallel. From the outset, it appears that Sangallo was to design a completely freestanding structure in the tradition of the ancient Roman *insula*.

The palace for Cardinal Farnese, which Sangallo began around 1516–17, contained many of the features of the executed structure. Taking advantage of its newly regularized setting, the repetition of aedicular windows, rusticated corner quoins, and lack of architectural orders emphasized the palace's massive scale and three-dimensional appearance. Yet within this essentially staccato framework there were emphatic architectural counterpoints. The rusticated entry portal leads to a basilica-shaped vestibule, itself the first realization of what many architects believed to be the form of an ancient atrium as described by Vitruvius. This was just the first in a series of spaces whose articulate forms and open spaces contrast with the neutral surfaces of the block-like exterior. Just beyond, lay the grandiose three-story courtyard with open arcades and superimposed orders derived from the Theater of Marcellus (73). In turn, the vaulted arcades were to lead to a grand staircase at the palace's northeast corner that directed the visitor to the state rooms and apartments on the *piano nobile*, a grand apartment composed of a linear suite of rooms descending in size.

Such was the condition of the Palazzo Farnese during the Sack of Rome in 1527. Shortly thereafter, Cardinal Alessandro appears to have requested from Sangallo a revised and enlarged design, a decision that took on new meaning after the Cardinal was elected to the papacy in 1534. According to Vasari, Sangallo was charged with making a papal rather than a cardinal's palace, and as a consequence, nearly the entire structure was rebuilt. Work proceeded slowly and major alterations were not begun until the next decade. The most

73

74

122

significant revision was the transfer of the main staircase to a position on the eastern, or side wing. Although this change resulted in awkward locations for blocked windows on the eastern elevation, it nonetheless permitted more generous chambers on the ground floor and on the *piano nobile*. More visibly, the height of the courtyard was increased by reconstructing the ground-floor vaults. If this meant that Sangallo's design would show an even greater sense of openness within its block, it also resulted in the extraordinary double moldings on the ground-floor piers, a detail sanctioned neither by antiquity nor by contemporary usage.

Sangallo's concept of a freestanding, insular palace brought about the restructuring of its urban setting, largely through the intervention of Paul III. In theory and practice, public squares were necessary adjuncts to palatial residences. In order to give greater visibility to the palace's imposing facade, the Piazza Farnese (1535–37) was created by demolishing the residences opposite it (74). However, the justification for building the piazza as a public ornament failed to take into account the protection of the palace and its princely inhabitants during periods of civil unrest. Visibility *from* the palace was now a concern, and in 1541, a proposal was made to realign the Via di Monserrato along an axis emanating from the apartments at the palace's northwest corner. The scheme was tinged with the same obsessive paranoia displayed by Paul III's plan to refortify Rome, and eventually nothing of substance was done. But the most extensive transformation of the surrounding area was begun in 1548, two years after Sangallo's death. Rights of way through existing blocks permitted the extension of the Via dei Baullari as far as the Via Papalis, thereby extending the impact of the palace far to the north. Originally, the goal of this ambitious urban perspective was to have been the Piazza Navona, but its intended course diverged from the geometry of the piazza and would have passed through the properties of some of Rome's most powerful families. Had this grandiose idea been executed, the Farnese under Paul III would have achieved what eluded the Medici under Leo X—the dominance of central Rome by a papal palace.

If Sangallo can be criticized for such a large and complex design, it would be for focusing his attention on individual sections of the building at the expense of the whole. The project took on a life of its own, and its numerous modifications suggests that Sangallo seems to have proceeded without a definite overall plan for the palace. The result was sometimes a contrast between parts, such as that between the aggressive Doric order on the ground floor of the courtyard and the meticulous Ionic order above it. In spite of a renewal of activity prior to Sangallo's death in 1546, Vasari wrote in the *Lives* that the palace "will never seem unified or by the same hand."

For example, the facade was nearly complete but the rear portion was barely begun. A competition was held to see who would build the cornice, and the commission was awarded to Michelangelo, who had been stymied in obtaining papal commissions by the Sangallo clique. In his designs for the cornice and the completion of the courtyard, Michelangelo emphasized bold contrasts over academic correctness to such an extent that Sangallo's estimable achievements appear to have been unmercifully satirized. But the most incisive cut at Sangallo's orthodoxy is the diamond pattern of brickwork on the upper floor of the facade that was revealed in a recent restoration. If this ornamental pattern was truly the work of Michelangelo, its capricious nature suggests that Michelangelo's subversion of Sangallo's design was now a matter of public spectacle.

Michelangelo's plans also called for an open loggia flanked by projecting towers on the garden front, an integral part of his proposal to link the Palazzo Farnese with the property on the other side of the Tiber. As conceived by Michelangelo, city and country would have been united by a single panorama passing through a palatial urban residence, but at the cost of much habitable space that was removed from the palace. It was replaced by the present form of the rear wing's lower stories, which were completed in 1568 under the direction of Vignola. Work on the palace continued until 1589, when Giacomo dell Porta completed the upper floor and its rear loggia.

Sangallo's design for the Palazzo Farnese defined the image of the Roman palace for the next four centuries. Its progeny was to be long and, for the most part, rather undistinguished. The Farnese's anonymous brick-faced exterior was to become as characteristic of early modern Rome as the *insula* was representative of the imperial capital. Its facade would eventually influence buildings as diverse as Domenico Fontana's uninspiring Lateran Palace, Carlo Maderno's ingenious Palazzo Mattei, and the several unremarkable government ministries designed by Gaetano Koch in the nineteenth century for Rome's new function as the capital of a unified Italy. By virtue of its eminence, the Palazzo Farnese created a new dimension of meaning that emphasized raw power. Such inferences were not lost on the English architect Charles Barry, who, as the architect of nineteenth-century "palaces" in London, gave this building type an aura of class privilege in the Reform and Traveler's Clubs. But in its transformation, the Roman type was deprived of its brute force, and its appearance became seemingly fussy and domesticated. As Karl Marx once said, "all great ideas come around twice, first as tragedy and second as parody."

125

In Architecture as in all other Operative Arts, the end must direct the Operation. The end is to build well. Well building hath three Conditions. Commodity, Firmness, and Delight.

SIR HENRY WOTTON,
Elements of Architecture, 1624

No person who is not a great sculptor or painter can be an architect. If he is not a sculptor or painter, he can only be a builder.

JOHN RUSKIN,
Lectures on Architecture and Painting, 1853

6
~
THE EMERGENCE *of the* ARCHITECTURAL PRACTITIONER:
SANGALLO THE YOUNGER, PERUZZI, & SERLIO

The dilemma that Wotton and Ruskin faced on the definition of an architect has its origins in the cinquecento. Throughout Europe, and particularly in Italy, an expansion of architectural knowledge was furthered by the appearance of the printed architectural book. Ancient ruins were no longer the exclusive purview of Humanist writers or the readers of their texts, which often lacked illustrations and were predominantly written in Latin. Instead, the architect now needed examples from antiquity that could be recast for contemporary needs. Beginning with the publication of Serlio's *Fourth Book* (1537), an utterly simple but effective concept governed architectural publications. The basic idea was to give primacy to architectural illustrations, which in turn were accompanied by a brief explanatory text. The publications that followed were not Humanist treatises for educated patrons but illustrated manuals for the practicing architect, written in a simple and direct Italian grammar, and copiously illustrated with woodcuts made from preparatory drawings by the author. Their impact was evident and immediate. As a consequence, antiquity was demystified through publications that simplified the application of the orders and illustrated a wide range of ancient and modern architecture.

The illustrated architectural manual demands attention for other reasons as well. A concept popular with historians and critics is that the architects of this era had little interest in architectural theory, and the new publications were anti-theoretical in outlook. The evidence seems to contradict the assertion; given the widespread interest in the study of ancient ruins, it seems impossible to believe that architects were not searching for guiding principles initially based in antiquity. Rather, their theoretical beliefs were expressed not in words but in powerful images. This kind of "unwritten" theory derives from the selection, description, and ordering of architectural images in order to articulate an idea. A more accurate assessment is that the authors of the illustrated manuals were perhaps disdainful of humanism and the admittedly obscure erudition found in Alberti, preferring instead to address real problems faced by architects of their time.

The appearance of the illustrated architectural manual—and such related devices as architectural prints—increased the importance of architectural drawing. Although today more drawings by architects exist from the Cinquecento than from earlier periods, the drawings' survival is not wholly accidental. The intensity of the study of antiquity demanded a systematic study of its remains. It is not surprising, then, to find Raphael advocating the use of plan, elevation, and section as the means of representing ancient Rome. Although Alberti had advocated the same drawings in his treatise, their significance for cinquecento architectural practice cannot be underestimated. The success of this form of architectural representation was linked to the efficacy of the illustrated manual; the systematic use of woodcut plans, elevations, and sections in Palladio's *Quattro Libri* is one reason for its immense impact. The new importance of architectural drawings was recognized by Antonio da Sangallo the Younger who began to systematically identify the projects illustrated on the sheets from his workshop and by collectors who began to acquire drawings for their importance as documents and as works of graphic art.

129

The new architect is also distinguished from his predecessors by an expanding context for architectural practice. In Rome, the most important professional institution was the workshop of St. Peter's, or *fabbrica*. From the time of Bramante, the scale of its endeavor was unprecedented, and in the case of Raphael's and Antonio da Sangallo's plans for St. Peter's, it actually increased. The execution of such a colossal project demanded a new, hierarchical, highly efficient organization composed of individuals who were capable of the project's conception, construction, and administration. Apart from matters of design, the responsibilities of the staff ranged from finances and record keeping to carpentry, masonry, and other specialties of building construction. Entrance into this powerful, exclusive organization was determined as often by prestige and connections as it was by competence. Even if the architects of St. Peter's were trained as painters, as were Raphael and Baldassare Peruzzi, the experience gained by any individual was sufficiently comprehensive to prepare him for a career as an architect. Although the existence of such a *fabbrica* was exceptional, those appointed to it dominated Roman architecture for the entire sixteenth century.

Elsewhere in Italy, the emergence of the new architect was conditioned by a variety of factors. As old states were consolidated and new ones created, their rulers sought peripatetic professionals to maintain and defend the boundaries of their dominions. Authority for the completion of projects consequently fell to trustworthy assistants, thereby contributing to the further separation of design from construction that was begun in Alberti's era. The concentration of architectural patronage in the hands of fewer, more powerful individuals meant that architects now had to fully understand the architectural ambitions of their patron. In Mantua under the Gonzagas, this role was filled by Giulio Romano, and in Medicean Tuscany, it was embodied in the architect-courtier *par excellence*, Giorgio Vasari. In the Veneto, architects such as Sansovino and Sanmicheli, on the other hand, derived their considerable power and authority from appointed positions as the overseers of projects, mostly for the procurators of St. Mark's or agencies of the Venetian Republic.

Three architects—Antonio da Sangallo the Younger (1484-1546), Baldassare Peruzzi (1481–1536), and Sebastiano Serlio (1475–1554)—best exemplified this new kind of practitioner. Although the architects' origins and artistic personalities differed in each case—and their success in obtaining commissions varied accordingly—their contributions to the development of the architectural profession cannot be denied. Sangallo's fame is primarily due to the establishment of an efficient family workshop that executed a variety of official commissions for Popes Leo X, Clement VII, and Paul III; of these projects, the Palazzo Farnese in Rome is Sangallo's built masterpiece. Peruzzi's career could be scarcely more different; his executed work in Rome amounts to two extraordinary structures separated by a quarter century. But for years, he also served as the architect of Siena, his native city, where his responsibilities included military architecture, hydraulic engineering, metallurgy, and espionage. Serlio, on the other hand, built little of consequence in Italy, and his most important executed works are found in France, where he lived for the last thirteen years of his life. But if influence is the measure of professional success, Serlio is the most important architect in this group, on account of his authorship of the first illustrated architectural manuals, and especially, his understanding of Italian and French preferences in domestic architecture.

ANTONIO DA SANGALLO THE YOUNGER

~

Antonio da Sangallo the Younger dominated Roman architecture for more than a quarter of a century. His professional ascendancy was due to four factors: a full mastery of the technology of building construction; a long tenure in the workshop of St. Peter's (which he directed for 26 years); an analytical mind that allowed him to seek out Vitruvian principles in imperial Roman buildings; and the unwavering patronage of Cardinal Alessandro Farnese, later Pope Paul III. No other cinquecento architect equaled the prodigious range of Sangallo's building activity, which included utilitarian works, military architecture, and city planning. In addition, other noted projects included the design of the most important palace of the era, the Palazzo Farnese, and the ambitious scheme for St. Peter's illustrated by his famous wooden model. Sangallo's career was made possible by a workshop of family members who collaborated on most projects, as well as a distant relative who administered business affairs. The result of this arrangement—in some ways similar to a modern architectural office—allowed for the absolute loyalty of assistants, which Antonio the Younger gave in turn to his patrons and their projects. Professional success was translated into financial success, as shown by his own palace on the prestigious Via Giulia.

131

Antonio the Younger was born into the famous Florentine clan of architects and builders (his mother was a sister of Antonio the Elder and Giuliano). According to Vasari, Antonio the Younger learned carpentry as a youth when he assisted his uncle Antonio on the construction of wooden ceilings in the Palazzo Vecchio. Around 1503, Giuliano took his nephew to Rome, where he assisted his uncle on a number of commissions. At the same time, Antonio the Younger's exceptional talent caught the eye of Bramante, and by 1509, the twenty-five-year-old Florentine was invited to join St. Peter's workshop. The experience gained by assisting Bramante on St. Peter's, the Belvedere Courtyard, and the palace and fortress at Civitavecchia was unparalleled, and around 1513, Antonio the Younger established his own practice. He was not yet thirty years of age when he began to prepare designs for two palaces already discussed, the Palazzo Baldassini and the Palazzo Farnese.

The architecture of Antonio the Younger was essentially an architecture of reconciliation. In all of his major projects, he sought to achieve a mode of design that unified two divergent attitudes of traditions without compromising their essential contributions. To Sangallo, a dialectical form of architectural thinking drew from contrasts such as ancient versus modern, structural versus ornamental, or Roman versus Florentine. The Palazzo Farnese is a clear example of such an approach. It reconciles a Florentine palace tradition that is characterized by the three-dimensional, block-like form of the

Palazzo Medici or the Palazzo Strozzi with its Roman preferences for elements of ancient derivation such as the atrium entry or the imposing scale of the courtyard of Bramante's incomplete Palazzo dei Tribunali. In his work on St. Peter's, Sangallo drew from these very same contrasts, but now with the additional task of reconciling the complex history of the church's reconstruction; a history which he knew first-hand.

As a member of the workshop of St. Peter's since the era of Bramante, Sangallo was fully trained to address the complicated problems faced in building this vast church. Famed for his technical expertise, Sangallo assisted Bramante by constructing the centering for the four arches that defined the core of the church. After the death of Raphael in 1520, Sangallo was named co-architect with Baldassare Peruzzi, but the title guaranteed little real authority over the project. Little had been built since the papacy of Julius II, and the Sack of Rome further delayed construction. To both pilgrims and professional architects, the building site appeared scarcely different from the remains of antiquity. Paul III, on the other hand, actively sought out contributions from the reigning monarchs of Europe. Over the course of a decade, 162,000 ducats were raised for the project and nearly half of this sum was contributed by Spain, the result of the plundering of the New World. After Peruzzi's death in 1536, Sangallo exercised sole authority over the church's design.

In designing St. Peter's, individual spaces, structural elements, and architectural details were worked out in isolation from surrounding elements. Not surprisingly, then, no overall plan of the church has been preserved among the many sheets from the Sangallo era. The only overall plan was engraved as part of five copperplate engravings (1546–49) that illustrate Sangallo's wooden model for St. Peter's (75–76). The engravings the largest, most elaborate, and most expensive of the wooden architectural models of the Renaissance. Built by craftsmen supervised by Antonio Labacco, Sangallo's assistant, the model is itself a small structure 7.36 meters long, 6.02 meters wide, and 4.68 meters high at its dome. Its cost, more than 5,000 scudi, could have paid for the construction of an actual church building, a fact not lost on the project's detractors. The model is a statement of Sangallo's overall vision for St. Peter's, and in the words of Giorgio Vasari, it was "utterly complete."

75 Rome, St. Peter's, wooden model by Sangallo, 1539–46
76 Rome, St. Peter's, engraving by A. Salamanca showing plan of
Sangallo's model, 1549

75

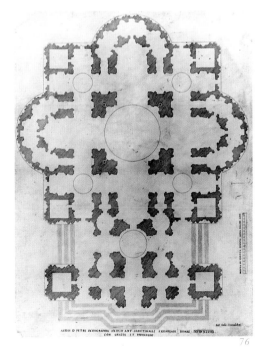

76

Sangallo's plan for St. Peter's is a kind of architectural hybrid, combining elements from both preceding centralized and composite schemes for the basilica. As a whole, the square central block owes its origins to Bramante's famous "Parchment" plan, but it is modified by a predilection of Raphael and Sangallo for spatial clarity and a duplication of elements. Yet, in adopting this arrangement, the facade has become disengaged from the main block of the church, creating a nearly independent, double-towered structure similar to the westwork of a Gothic cathedral. The most unusual feature is a tall, domed vestibule that joins the facade to the body of the basilica. Presumably, this chamber would serve as the resolution of the different approaches from the square and the Vatican, just as the public entering through the atrium and processions from the Imperial Palace meet in the narthex of Hagia Sophia in Constantinople. Otherwise, this link has no identifiable liturgical purpose, and it stands unique in the history of St. Peter's plans.

Similarly, the exterior of Sangallo's design fuses multiple (and often contradictory) images. If the bell towers resemble the Temple of Porsenna near Chiusi, and the double drum recalls the Mausolea of Augustus and Hadrian, the dome's pointed section is a compromise between the pointed profile of Florence Cathedral and the semicircular dome Bramante envisaged for St. Peter's. Recently, it has been suggested that the towers in Raphael's scheme for St. Peter's resemble funerary pyres and that Sangallo's continuation of this scheme recalls the traditional burial site of St. Peter between two such forms usually found on the spine of ancient racecourses. Yet the integration of recondite allusion must have contributed to the qualities of uniformity and repetition that permeate the design. Michelangelo, after all, criticized the scheme for its many nooks and crannies suitable for "delinquency, forging money, raping nuns, and other such roguery." Vasari also relates Michelangelo's dislike for multiplicity of the model's many levels, with "arches placed upon arches and cornices above cornices." In the minds of his critics, Sangallo may have captured the immense size of the new basilica without addressing the greatness embodied in its architectural scale.

The single most important change Sangallo made to existing construction was the raising of its floor level by about 3.2 meters. Surprisingly, for Sangallo, the change was motivated by aesthetic concerns regarding the extreme verticality of Raphael's nave rather than structural necessity. By setting the floor at a new, higher level, Sangallo dispensed with the need for the tall pilaster bases that had been designed by Bramante. With this change, the observer stood squarely on the same level as the system of architectural orders, no longer being required to look up into the building from below. If something of Bramante's characteristic spaciousness was lost, perceptual clarity was gained. Similarly, the orders could now be understood as part of a skeletal framework instead of parts of a continuous, space-defining wall. The repetition of clearly defined units was to become both the intellectual strength and the visual weakness of the project.

Otherwise, Sangallo's great model failed to influence St. Peter's in any way whatsoever. This was not the case in his other ecclesiastical projects, which often broke new ground within their clearly defined limits. Along with Raphael, Sansovino, and Peruzzi, Sangallo participated in the competition for S. Giovanni dei Fiorentini (1520), the Florentine church built in Rome for the glory of the Florentine pope, Leo X. An initial sketch proposed alternative longitudinal and centralized schemes (77), but the latter must have been clearly preferable for a visible site along the Tiber at the head of the Via Giulia. As engraved, the design clearly took its temple-front facade from Raphael's scheme for St. Peter's and adapted it to a circular plan with sixteen chapels, which in turn was a centralized version of a basilical plan. On the other hand, his most influential church addressed issues of ecclesiastical reform brought on, in part, by the Sack of Rome in 1527. S. Spirito in Sassia (1539), the church attached to the famous eponymous hospital near the Vatican, was among the very first to adapt to liturgical demands for multiple chapels, space for preaching, and the separation of clergy and laity (78). The box-like shape of this unassuming design recalled Florentine tradition (S. Salvatore al Monte) and paved the way for later developments in Rome (Il Gesù and its many variants).

Conspicuous as they are in the history of cinquecento architecture, the Palazzo Farnese and the model for St. Peter's form a small (and in many ways, atypical) part of Sangallo's architectural output. Among the thousands of drawings from the Sangallo workshop now preserved in the Uffizi, there are numerous schemes for smaller palaces, churches, and chapels throughout central Italy. No project was beyond the range of his estimable talent. The Pozzo di S. Patrizio (1527–35) in Orvieto perhaps represents the best illustration of a

135

professional readiness to take on any sort of project. Clement VII and his court took refuge in the famed hilltop city during the Sack of Rome, and Sangallo was ordered to provide water in case of attack. The well that Sangallo dug is a cylinder 13 meters wide and 63 meters deep, into which two independent and interlocking horse ramps are placed around a smaller, window-pierced shaft. Interlocking stairs of this sort had been drawn by Leonardo da Vinci and employed at Chambord, but in Orvieto their purpose was completely utilitarian. Horses could descend along one ramp, draw water, and return along the other without changing direction.

Antonio da Sangallo the Younger practiced architecture at a moment when there was no agreement on the form of the architectural profession. Trained by his uncles, who in turn were trained during the quattrocento, it comes as no surprise that there is a strong medieval heritage in Sangallo's full knowledge of technique and material. At the same time, the necessity to simultaneously direct several projects from his base in Rome contributed to the separation of design and construction that lay at the core of Alberti's vision of the ideal Renaissance architect. Yet Sangallo, for all his knowledge of antiquity, was no mere scholar-architect. As his architectural drawings repeatedly show, his architectural decisions were systematic and thoughtful. His view of professionalism addressed external factors that impinge upon design considerations—the symbolic and actual needs of powerful patrons, new forms of fortified architecture—to name a few. Baldasssare Peruzzi would address many of the same issues, but his artistic background and the context of his commissions would make him draw totally different conclusions.

BALDASSARE PERUZZI

Baldassare Peruzzi (1481–1536) may seem an unlikely candidate to be considered as a professional architect. Trained as a painter in his native Siena, Peruzzi arrived in Rome in 1503, and remained there for most of his life. Throughout his career, he stood in the shadow of Bramante, Raphael, and Antonio da Sangallo the Younger and never achieved the social or economic status of his peers. In comparison to the prolific output of the Sangallo family firm, Peruzzi left few completed architectural projects. Both unfairly and inaccurately, his

77　A. da Sangallo the Younger: Rome, San Giovanni dei Fiorentini, plan
　　showing superimposed longitudinal and central plan schemes, circa
　　1521
78　A. da Sangallo the Younger: Rome, S. Spirito in Sassia, begun 1539,
　　drawing showing facade and sketch of plan

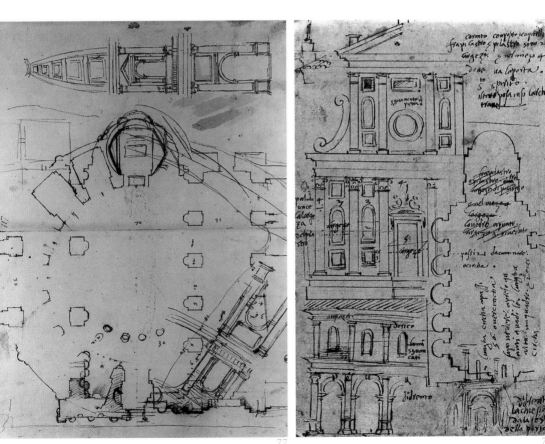

77   78

79 Peruzzi: Rome, Villa Farnesina, begun 1505–08
80 Villa Farnesina, plan

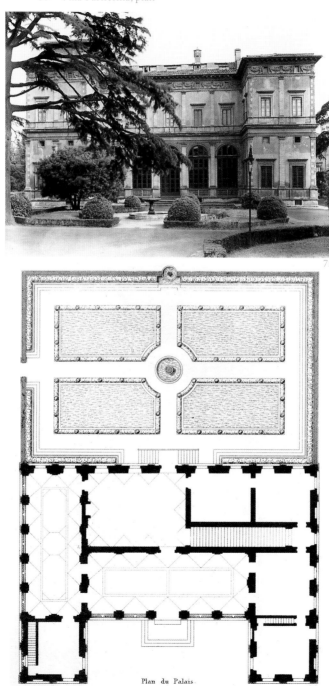

Plan du Palais

79

80

achievement has been measured by only two buildings, the Villa Farnesina and the Palazzo Massimo, which mark the initiation and conclusion of a career that brought little financial success or public recognition. Some his most innovative designs remain unfinished (like the Villa Trivulzio at Salone) or had little chance of being built (like his schemes for St. Peter's).

Yet Peruzzi's reputation rests on other accomplishments. A gifted architectural draftsman whose architectural plans cleverly disguised the difficulties posed by irregular sites and preexisting construction, Peruzzi's greatest ideas often remained on paper. The true measures of Peruzzi's professionalism, then, are his evocative architectural drawings and the full range of his varied endeavors—building design, military architecture, stage design, hydraulic engineering, metallurgy, and architectural theory.

Perruzzi's debt to the artistic traditions of his native Siena was considerable. Lacking the quasi-scientific perspective that had become a characteristic of Florentine art, Sienese painting traditionally showed a tenacious survival of Gothic motifs and Byzantine effects. If judged by Florentine standards, it could be seen as deeply conservative and even illogical. There was never any figure comparable to Brunelleschi or Alberti, and consequently, Sienese quattrocento architecture was never much constrained by theory or by a dogmatic appreciation of antiquity. This posed a dilemma of sorts to Francesco di Giorgio, the only Sienese prior to Peruzzi who displayed considerable talent as both a painter and an architect. Di Giorgio's churches show an austere geometry so close to that of Alberti, while his paintings display a medieval-like personality. If there was a virtue to Siena's artistic isolation, it was that unusual and unconventional solutions resulted from the reluctance to adopt new formulae employed elsewhere.

Peruzzi's archaizing but freethinking training, so characteristic of his Sienese background, was put to use in the design of the Villa Farnesina (begun 1505–08), the palatial villa of Agostino Chigi, the affluent Sienese banker who had become a close friend and financial advisor to Julius II (79–80). In type, the concept of the residence was that of a suburban villa, the informal pleasure retreats that were usually set among vineyards on the hills close to the center of Rome. Chigi's *vigna*, which acquired its present name after the

Farnese family who later purchased the property and incorporated it into their adjacent residence, was composed of four principal parts. They included Peruzzi's palatial residence, smaller and larger formal gardens surrounding it, a dining loggia overlooking the Tiber River, and a combination guesthouse and stables designed by Raphael. By virtue of its location on the Via della Lungara, the street that was the extra-urban counterpart to the Via Giulia, Peruzzi's design is usually characterized as a suburban villa.

The villa was primarily used for entertainment on a scale that invited comparison with the great banquets of antiquity. From the outset, the villa was employed to amuse the reigning Pope. Julius II visited the Farnesina twice, as if to ascertain Chigi's status as a rival in splendid patronage. Leo X was also a visitor to the Farnesina, where, after a banquet on August 28, 1519, he performed a marriage ceremony of Chigi and his long-standing mistress. The honored guests for the wedding were each given a silver plate used in serving the meal, and in another instance, the silver was tossed in the river, only to be retrieved by hidden nets after the visitors had departed. With fresco decorations by Raphael, Sodoma, and Peruzzi himself, the Villa Farnesina exuded the air of luxury and hedonism, especially in the grand fetes given there.

If the concept of a structure for such lavish purposes ultimately derives from antiquity, the Villa Farnesina's layout had its roots in more recent developments. While it was not the first suburban villa in Rome, it was clearly the most splendid and the most luxurious. The formal typology of its arrangement of a central loggia flanked by corner towers has been traced back ultimately to antiquity, by way of both Venetian palaces and vernacular structures throughout northern Italy. But Peruzzi's sights were set less high. Through the villa's U-shaped plan and back-to-back loggias, the Farnesina emulated Villa Chigi alle Volte near Siena (circa 1480–1505), which had been built for Agostino's brother Sigismondo. If this accounts for the Farnesina's links to traditions in non-urban architecture, its applied orders reflect a tradition of palace facades developed in Rome and Urbino that are best expressed in Rome by the imposing exteriors of the Cancelleria. Originally, the Farnesina's appearance was nowhere as austere as it appears today. Peruzzi frescoed the entire facade with figures in a terra-cotta-colored chiaroscuro, giving the orders a function of a frame around an illusionistic view.

81

82

Peruzzi was particularly adept in expressing architectural ideas through his paintings, decorations, and stage design—the three areas that occupied his time during the second decade of the sixteenth century. Unlike other designers, whose urban representations sought to display a part of an ancient city as they imagined it, those of Peruzzi—irregular in the shape of its public spaces and containing buildings of different character from diverse periods—could easily be mistaken for a corner of Rome. Even when dealing with exalted subject matter, Peruzzi conceives of architectural settings in a flexible manner usually associated with his comic scenes. The frescoes he painted in the Sala delle Prospettive (circa 1515), the main *salone* of the Villa Farnesina, give the illusion of looking outward through a portico to the actual city beyond (81). The same ideas are repeated on a grand scale in the *Presentation of the Virgin* (1518), where an imaginary forum is composed of an asymmetrical arrangement of two classical temples, a mausoleum inspired by the campanili in Raphael's proposal for the facade of St. Peter's, and a contemporary palace whose powerfully rusticated columns anticipate those of Giulio Romano's house in Rome and Sansovino's Mint in Venice (82). At the rear, a street leads into a medieval quarter, as suggested by the bell tower in the distance. When seen in comparison to Raphael's *Fire in the Borgo*, the *Presentation* may appear to historians of painting as less dramatic and disciplined. But to architectural historians, the setting reveals Peruzzi's considerable imagination in inventing buildings of different styles and epochs.

Although Rome was the focus of Peruzzi's career as an architect and painter, his fame brought him commissions elsewhere in northern Italy. In 1514–15, he may have made two trips to Emilia where Alberto Pio was seeking to transform Carpi into a model princely court. Peruzzi's first project, a new facade for the Cathedral of Carpi (La Sagra), emphasized the contrast between small and large orders in a coherent design for the facade of a basilical church plan (83). If the origins for the scheme are found in Bramante's facade for the parish church at Roccaverano, then Peruzzi's interlocking temple fronts suggest the solutions employed later by Palladio in Venice. A design for a new cathedral shortly followed, and again Peruzzi turned to Bramante for inspiration, this time transforming the most recent longitudinal plans for St. Peter's by emphasizing a more plastic treatment of crossing piers. The final project, the completion of the church of S. Nicolò, only involved work on the church's three-bay nave. Northern Italian craftsmen executed all projects in Peruzzi's absence, and the present condition of these buildings does not fully reflect the richly innovative ideas of their architect.

When Peruzzi returned to Northern Italy for a second visit in 1521–23, he encountered one of the most unusual commissions of his career. The immense Gothic church of S. Petronio lacked a completed facade, as only a few levels of marble encrustation had been laid since 1394. To complicate matters, the central portal contained figures by Jacopo della Quercia in the jambs and tympanum. An initial proposal by a local architect was unsatisfactory, and Peruzzi in turn provided three alternative proposals. In two contrasting schemes, Gothic motifs such as a central rosette, bifora windows, and various forms of tympana are employed in what is essentially a closely knit, classical three-story scheme (84). Peruzzi builds up the schemes with superimposed rectangular panels, and in one, he presents radically different alternatives for the towers: a telescoping octagonal shaft on one side and stunted turrets on the other. From these schemes, it is clear that Peruzzi had wished to recast Raphael's ideas for the facade of St. Peter's in the medieval forms found in the cathedral of his native Siena. Eventually, the projects were criticized for failing to conform with the architecture of the church, a problem that was to haunt subsequent proposals by Giulio Romano, Vignola, and Palladio, among others.

The Sack of Rome (1527) profoundly altered the direction of Peruzzi's career as an architect. He was captured by the invading troops, and his freedom was obtained only after the payment of a ransom by a Sienese ambassador. Indebted to his compatriots and with little immediate opportunity to paint or build as he had done in Rome, Peruzzi returned to Siena, where he was immediately appointed as city architect. Although other cinquecento architects such as Giulio Romano in Mantua and Giorgio Vasari in Florence wielded great authority over extensive building programs, they essentially served as courtiers responsible to a single ruler. In the tradition of the medieval city states, of which Siena was among the very last, Peruzzi answered directly to the government and was put in charge of the modernization of Siena's fortifications (1527–32). His

143

83 Peruzzi: Carpi, Cathedral (La Sagra), 1514–15
84 Peruzzi: Bologna, scheme for facade of S. Petronio.

83

84

true peers were medieval artist-architects such as Giotto, who was employed on the construction of Florence's third circuit of walls, rather than his own contemporaries.

As we have already seen, the Palazzo Massimo shows Peruzzi's professionalism at its most inventive (67–68). Whenever he was faced with difficult sites or existing construction, he found ways of conveying the apparent effect of regularity whenever it could not be achieved as an absolute fact. While Palladio and others designed buildings according to recognizable typologies of form, Peruzzi delighted in providing alternative solutions to unique challenges. This is indicated by many of his projects—the numerous schemes for the rebuilding of S. Domenico in Siena, the facade of S. Petronio, the Palazzo Ricci in Montepulciano, and a dam on the Bruna River near Siena—for which three or more schemes survive. Although Peruzzi left no mark on St. Peter's during his tenure in the workshop, his sketches convey a concern for graphic representation and a tendency to see spaces as independent geometric shapes with an architectural identity all their own. The oval particularly intrigued Peruzzi as a way of reconciling the ideal shapes of centrally planned structures with the response to circumstance found in longitudinal church plans. This addition to the repertoire of architectural shapes can be found in structures of all sizes and types—the small church of S. Giacomo in Augusta for the Hospital of the Incurabili in Rome, larger ideal churches, and even a garden for the Villa Trivulzio near Salone.

Peruzzi was a learned student of antiquity who made an extensive survey of its remains. Yet he was also critical of Vitruvius for a lack of appreciation of visual qualities in architecture. In contrast to equally professional architects such as Antonio the Younger who found discipline in Vitruvius and archaeology, Peruzzi was attentive to the remains of unconventional ancient buildings and was notably flexible in his application of their motifs. He was among the first architects to study Hadrian's Villa, as shown by his sketches (in Uffizi, A 553 recto) of the nympheum of the Water Court—also known as the Piazza d'Oro—that capture the structure's complex curved systems of enclosure. Early Christian remains also caught Peruzzi's imagination and were to reappear in his architecture. *Vestibula*, like the narthex of the Lateran Baptistery, seen in Uffizi, A 457 recto, were seminal ideas for his reshaping of the portico on the facade of the Palazzo Massimo, and the curved corner piers of the Oratorio

145

della Croce (Uffizi, A 438 recto) were to reappear in the crossing of the Carpi's new cathedral. Of all of Peruzzi's experimental sketches based on antiquity, the most intriguing is for a central plan church composed of interpenetrating triangles with alternating semicircular and trapezoidal recesses (Uffizi, A 553 verso). The hexagonal shape for a ground plan was indeed rare in the Renaissance, but the essential features of Peruzzi's sketch were to emerge a century later in Borromini's plan for S. Ivo della Sapienza. Although the buildings of these two great architects were fundamentally different in every conceivable way, what they shared was a creative license in articulating non-Vitruvian forms.

The best evidence for Peruzzi's thoughts on architecture—the limitations of Vitruvius, ground plans for irregular sites, the creative limitations of preexisting construction—is found in his actual buildings and especially in his expressive drawings. Several contemporary sources indicate that Peruzzi may have intended to prepare a treatise touching on the subjects of ancient buildings, a comparison of Vitruvian doctrine with ancient practice, and even perhaps, contemporary buildings, including his own. Sadly, there is no evidence as to how he had planned to publish his theoretical writings and their illustrations. When seen in the context of the full body of Renaissance architectural theory, Peruzzi's hypothetical treatise would have represented a middle ground position, tempering Alberti's and Palladio's blind faith in antiquity with the common sense and professionalism of his own experience and that of his teacher, Francesco di Giorgio. The greatest beneficiary of Peruzzi's architectural thought was Serlio, who inherited a share of Peruzzi's drawings, and in turn, used them as inspiration for a completely new kind of treatise, the illustrated architectural manual written for architects by a professional colleague.

SEBASTIANO SERLIO

Sebastiano Serlio was the author of the first illustrated architectural manual for both architects and the general reader. Unlike Alberti, whose ten books in *De re aedificatoria* formed a coherent text in Latin that contained no illustrations, Serlio's pages are copiously illustrated with woodcuts of ancient buildings, contemporary examples, and projects of his own design. Nor was the endeavor the publication of a book in the commonly accepted sense of the term. Rather, it was to have been composed of seven volumes whose content appears to have changed over the course of its complicated history of publication. A first volume on the orders of architecture, the *Fourth Book*, was published in Venice in 1537. The *Third Book* on antiquities appeared three years later, also in Venice. Serlio then moved to France, where he published his *First Book* on geometry, his *Second Book* on perspective (1545), and a *Fifth Book* on temples (1547). A supplementary volume devoted to gateways, the *Libro estrordinario* (1551), was the last published work in Serlio's lifetime. Two manuscripts for the *Sixth Book* on housing exist in Munich and the Avery Library at Columbia University. A *Seventh Book* on unusual design circumstances was acquired by the Mantuan antiquary Jacopo Strada and published posthumously in Munich (1575). Another supplementary volume, the so-called "Eighth Book" on Roman military camps as described by Polybius also exists in manuscript in Munich but was not published until recently. No contemporary can equal Serlio in the breadth of his architectural interests and the variety of architectural traditions encountered in his long and productive life.

For a figure of such importance, it is surprising that the first half-century of his life is still something of a mystery. Serlio was a native of Bologna, and his origins were exceedingly humble; his father was a furrier. In all probability, Serlio was apprenticed to Bolognese painters from whom he learned the skill of painting architectural backgrounds in perspective, which served him well in the preparation of his treatises. He acquired his knowledge of contemporary developments in Roman architecture during his apprenticeship to Peruzzi, which lasted from 1515 to 1520. The contemporary buildings published in his treatise are highly selective, and there are errors, such as the implications that the projects for St. Peter's by Raphael and Peruzzi were executed during the reign of Julius II, or that the courtyard under execution in the Villa Madama was rectangular. The omissions are even more startling, if Serlio's desire to illustrate buildings that complement his vision of antiquity is taken into account. For example, Bramante's scheme for St. Peter's is represented only by its cupola, while plans by Raphael and Peruzzi deriving from Bramante are shown. Domestic structures—Bramante's Palazzo Caprini, Raphael's palaces, and the Palazzo Farnese, whose incomplete hulk would have startled any visitor—

are conspicuously absent. Even more inexplicable is Serlio's failure to illustrate Peruzzi's Villa Farnesina, which is discussed primarily in terms of its decorations.

Serlio returned to Bologna in 1520, and by the summer of 1522, he assisted Peruzzi by preparing two plans of S. Petronio, which were likely made in conjunction with Peruzzi's proposal for the church's facade. Sometime before 1528, Serlio left for Venice to begin publishing a series of engravings of the classical orders, for which the copyright was granted by the Venetian Senate in 1528. Even after his move to Venice, Serlio may have returned to Bologna and traveled to Rome for study.

Serlio was undoubtedly attracted to Venice for its tradition of publishing quality books and woodcut engravings. In his adopted city, he became its first spokesman for a new class of architectural ideas involving the systematic use of the architectural orders based upon the proportion of a column's diameter to its height. While Serlio's selection of examples was governed by Vitruvian orthodoxy, his critical point of view was sufficiently flexible to allow for the individual judgment of the architect. Serlio is particularly attentive to the coherence of the orders and the visibility of all their parts without obstruction from below. In this sense, variations such as the reduction of moldings in the Pantheon's upper order, could be justified because they would have appeared diminutive and chaotic when seen from below. Similarly, Serlio eschews the Vitruvian association of the Corinthian order with Venus in favor of Vesta, the goddess of virginity, because of the potential association with churches dedicated to the Virgin Mary.

In Venice, Serlio's circle of friends was notable for the both the range of their interests and their own intellectual independence, and it is certain that unpublished drafts of Serlio's treatises circulated among them. For instance, Pietro Aretino's interest in architecture can be attributed to Serlio, just as Titian's paintings from the 1530s onward reveal architectural backgrounds full of Serlian ideas. Serlio is thought to have held anti-papal ideas, and his avoidance of classical orders has been linked to the rise of a new spirituality based on the reformist ideas of Luther, Erasmus, and Calvin. Serlio's religious beliefs also helped to attract patronage in France. From 1541 to 1549, he received a pension from Marguerite of Navarre, the sister of King Francois I, to whom the *Fifth Book* was dedicated. It is, in fact, in the dedication of this book where Serlio boldly paraphrases the new evangelical ideas of the Reformation.

A logical consequence of the intellectual stimulation provided by his contemporaries was Serlio's attention to Venice, which he likely saw as the initial market for his publications. In the *Fourth Book*, Serlio states that Venetian building practice differs from all other cities on account of its dense population. As a consequence, sites are narrow and buildings must be laid out with the greatest care. Serlio was, of course, speaking about the Venetian palace as a recognizable type, and if he does not mention its conflicting orientations to water and land, lack of an impressive courtyard such as those of Florence and Rome, or the tendency of its tripartite plan to be reflected throughout the structure, these factors are taken for granted in the discussions and engravings that follow. Another unstated principle is how the characteristic tripartite rhythms in turn influenced architectural membering of palatial facades. The visible portions of the palace matter most. All of the facade's major elements—the width and height of doors and windows, their spacing, and their parapets—are all based on a single unit of measure, the width (that is, the diameter of the base) of its columns. The most notable departure from Roman and Florentine tradition is the suggestion that the height of the palace's stories be reduced by one quarter for each successive floor. Those palaces with rusticated ground floors form an exception in that their heights are the same as the floor above.

In the course of his discussion of the architectural orders, Serlio provides the reader with designs for three palace facades (85–86). While each scheme in some way employs Doric, Ionic or Corinthian columns, they illustrate different kinds of facade types, all of which can be understood as Venetian. In the first two examples, the reduction in the height of the uppermost story is demonstrated. From the evidence provided by the illustration, the subject of the first is the assimilation of Roman motifs into the tradition of flat relief found in Venetian palaces of the late quattrocento. For this reason, it is the best known of the three and perhaps the most influential. Yet in the second scheme, architectural orders are given a secondary role in the *serliana*, and an emphatic role is assigned to blank panels and windows. Of all schemes, it is the one most closely tied to conventions of use and comfort. Serlio remarks emphatically upon the Venetian custom of employing several balconies for viewing the canals and

149

85   Serlio: Facade for a Venetian palace
86   Serlio: Facade for a Venetian palace
87   Serlio: Fontainebleau, Grotte des Pins, 1541–43

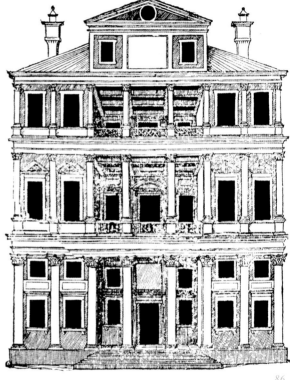

85

86

87

enjoying cool breezes, and in this instance, he seeks to maintain the facade's structural integrity by placing them on projections of the wall below. The position of the elaborate chimneys above the panels also indicates that Serlio had studied vernacular housing in Venice, where fireplaces were customarily located between paired windows. The final scheme is the most idiosyncratic, since it bears little relation to the text. At the same time, it is also the most overtly antiquarian of the facades in its use of a flat entablature over columns echoing both a Roman basilica and Peruzzi's Palazzo Massimo. It is also the most deliberately archaic in its accommodation of post-and-lintel construction in wood, the technique in which most upper-story floors were constructed. This peculiar conjunction of bold design and local tradition was recalled two decades later in Palladio's Palazzo Chiericati in Vicenza.

As an architect, Serlio held no official position in the Venetian government, and thus, he was involved primarily in consultations with private clients. The only structure of consequence attributed to him, the Palazzo Zen (1538), bears little relationship to those illustrated in the treatise. What makes this exterior so astonishing is the alternation of round classical arches with Byzantine ogee arches on the *piano nobile*. This unusual combination of Byzantine and classical elements has been explained as a reference to the diplomatic missions undertaken by its patron to Constantinople. For Serlio, this experience was a preparation for the mixture of medieval and classical forms illustrated in the *Sixth Book* and the *Seventh Book*.

Serlio sought and obtained the critical approval of his Venetian friends, but financial support was more elusive. Once more, he had to seek support for his treatise. An appeal in 1539, to Henry VIII of England came to nothing. With the assistance of the French ambassador in Venice, he obtained the support of Francois I of France for the publication of the *Third Book*. Following an appeal to Marguerite of Navarre, Serlio departed for France in 1541, primarily to publish the remaining books in his treatise. Shortly after Christmas that year, Serlio catered into the service of King Francois I at Fontainebleau.

As the king's architect, Serlio made two contributions to Fontainebleau. The first was the Grotte des Pins (1541–43), a rusticated grotto underneath a pavilion at the end of the Galerie d'Ulysse (87). Although Serlio may have also provided designs for illusionistic architecture of the grotto's vaults, all that remains today is the exterior of its three-bay loggia. The design must have appeared strange to a court already permeated by Italian culture. Figures of muscular giants merge with each of its boldly rusticated piers, which in turn, support roughly hewn gables. The design has the character of a satirical commentary on art and artists at court; the giants and their surrounding architecture being the uncouth country relations to the elegant and refined stucco figures by Rosso and Primaticcio inside the chateau.

As befitting its purpose, the Salle de Bal (begun 1541) on the Cour Ovale was meant to be more formal and luxurious. Its exterior was meant to recall the portico-villas with corner towers that Serlio had known in Italy, and its interior contained a rectangular hall with great apses at each end. The hall was to have been covered by a barrel vault, a concept that was probably inspired by Sansovino's library in Venice. After the death of Francois I in 1547, Serlio was replaced by Philibert de L'Orme, who completed the project with a flat wooden ceiling.

At the same time, Serlio was able to take on independent architectural commissions. In his design for the chateau of Ancy-le-Franc in Burgundy (1541–46), he faced the problem of combining the image of an Italian building with the closed form of a fortified French chateau (88). Although Serlio at first desired to make a building that was Italian down to the final detail, the patron intervened in architectural matters and made decisions that his architect was obliged to follow. Serlio presented three separate designs, all subsequent changes emphasized traditionally by French architectural values. With the removal of the ground level rustication and its replacement with attached pilasters on all exterior surfaces, the orders were disengaged from the body of the building and became a form of architectural decoration as had been done at Chambord. Further changes included the substitution of a pitched French roof for a lower Italian one and the transformation of the ground-floor loggias into a solid wall whose elevation unimaginatively restates that of the Belvedere Courtyard.

It is not surprising that Serlio's most successful French project was designed for an Italian patron. Le Grand Ferrare (1544–46) was a residence at Fontainebleau for Ippolito d'Este, archbishop of Lyons and the future patron of the Villa d'Este at Tivoli (89). Serlio's plan is

88   Serlio: Ancy-le-Franc, chateau, 1541–46
89   Serlio: Fontainebleau, Le Grand Ferrare, 1544–46
90   Serlio: A House for a Merchant in France

88

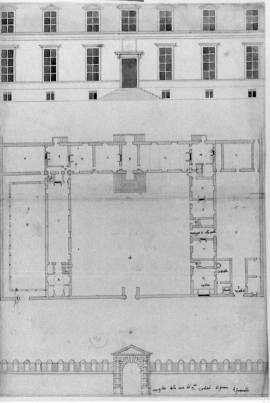

89

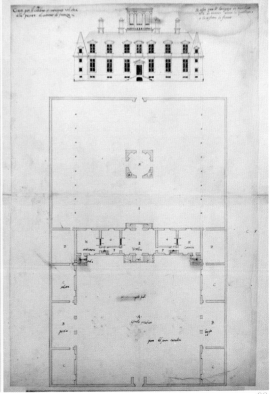

90

one of utter clarity, and it fuses divergent formal traditions in a way he was prevented from doing at Ancy-le-Franc. Three wings surround a roughly square courtyard, which is enclosed on its fourth side by a wall. Of the wings, the main block is the *corps des logis*, which is set at the back and opens to a garden. Although Serlio's layout was derived from late medieval French residences such as the Hotel Cluny in Paris, it now showed a new regularity in its arrangement and an unambiguous hierarchy of its parts. Unfortunately, only the rusticated portal from the main entrance is all that remains of a design that became a distinct type in French domestic architecture.

Serlio's affinity with French architecture is best illustrated by his *Sixth Book*. By far the most original chapter of the treatise, it is a nuanced comparison of housing types found in both Italy and France. It contains the designs for nine types of country residences and eleven types of urban residences, which are organized according to two related principles—an ascending social hierarchy according to the status of the occupant and divergent traditions of design and decoration in Italy and France. Their range of scale and complexity is extraordinary, varying from the house of a poor farmer or artisan to palaces fit for a merchant, governor, prince, or king (90). If Serlio's role in France was that of a purveyor of Italian style, throughout the book, he also departs from Italian norms in order to accommodate French concepts of comfort and climatic conditions. It differs from preceding treatises in its concern for buildings for all classes of citizens and the vernacular structures that they would inhabit. Although Serlio provides no overall plan for a city in which these structures would be placed, it has been assumed that they would be located in a non-hierarchical fashion throughout the city.

The influence of the *Sixth Book* demonstrates the complex interrelationships between French and Italian architecture. Although the book was never published until recently, it was well-known in both countries, having circulated through copies after the original manuscripts. Almost certainly, the book influenced Palladio's design for the Villa Rotunda, as indicated by its similarity to two designs for pavilions that combine domes and temple fronts. The Avery version of the *Sixth Book* was once owned by Jacques Androuet du Cerceau, who copied several of its designs for his *Temples et habitations fortifies*, and the same manuscript may have influenced Ledoux in his design for the salt works of Chaux.

So books rather than buildings are the measure of Serlio's achievement. In terms of ideas, he seems consciously intent on protecting architectural traditions rather than deliberately overthrowing them. The achievement of this deliberate archaizing was more than just an appeal to taste; it represented a central element in Serlio's approach to architecture. Just as Serlio's Bolognese origins stand apart from Rome and Florence, the traditional centers of Renaissance architecture, his status as an outsider contributed to his appreciation of regional architectural traditions. In the *Seventh Book*, the urban form of Bologna, his native city, is described being for the most part, defined by porticoes, a characterization that meets with universal approval. No other architect maintained such a critical detachment from the classical tradition, which he employed on its own terms, or accepted non-classical architecture as the equal of antiquity.

Peruzzi, Sangallo, and Serlio represented what Catherine Wilkinson Zerner has called the "new professionalism" in cinquecento architecture. Neither a *uomo universale* nor a practitioner in the modern sense, each of these three architects was to a great degree conditioned by the new kinds of information that were put at his disposal. A working knowledge of Vitruvius's treatise was necessary because the architect could find for himself an adequate explanation of the buildings and principles of Roman antiquity. But his observations were entirely superseded in time by the intense study of ruins by the architects themselves. As assisted by the numerous sketchbooks, drawings, and copies made after them, architects followed a systematic and scientific archaeological approach, and the illustrated book was thus the perfect means for dispersing and preserving their information.

But antiquity alone did not ignite an architectural revolution. In effect, the achievements of Bramante and Raphael brought about a fundamental change in the appreciation of ancient architecture. Their achievements were now illustrated in the publications of Serlio, where they were interspersed with the designs made by the author himself. Eventually, Serlio's own designs came to predominate in the later books, and in Palladio's *Quattro Libri*, the career of an individual architect was presented in the context of a didactic exhibition. From these antiquities old and new, a different kind of architect emerged. To borrow a concept from Burckhardt, architectural practice was now a work of art.

Venetian architecture, indeed is stage architecture, caring little for principle (up to Palladio) and concerned mainly with effects. Venice is the world's loveliest city, but it produced only one architect—Palladio—who worked along conceptual lines. Intellectual power, the posing and solving of architectural problems, is missing from Venetian buildings, which captivate the eye by tricks and blandishments, as Venice's detractors have perceived....later in the 16th century they made use of a somewhat degraded Florentine, Jacopo Tatti, called Sansovino, to revamp the city in the High Renaissance style.

MARY MCCARTHY,
Venice Observed, 1956

z

THE MOST SERENE REPUBLIC:
OPULENCE & RETARDATION

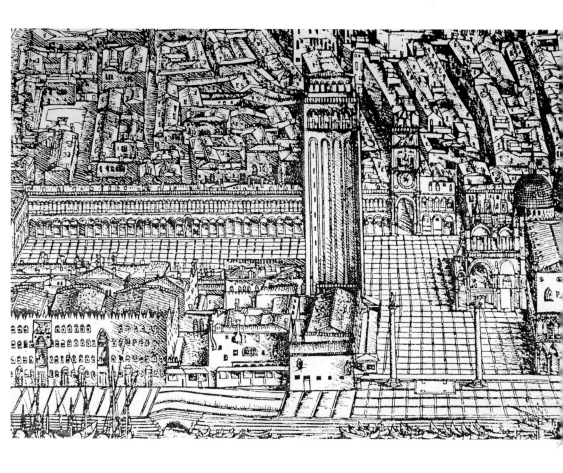

91   J. de' Barbari, perspective view of Venice, 1500,
detail showing Piazza San Marco

Mary McCarthy, the great American writer and observer of Italian culture, felt uncomfortable with public display as a principle of architectural expression. If her taste in Venetian architecture was formed by the austere classicism of Palladio, then there was little room for critically accepting buildings displaying a sense of theatricality.

This does not suggest that Venice's buildings were designed according to scenographic principles, although the structures' appearance is seen in a context that shares many features with stage design. Nor are the buildings theatrical in the sense of the Italian term *teatro*, which was frequently employed to describe large and impressive architectural designs. Theatricality in Venetian architecture exists at both grand and intimate scales. It is instead the means by which Venice created a self-conscious urban life full of spectacle and ceremony around which its buildings were formed. The architecture is manmade but sea-borne, and by its separation from the Terraferma, the experience of Venice's architecture takes on the unreal quality of a theatrical production.

If Venice's physical setting contributed to architectural opulence, its long history as an independent republic fostered a tradition-bound architectural patronage. After all, the first doge was elected in 697, and the last doge abdicated in 1797. More than a millennium of unbroken self-government led to the belief that Venice was the "eldest child of liberty." The sense of permanence ensured by the elaborate, five-stage procedure employed in the election of a doge was the complement to the archaisms so prevalent in Venetian art. The earliest and best known of these is the eleventh-century church of S. Marco, the private chapel of the doge and the patronal church of the city, which was built in emulation of Justinian's sixth-century Church of the Holy Apostles in Constantinople. A revival of interest in eastern church types also occurred after the Ottoman conquest of Constantinople in 1453, when thousands of Venetians returned home with a full knowledge of Byzantine architectural traditions. Yet this revival of Byzantine forms, like all other revivals in Venice, was not sentimental; it was merely efficient.

The theatrical experience of Venice's architecture is the natural consequence of a taste for visual opulence and a retardation in accepting the formal vocabulary of Florence and especially Rome. The roots of these effects are to be found in Venice's unique setting, a series of islands that coalesced to form the apparently homogeneous city we know today. Dualities exist on all levels. Venetians understood the island settlements as independent entities defined by the canals that surround them, but the body of the city is knit together by a tapestry of interwoven passageways and bridges. In Venetian architectural parlance, there are many squares, or *campi*, but there is only one piazza, the Piazza S. Marco (91). There are many palatial residences that the Venetians call a *Ca'* (a diminutive of *casa*), but there is only one palazzo, the Palazzo Ducale, known in English as the Doge's Palace. Venice's urban structure becomes apparent after many changes of direction in its maze of narrow, dark *calle* and their contrast with the brilliant, open *campi* with their parish churches and wellheads. Throughout the city, facades take on a special importance because of frontal viewpoints offered by broad bodies of water. Their material presence is sharpened by light reflected from the water, and the contrasts in their surfaces are heightened by precisely defined shadows. On the Grand Canal, a street of water flanked by aristocratic residences, palaces appear unapproachable by water, but on land, they are aggressively accessible. The visible theatricality of Venice's buildings is, in fact, the architectural counterpart to a sensuality of light, color, and texture in its paintings.

Precisely how theatricality extended to the private domain is demonstrated by the palaces of Venice's noble families, the most visible symbols of the city's wealth and stability. In terms of their use, Venetian palaces were part family residence for one or more members of a merchant aristocracy, and part warehouse, where the fruits of its trading ventures were sometimes stored. What made Venetian palaces different from those in Rome or Florence, which are organized around a large courtyard, is their tripartite floor plan where smaller rooms flank a long, narrow hall (92). This arrangement was ideally suited to building sites that were typically narrower along the water's edge than they were deep. Such a configuration meant that the Venetian palace usually had two entrances, one an important part of the building's facade facing the water, and the other, leading to a small courtyard where an open staircase led to the upper story. As a type, the Venetian palace was distinct from all others in Italy, and its origins are to be found in early Veneto-Byzantine residences.

The technical constraints that influenced palace design were also characteristically Venetian. Building on wooden poles sunk deep into unstable, muddy soil required that the physical structure be as light as possible (93). Bearing walls were nominally constructed with brick, which was usually covered with stucco and often frescoed with painted decorations by painters such as Giorgione. Even the Venetian love for richly veined polychrome stone facing on luxury residences was a veneer applied to a brick core. For the same reasons, masonry vaulting was avoided, and wooden floor construction covered by terrazzo was preferred for its lightness and flexibility.

If typology is read in a building's plan, a palace's exterior and interaction with its urban setting are the measures of its theatricality. With rare exceptions, palaces on secondary canals located within the city's dense urban fabric are never visible in their entirety. But the Grand Canal allowed for the uninterrupted visibility of palace facades, and their architects responded by developing complex, interlocking rhythms that elaborated (but never totally obscured) the tripartite arrangement. These principles of palatial design were largely independent of architectural style (and to a surprising degree of scale as well), remaining just as valid for the grand Baroque palaces of Longhena as they were for smaller medieval residences.

The palaces of Mauro Codussi (circa 1440–1504) marked the arrival of the kind of Renaissance architectural style normally associated with buildings in Rome or Florence. Rather little is known about Codussi's seminal contributions to palace design, the Palazzo Lando (circa 1485–90, later Corner-Spinelli) and the Palazzo Loredan (circa 1500–08, later Vendramin-Calergi), though both can be clearly attributed to Codussi on account of the sophistication and coherence of their design. In the Palazzo Lando, the taller ground story is rusticated, serving as a base for the two shorter stories above. Although classical elements are limited to the pilasters at the corners of each floor, the culminating entablature with garlands and roundels, and the columnar mullions of the windows, the design as a whole conveys a deliberately classical sense of elegance and refinement. In the Palazzo Loredan, on the other hand, the facade is fully developed in three dimensions, marking the first instance where Roman grandeur can be seen in a Venetian palace (94). Paired pilasters flanking the outer bays and single pilasters in the central bays again form a base for the upper two stories, which are now delineated by fluted columns and entablatures—the imposing entablature of the upper story gives the facade a sense of weight and mass unprecedented for a Venetian exterior. Although both palaces represent an assimilation of

161

92   Venetian palace type, Diagrammatic plan
93   Typical Venetian building foundation, section
94   Codussi: Venice, Palazzo Loredan (Vendramin–Calergi), circa 1500–08

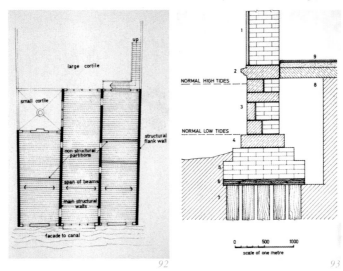

92

93

94

classical motifs into the system of a Venetian palace facade, they also define the two broad trends followed by cinquecento architects—the flat relief of the Palazzo Contarini delle Figure (rebuilt 1545) or the Palazzo Balbi (1580s) by Alessandro Vittoria, and the deep relief of Sansovino's Palazzo Cornaro or Sanmicheli's Palazzo Grimani.

Revolutionary as these exteriors may have been in terms of announcing a new era in architectural design, Codussi's palaces never completely overthrew Venetian practices. The tripartite division so typical of Venetian palaces can be discerned behind their classical masks; the layout of the Palazzo Loredan, for instance, employs a T-shaped loggia and central hall on the ground floor. In their own ways, each palace facade displays a concern for sumptuous effects. For example, the Palazzo Lando for the overall textural relief of its rustication, windows, and ornaments, and the Palazzo Loredan for the coloristic effects of its marble revetment and porphyry roundels—the complementary effects of shade and shadow that are the logical result of its deep relief. The lesson of how these buildings assimilated Renaissance ideals and local traditions was not to be forgotten by Serlio or Sanmicheli.

To Venetians, theatricality was just a part of a larger myth that occasioned Venice's identity—the myth of Venice as The Most Serene Republic. The principal item was the belief in the continuity of old and new Roman law and culture, of which Venice was the primary exponent. So prevalent and so longlasting was this tenet that Lord Byron characterized Venice as "the last Roman vestige from the overwhelming Attila." Venice's aspiration to be the true successor to Rome was commonplace from the Middle Ages onward, however, its validity for architecture was open to question. Venice, after all, had no Roman ruins or Christian relics—the body of St. Mark was stolen from Egypt. The traditions of Byzantium and Islam, on the other hand, were pervasive and to be seen in its public and private structures down to the arrival of a self-conscious Romanism in the sixteenth century. Yet belief in a mythical Roman continuity in Venetian culture and the non-Roman appearance of its buildings posed a contradiction to which no Venetian would admit.

The second tenet in the myth was the independence of the Venetian Church from Rome. In Venice, the structure of church authority was assumed by the state. Venice's cathedral, S. Pietro in Castello, displayed no visible sense of authority because of its distant

163

location far from the center of Venice (S. Marco became a cathedral only in 1807). Parish priests were not appointed by the bishop but elected by a majority of the male parishioners. In this light, it was important to realize the civic roles of Venice's three most important sixteenth-century churches. The initial cost of building S. Salvador was paid by the Venetian government on account of its central role in the myth of Venice as a city dedicated to Christ. S. Giorgio Maggiore was built by a powerful religious order that assisted the state in its conflicts with the Turks, and the Redentore was effectively a church of state because of the annual congregation of the Senate in its tribune during the Feast of the Redeemer. In the seventeenth century, traditional Venetian religious independence was so strong that James I maintained the hope that Venetians would forsake the papacy and join the Church of England.

That Venice remained uncorrupted by papal interference was to a large degree true. Venice's status as a pariah in the eyes of Rome was proven by the League of Cambrai, which was formed in 1509, when the Papal States joined with France and Spain in an attempt to counter Venetian expansionism on the mainland. While the war that followed resulted in little loss of territorial power, it was a watershed event for both architectural patronage and stylistic development. For more than a decade, no major new commission was begun, and although older projects were slowly completed, the result was an increase in Venice's isolation from architectural developments elsewhere. The influence of Codussi and the succeeding generation of architects lapsed into atrophy, and as a result, Venice was not reinvigorated by a generation of new architects and their new ideas until after the Sack of Rome.

The recognition of traditional independence was a major factor in the development of Venice's urban fabric. Unlike Rome, where the *maestri di strada* oversaw the development and maintenance of city streets, in Venice there was no comparable authority for the construction of bridges or the upkeep of its squares. Jacopo de' Barbari's famous aerial perspective of the city shows that many of its embankments and public spaces were unpaved at the outset of the sixteenth century, some of which were privately owned (95). Most bridges were still constructed of wood—like the Rialto bridge that connected the city's market with its commercial and administrative center around Piazza S. Marco—and built by private owners who could

95 J. de' Barbari, Perspective view of Venice, detail showing
    Campo Santa Maria Formosa, 1500
96 Scarpagnino: Venice, apartments adjacent to
    Corte di S. Rocco, 1547

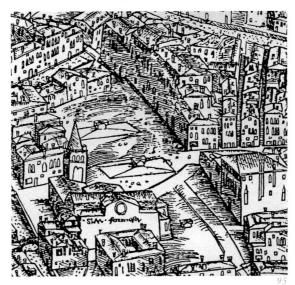

95

96

restrict access across waterways. Although the Senate decreed new projects and state authorities financed their construction, responsibility for subsequent upkeep fell to neighborhoods or religious orders. In this way, Venetians were entrusted with the power of shaping their urban destiny.

De' Barbari's aerial perspective also shows many of the housing developments that contributed greatly to the consistency of Venice's urban fabric. Already in the Middle Ages the scarcity of land, the high cost of construction, and the need for housing for all classes favored the development of groupings of compact residences. Private individuals and charitable societies initiated housing projects for both profit and the benefit of those who could not afford a residence. If their external appearance was consistently austere in the avoidance of any architectural orders, they achieved a richness comparable to palatial residences through painted decoration, now lost, and the unrivaled sophistication of their design. The simplest and most ubiquitous form was a series of row houses on one or both sides of a street.

In some instances, shops were included on the ground floor and the block linked by a tympanum (as in the Calle del Paradisio that connected a major commercial street, the Salizzada di. S. Lio, with the Campo S. Maria Formosa) or an archway. If the upper story apartments were little more than a cluster of rooms, they almost always had their own entrances from ground level. Other projects (such as the Corte di S. Rocco in the parish of S. Maria Maggiore) took the form of a courtyard surrounded by a series of residences, an arrangement that was effectively a microcosm of the islands and squares that were the basic unit of Venice's urban form. Apartment buildings sometimes reached the size of a small palace, thereby providing those with greater means spacious residences with features found in patrician palaces, such as exterior frescoes and a display of architectural orders (96). In certain instances (as in Sanmicheli's extraordinary Palazzo Cornaro), entire floors of palatial residences were designed from the outset as luxurious apartments (108). Theatricality in domestic architecture was not limited to the nobility.

Venice's urban fabric is composed of numerous self-sufficient neighborhoods, with each usually having a *campo* and parish church as the focal points of insular communities. But the tendency to focus on the city as shapes and patterns creates the illusion of a spatial continuity and social homogeneity that Venetians never would have understood. Venice was a city of foreigners, and each group of foreign nationals had its own enclave, in part, because of governmental decree, and in part, because of a desire for self-protection. Of these, the most famous is the Ghetto, the place of enforced residence of the Venetian Jews, which established a specific architectural form of segregation.

Venice's unique physical setting, urban layout, and social customs allowed theatricality to flourish at every level of the city's existence. Theatricality nominally involves the presence of an observer and the observed and the relationships between them. In the case of the Ghetto, theatricality was defined in contrast by the absence of the observed.

167

... the Library in Venice [is] the most splendid secular work of modern Europe. ... For the Venetians satisfaction lay in the true Roman formal idiom, the Renaissance being for them until then a matter of hearsay.

JACOB BURCKHARDT,
The Architecture of the Italian Renaissance, English edition, 1985

8

THE MOST SERENE REPUBLIC:
SANSOVINO & SANMICHELI

Nikolaus Pevsner, the historian of modern architecture and apologist for the Arts and Crafts movement, made no mention of the Library of S. Marco (begun 1537) or its architect, Jacopo Sansovino, in his *An Outline of European Architecture,* the most important handbook of architectural history in the post–World War II decades. Similarly, no discussion of Venice's most visible Renaissance building occurs in Goethe's account of his Italian journey, where there are numerous references to Palladio but none to Sansovino or his buildings. But all of this is puzzling when sixteenth-century opinion is taken into account. In the second edition of the *Lives of the Artists* (1568), Giorgio Vasari remarks why the Library was considered most beautiful and rich and how knowledgeable individuals regarded it as without equal. To Andrea Palladio, the Library was the most ornate building in Italy. Even in the nineteenth century, the building was the subject of the most extravagant acclaim from the otherwise cautious Jacob Burckhardt whose observation captures the *romanità* of Sansovino's greatest architectural achievement.

171

But the omissions could not have been the result of ignorance of Sansovino's buildings. His structures on and around the Piazza S. Marco—the Loggetta, the Library, and the Mint—have captivated visitors for more than four centuries, and similar echoes can be found in Wren's library for Trinity College in Cambridge, the clubs of Victorian London, and the cast-iron facades of lower Manhattan. But it is not visual consistency, but in fact, stylistic variety that characterizes Sansovino's Venetian buildings. In addition to the buildings famous for bringing the forms of the Roman High Renaissance to Venice, Sansovino's buildings include a monastic church modeled on quattrocento Florentine architecture (S. Francesco della Vigna), a parish church derived from Veneto-Byzantine Greek-cross churches (S. Martino), and several utilitarian buildings with little or no pretense to architectural style.

The Sansovino Library announced a new direction for Venetian architecture in its homage to both ancient and modern Rome (97). In terms of architectural style, the structure demonstrates a Roman preoccupation with the application of architectural grammar and contributes to what has been called the Roman legacy in Sansovino's Venetian architecture. With its luminous, porticoed facade of Istrian marble opening to a public square, the building has been understood as a modern equivalent of an ancient basilica. Its primary architectural system—superimposed Doric and Ionic columns attached to piers—originated in ancient monuments such as the Theater of Marcellus and was revived by Bramante and members of the Sangallo family. There is even a hint of erudition; the Library's eastern orientation may have been determined by Vitruvius's suggestion that ancient libraries should face east to permit the morning light.

Other features reflect the influence of Sansovino's contemporaries in Rome, and particularly, those buildings designed by members of the Sangallo family. The Library's rectangular pier with engaged columns occurs in the Palazzo Farnese, which Sansovino would have known from his second visit to Rome. At the same time, he would have also become familiar with Antonio da Sangallo the Elder's S. Biagio in Montepulciano (4). Here, the arrangement of pier, column, and entablature inspired the Library's own corner detail, which complies with the Vitruvian recommendation that a half metope should occur at the end of a Doric frieze.

In no other cinquecento building is visual opulence quite so fully the complement to the discipline provided by antiquity. The Library's densely ornamented surfaces seem to dissolve in the Venetian light, just as human figures merge with shadows in a painting by Giorgione or Titian. At the same time, the superimposition of the arcaded facade above the ground floor portico creates a remarkably open and spacious structure that harmonizes with the two-story Gothic arcade on the Palazzo Ducale. In this context, the obelisks and statues of gods and goddesses that animate the building's roofline are classical transformations of crenellations traditionally found on the skyline of Venetian buildings.

Sansovino's emergence as an architect occurred within the framework provided by the Florentine patrons of building projects, mainly in Rome. Born Jacopo Tatti, he took the surname of the sculptor Andrea Sansovino to whom he was apprenticed. From 1506 to 1511, the architect Sansovino lived with Giuliano da Sangallo in Rome, where he, like Sanmicheli and other architects of his generation, acquired first-hand knowledge of both ancient and modern buildings. After returning to Florence, Sansovino participated in the design and execution of temporary structures erected for the entry of Pope Leo X in 1515. By far, the most visible was a facade in the form of a triumphal arch placed in front of the Duomo's unfinished exterior. During a second visit to Rome after 1518, Sansovino obtained two commissions for permanent structures—a church for the colony of wealthy Florentines in Rome, S. Giovanni dei Fiorentini, and a superb palace for the Florentine banker Giovanni Gaddi.

JACOPO SANSOVINO AND THE RENEWAL OF PIAZZA S. MARCO
~

When Sansovino departed for Venice in 1527, after the Sack of Rome, he was a mature architect who had built little. Shortly after his arrival, he began to work on reinforcing the domes of St. Mark's, and by 1529, he had been appointed as proto to the procurators of St. Mark's, the body responsible for the famous Byzantine church and its numerous properties surrounding the Piazza S. Marco and the adjacent Piazzetta. Almost immediately, Sansovino began to improve the appearance of properties under his authority by removing miscellaneous accretions of shops, merchants' stalls and other notable eyesores. He also sought to improve the financial return to the procurators, as indicated by the five Doric shops (1531) built on a bridge just west of the Piazzetta, his first architectural project in Venice. Even though Sansovino had demonstrated his concern for urban environment around St. Mark's, there is no evidence that he had ever formulated a comprehensive plan for its renewal.

Sansovino's ambitious renewal of the area around Piazza S. Marco was preceded by four centuries of concern for the square's visual appearance. The structure of its spaces was determined in the 1170s, when Doge Sebastiano Ziani extended the square to the west, doubling its size and roughly establishing its dimensions that exist today (98–99). A new ducal palace with two stories and flanking towers replaced the random collection that stood adjacent to St. Mark's, the personal chapel of the doge. Even more significant for the square's future appearance was the reclamation of the inlet of water that led to the square, thereby creating the Piazzetta as an extension of the ducal palace. At the water's edge of this new public space, Ziani erected the two monolithic columns of granite that support statues of the Republic's two protectors—the Greek Saint Teodoro, and the Winged Lion of St. Mark, which is actually an ancient bronze chimera to which wings were added (100).

With these transformations, Ziani created the ceremonial entry into the city and established the tradition of visibility accorded to the church of St. Mark. Its setting was now two interlocking squares,

98 Venice, Piazza San Marco, plan prior to Sansovino's renovations
99 Venice, Piazza San Marco, plan after Sansovino's renovations
100 Venice, Piazza San Marco, Piazzetta towards *bacino*

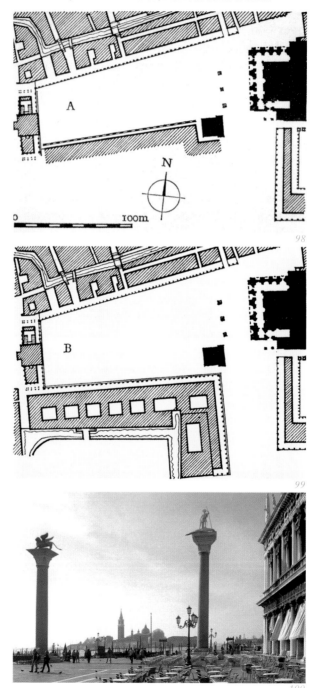

98

99

100

S. Marco being rhomboidal in shape and the Piazzetta trapezoidal. Differences in size and shape were reinforced by distinction in use and symbol. The Piazza S. Marco was effectively an extension of the church that served primarily as the setting for religious ceremonies, although its size and location made it the site of Venice's annual trade fair. The Piazzetta, on the other hand, was its civic counterpart, serving as the state entry to the ducal palace and all of Venice. Subsequent emendations respected the new arrangement. The reconstruction of the ducal palace in distinct stages, begun in 1340, and continued into the next century, was itself a mirror of the area's evolutionary development. The clock tower (1490) designed by Mauro Codussi, which terminates the panorama framed by Ziani's columns, heightened the triumphal aspect of the visitor's passage from water's edge into the city. Even the three-story structure containing shops and houses of the procurators on the west side of the square follows the design of its two-story Byzantine predecessor, which was rebuilt after a disastrous fire in 1512.

Sansovino's renewal of the S. Marco area began at its periphery. In 1535, the Council of Ten, a quasi-independent state body responsible for internal security, approved the reconstruction of the Mint. Its narrow, trapezoidal site was constricted by the state granaries on one side and the meat market and various hostelries on the other. Its greatest architectural potential was a splendid panorama toward the lagoon. Yet the area as a whole was unseemly, and its visual potential, however, remained unfulfilled because of the array of cheese stalls located on the lagoon side of the Mint.

Sansovino's design for the Mint was approved a year later (102). The basic idea for the exterior was the creation of a richly textured stone facade that could be seen at a considerable distance. The nine bays on the ground floor contained shops, replacing the cheese stalls destroyed when the facade was moved closer to the water to gain additional space on the upper floor. In a curious reversal of the expressive system of Bramante's Palazzo Caprini, the lower floor is articulated in refined, drafted masonry. Here, however, the texture of the facade changes drastically when the mural quality of its rusticated lower floor gives way to the skeletal arrangement of banded columns, deep entablature, and boldly projecting lintels on the *piano nobile*, where scarcely any wall surface is visible. In contrast to Antonio da Sangallo the Younger's almost contemporaneous papal

175

Mint in Rome (1530), in which an elegant refined arch motif terminated the view along the Via de Banchi, the upper floor of Sansovino's Mint declares an almost brutal sense of strength and security befitting its purpose. Familiar as this facade has become, Sansovino's original differs from what is seen today. The third story, which was begun in 1558, is a pale reflection of Sansovino's vocabulary and cannot be considered as his own.

Other architects also employed the unorthodox contrast between rough and smooth elements to enhance the visual complexity of facades, as Giulio Romano had done in Rome and Mantua. But what differentiates Sansovino's approach to rustication from that of his famous contemporary is its rhetorical role in conveying impregnability, as first justified by Serlio in the *Fourth Book* and later taken up by Sanmicheli in his fortifications and gateways. Its link with the meaning of *fortezza* as both a fortification and the more abstract quality of strength is appropriate; Serlio uses the term repeatedly in the context of rustication. In fact, the term *fortezza* was used by Jacopo's son Francesco Sansovino to describe the Mint as a prison-like fortress for gold, suggesting perhaps that this conceit was his father's intention. The collision with the Library's *romanità* is as jarring as the Mint's rustication is provocative.

The Library changed the shape of Venice by determining the future appearance of Piazza S. Marco and the Piazzetta (99). Prior to the Library's construction, the Campanile was embedded into the mass of buildings at the intersection of the two open spaces. Sansovino's design for the new structure firmly disengaged it from the Campanile, which became a isolated, freestanding element at the point where the spaces meet. Evidence is ambiguous whether Sansovino wanted the Library to extend only seventeen bays or the full twenty-one as it stands today. The new arrangement also did not account for the medieval hospice that stood on the southern side of the square, and in his guidebook, Francesco Sansovino indicates how his father planned to complete the remainder of the square. The Library's facade would continue along a new line to the southwest corner of the square, then turn along the narrow western side until it reached the church of S. Geminiano, whose interior would then be completed by Sansovino and given a facade (1557).

Unfortunately, the Piazza S. Marco was completed at a considerable cost, far from what Sansovino had originally envisioned. In

1582, twelve years after Sansovino's death, Scamozzi provided a design for the Procuratie Nuove (1582), which followed the general outlines of Sansovino's proposal. But the design included a third story for the tract along the southern side of the square. The increase in height was brought about by the procurator's desire for additional space, and Scamozzi responded predictably by adding a Corinthian order to the Doric and Ionic orders below. If the solution could be justified by an appeal to classical precedent, it nonetheless overpowered Sansovino's carefully considered response to the square's scale.

The isolation of the Campanile also occasioned Sansovino's design for the Loggetta (1537–45), which has often been called the "least architectural" of any building by Sansovino (101). Like other Northern Italian cities, Venice had a small loggia where members of the nobility could meet before attending to the republic's business in the Palazzo Ducale. Just as shabby as the hostelries that stood near it, the old lean-to structure at the foot of the bell tower would have appeared unseemly in this new, self-consciously Roman environment.

More than any of Sansovino's other buildings, the new Loggetta directly evokes the architecture of Imperial Rome. Its similarity to triumphal arches like that of Constantine is undeniable, and like its classical prototype, it was primarily an architectural framework for the display of sculpture. The reliefs in the attic are particularly triumphal in their subject matter. They include a representation of Venice as Justice flanked by personifications of Cyprus and Crete, two of the most important islands under the republic's dominion. The niches below contain Sansovino's own figures of Minerva, Apollo, Mercury, and Peace.

For all of its overt *romanità*, the Loggetta is emphatically Venetian in its opulence and rhetoric. It draws substance and symbol from surrounding buildings, and its location is firmly anchored in the calculus of interlocking visual relationships that define the experience of a public square. As in the facade of nearby S. Marco, the Loggetta's coloristic hue is more Byzantine then Roman. Stone plays a predominant role in setting a triumphal tone. Oriental marbles, such as those displayed on the church's exterior, were selected for the projecting columns. The white Istrian stone and the red marble from Verona harmonize with the Campanile behind it and the Ducal Palace across the square. In thematic terms, the Loggetta's emphasis on Venice as a mighty sea power complemented the allusions to its power on land expressed by the four horses on the facade of S. Marco. In political terms, the Loggetta is an extension of the Palazzo Ducale because of its location on an axis that begins with the Scala dei Giganti, the site of ducal coronations, and passes through the Arco Foscari. As one proceeds along this axis, which was employed in both daily activity and public ceremonies, the myth of the Venetian as the perfect political state is revealed in its entirety. Although architecture alone was incapable of expressing the myth of the most serene republic, it provided the spatial and temporal frame-work through which it could be understood.

MICHELE SANMICHELI AND THE ARCHITECTURE OF CIRCUMSTANCE

In our era, Michele Sanmicheli's achievement as an architect has been overshadowed by those of his contemporaries. Unlike Sebastiano Serlio or Andrea Palladio, he wrote no treatise that would assure lasting fame throughout Europe. Unlike Jacopo Sansovino, whose buildings have determined the appearance of Piazza S. Marco, Sanmicheli's contributions to urbanism never involved the reshaping of a city center. Above all, Sanmicheli was a circumstantial urbanist, an architect who by fate had to resolve the richness and complexities of urban sites in the designs of his buildings. And if Sanmicheli's knowledge of fortifications resulted in requests from the rulers of France and Spain for his services, he never luxuriated in the courtly patronage and princely splendors bestowed upon Giulio Romano by the Gonzaga in Mantua.

Yet Sanmicheli's designs are inherently more interesting in their reconciliation of architectural circumstance with precedents both ancient and modern than any of his contemporaries. The plans of his palaces can be appreciated for their clever adaptation to the con-straints of urban sites. The buildings' exteriors are austere and con-ventional at first glance, yet their arrangement of architectural membering creates an enchanting web of patterns and rhythms that demand contemplation. Sanmicheli's approach to antiquity is both inventive and rigorous but never pedantic. Few of his contempo-raries had Sanmicheli's capacity to define problems of architectural expression so that they could simply be solved. In this way he is to be understood preeminently as an architect's architect.

101 Sansovino: Venice, Loggetta, exterior, 1537–45
102 Sansovino: Venice, Mint, begun 1535
103 Sanmicheli: Orvieto, S. Domenico, Petrucci Chapel, circa 1516

179

101

102

103

Sanmicheli received his first training from his father and uncle, who belonged to a family of stonemasons from Lake Como who had settled in Verona. Around 1500, he left the Veneto for Rome. The impact of the visit on an impressionable sixteen-year-old must have been considerable. Here, Sanmicheli acquired a comprehensive knowledge of ancient monuments, presumably recorded in a now-lost sketchbook. At he same time, he would have become familiar with both the epoch-making buildings of Bramante and the conservative designs of Giuliano da Sangallo, the two architects who were central to the formulation of Sanmicheli's architectural style. By 1509, Sanmicheli's technical knowledge and skill as stonecutter were sufficient to earn an appointment as the chief architect of Orvieto Cathedral. Yet the position did not prevent Sanmicheli from taking on other commissions, both in Orvieto and elsewhere in the papal states. Of these, the most extraordinary design is the cloister of S. Agostino in Bagnoregio (circa 1524–25). The design is both archaic and modern, with octagonal columns recalling quattrocento Roman courtyards and Doric capitals, anticipating the bold relief of Sanmicheli's Veronese city gates. Throughout this period, he maintained contact with architects at the papal court; in 1513, he sought advice from Sangallo the Younger in Rome on the cathedral's facade and accompanied him in 1526, on an inspection of fortresses in Parma, Piacenza, and other Northern Italian cities. When Sanmicheli returned to his native city in 1530, few architects could match the range and depth of his professional expertise. It is unfortunate that Sanmicheli was never invited to submit a design for the facade of S. Petronio in Bologna, a task for which his talents were admirably suited.

Another project stands out among those from Sanmicheli's years in Orvieto. The burial chapel for the Petrucci family in S. Domenico is composed of an underground octagonal chamber and attached altar house connected by two symmetrical flights of stairs to the church above (103). Although the patron, Girolamo Petrucci, was in close rapport with the administrators of the cathedral, a site in the Dominican church offered fewer restraints of size and expression. The resulting design was fully in the spirit of both pagan buildings and the catacombs of Christian Rome. Both the chapel's shape and ancillary spaces suggest that Sanmicheli was familiar with the recently rediscovered octagonal hall of Nero's Domus Aurea. By locating the chapel below the church's main altar and choir, the design also forges a link with the tomb of St. Peter underneath the Constantinian basilica, certainly the most fabled example of an underground burial. The tiny size of this space belies the importance of this chapel for later projects. The dramatic potential of the vista created by the longitudinal arrangement of its chambers was first achieved in Sanmicheli's Madonna della Campagna outside Verona and then realized a century later on a grander scale in Longhena's S. Maria della Salute in Venice.

181

The palaces Sanmicheli designed after his return to Verona reflect conspicuous display and the elaboration of architectural circumstances, but now at the scale of the single building. Facades are their most distinctive features, and they are the earliest and most direct examples of the impact of Bramante and Raphael in the Veneto. Certain traits are found in their design. All enjoy unconstrained visibility and can be seen in their entirety from a considerable distance across broad streets or public squares. As a whole, the Terraferma palaces reflect the fundamental influence of Bramante's epoch-defining facade of the Palazzo Caprini in the employment of rustication on the ground floor and engaged orders above. With one exception, they are typically constructed out of richly carved stone, a Venetian precedent established by Codussi. The round-headed windows on all facades are flanked by paired or coupled architectural orders. Although Sanmicheli's Venetian palaces exhibit many of these characteristics, they form a special group unto themselves due to their unique sites and the particulars of their commissions.

If Sanmicheli was not as single-minded as Palladio in approaching palace facades as a distinct architectural problem, he demonstrated a similarly wide range of solutions. As a whole, his designs are heirs to the Roman facades of Bramante and Raphael, but with significant variations. In the Palazzo Bevilacqua (1530), Sanmicheli's first palace and most elaborate palatial exterior, the facade is little more than a kind of architectural scrim that serves as the ornament of a screen wall along the street (104). It is physically distinct and stands apart from the actual residence, which is separated from its pseudo-facade by a courtyard. The lack of any physical, true and proper connection to the palace may have suggested to Sanmicheli

182

104

105

its function as a richly ornamented screen. Although only seven bays are standing today, it seems probable that the facade would have been composed of eleven bays, forming a symmetrical arrangement of alternating units.

Although the Palazzo Bevilacqua's facade is Roman in its architectural language, its dialect is specifically Veronese. In order to emphasize the manifest complexities of his design, Sanmicheli adapted the effects of the nearby Porta dei Borsari, the preeminent Roman city gate of Verona. Seeking to avoid the monotony of the strict A-B-A alternation of bays, Sanmicheli made clusters of three bays the basis unit of design. In each unit, pride of place is logically given to the wider bays with their taller arches, which are flanked alternately by columns that are vertically fluted or with spirals turning inward. The horizontality of the scheme is thus counteracted by a rhythmic pattern that both links the units into a harmonious design while maintaining the visual independence of its bays according to variations in the form of fluting.

The Palazzo Canossa (1532) is commonly acknowledged as the most impressive of Sanmicheli's palaces in Verona (105). It draws its effect not from its great size but from the ingenious application of its razor-sharp detail. Here, the Bramantesque formula has been reinterpreted in the spirit of Giulio Romano, as evidenced by its three-bay loggia, rusticated voussoirs, and deep incisions surrounding individual blocks. In contrast to the flatness of the exceptionally tall ground level, the upper floor is made of four densely-packed planes. At the corners, the primary Corinthian orders overlap to form a two-layer cluster of architectural membering, one of which continues as the paired pilasters that define each bay. Along the entire facade, a molding without any order passes behind the pilasters and over the arched windows, creating a series of framed panels that reveal the actual bearing wall within their confines. As in the Palazzo Bevilacqua, Sanmicheli's ingenious system binds together elements on an expansive, horizontal facade without denying the vertical emphasis suggested by each of its bays. Recently, the similarity of these features to Giulio's Mantuan work has been explained by the link of the Canossa family to Mantua and has led to the proposal that the palace was either wholly designed by Giulio or based initially on a proposal by him. While there is evidence to support this suggestion, an attribution to Giulio has not met with universal approval.

183

The facade of the Palazzo Canossa also masks an intelligent layout to be seen from the city and the countryside. Following the tradition established in Venice, the Palazzo Canossa's plan is composed of three broadly linear zones around a long courtyard facing the Adige River. Although this holds true for most of Sanmicheli's Terraferma palaces, circumstances of the commission or preexisting construction limited the options at the architect's disposal. No such constraints existed at the Palazzo Canossa, where Sanmicheli was free to adapt the sequence of spaces found in an ancient house described by Vitruvius—vestibule, atrium, peristyle courtyard—to a plan deriving from a completely different historical tradition. The Palazzo Canossa is unique among Sanmicheli's palaces in its response to the surrounding countryside. When seen from the Adige River or the open fields farther to the west, the Palazzo takes on the appearance of a villa with its central loggia and flanking wings. The fusion of urban and suburban building types would naturally appeal to Palladio, who faced a similar challenge in the design of the Palazzo Chiericati (1555) in Vicenza.

Sanmicheli's palaces also demonstrate the continuous interchange of ideas and reciprocal influence among architects in Venice and the Veneto. Although Sanmicheli, Sansovino, Giulio Romano, and Palladio are usually portrayed as independent architects working in different cities, there was much that bound them together. Palladio's architectural origins in the work of his teachers in the Veneto is well-known, but the interconnections between his architectural elders need to be stressed. One link shared by all is, of course, the experience of Rome. Another is the geography of the Veneto, in which Verona lies closer to the Mantua dominated by Giulio Romano than to Vicenza or Venice. Just as Bramante and Raphael had created a Roman High Renaissance in architecture under Julius II and Leo X, the architects working in an atmosphere of mutual inspiration and cross-fertilization achieved a marriage of classical discipline and overt theatricality that was to characterize Venetian architecture for the next three centuries.

The strongest bond was between Sanmicheli and Sansovino, who shared common experiences in their architectural training under the Sangallo in Rome, and later, their employment by the Venetian state. Familiarity with the work of one often provided the seeds for the other's ideas. During his years in Orvieto, Sanmicheli became familiar with Sansovino's Palazzo Gaddi in Rome, whose long, narrow courtyard likely influenced the layout of the Palazzo Canossa. Sanmicheli was, in turn, to exercise a clear and direct impact on Sansovino. Two hallmark features of the Palazzo Cornaro in Venice (begun 1545)—the effect of its facade as a monumental screen and the imposition of a Roman court on its characteristically Venetian plan—owe their inspiration to Sanmicheli's Veronese palaces.

185

SANSOVINO AND SANMICHELI
AS THE DESIGNERS OF VENETIAN PALACES
~

All sorts of domestic buildings form a major part of Sansovino's private commissions. The difficult problem of planning a palace for a trapezoidal site was a challenge first faced by Sansovino in an unexecuted plan for a palace for Vettor Grimani (1527) on the site of the Ca' del Duca (106). Here, the sequence of courtyards and loggias that distinguished the constrained arrangement of the Roman residence was now deployed in two distinct zones, one whose orientation was determined by the facade block on the Grand Canal and the other by the adjacent *rio*. By inserting a wedge-shaped wall between the two blocks (a device employed by Bramante in the Cortile del Belvedere and Raphael in his project for a palace on the Via Giulia), Sansovino resolved the divergence of orientations so cleverly that a visitor never would have realized that any difficulty existed. With its pair of grand staircases and a vista unbroken through the entire length of the palace, the scheme would have been the first grand palace in cinquecento Venice. Yet the scheme also demanded the virtual elimination of the long central *salone* commonly found in Venetian palaces, thus providing the patron with considerable splendor but little habitable space. Venetians were accustomed to getting more for their money.

Sansovino's grandest palatial residence is the Palazzo Cornaro in the parish of S. Maurizio, also known as the Palazzo Corner della Ca' Grande (107). The history of the commission is complex and must be explained in some detail, because it is intertwined with that of another Cornaro palace designed by Michele Sanmicheli. As early as 1517, Zorzi Cornaro acquired houses and a boatyard adjacent to his palace, presumably providing for the construction of a larger residence at a later date. The property was understood to be an emblem of the family's wealth and prestige, and in his will, Zorzi stipulated that the property was to always remain in the ownership of his family. In 1532, five years after Zorzi's death, the palace was destroyed by fire. In preparation for its reconstruction, the Cornaro heirs sought and ultimately obtained funds that the Venetian Republic had previously acquired from the dowry of Caterina Cornaro, the Queen of Cyprus and Zorzi's sister, who was persuaded to hand over the island to Venetian rule. With the return of funds deposited to the republic, the unbuilt structure became both a palatial residence for the Cornaros and a palace of state. The affairs became more complicated when a second Cornaro palace, this time in the parish of S. Polo, was destroyed by fire. The properties were divided among the Cornaro heirs only in 1545, which is when reconstruction was begun in earnest on both palaces. Zorzi Cornaro, a grandson of the elder Zorzi, became the patron for Sansovino's palace at S. Maurizio; Zuanne Cornaro, son of the elder Zorzi, engaged Michele Sanmicheli to design the palace at S. Polo.

The ambitions of the Cornaro both challenged and exceded Sansovino's capacity as an architect. When seen at a distance from the direction of the Doge's Palace, the facade of the Palazzo Cornaro in S. Maurizio (begun 1545) appears to be a three-dimensional block projecting from the palace and dominating the lower sector of the Grand Canal. This is Sansovino at his most forceful and theatrical. But further inspection reveals a less compelling design. Its basic formula comes from the Palazzo Caprini, but lacking Bramante's bold rustication and the deeply shadowed orders that captivated generations of architects. Sansovino also drew on his own experience of the S. Marco buildings, but to little profit. In comparison to the richly ornamented surfaces of the Library, from which it derives many features, the facade of the Palazzo Cornaro is tame. The emphatic banded blocks on the Mint's columns are now merely ornamental additions to the ground floor windows; the simplicity and directness of the Mint's courtyard now becomes a potpourri of contradictory motifs in that of the palace. There are echoes of Michelangelo in the superimposed windows on the facade's ground floor and of Mauro Codussi in the rusticated pilasters in the courtyard. For each idea, there is an identifiable source, but there is no consistent theme to the whole.

Sanmicheli's Palazzo Cornaro in S. Polo (1545) speaks an entirely different idiom altogether (108). Unlike Sansovino's palace, which

106 Sansovino (attr.):Venice, plan for Palazzo Grimani
     on site of Ca' del Duca, 1527
107 Sansovino:Venice, Palazzo Cornaro (Ca' Grande), begun 1545
108 Sanmicheli:Venice, Palazzo Cornaro (S. Polo), 1545. Exterior view
109 Sanmicheli:Venice, Palazzo Grimani, begun circa 1556

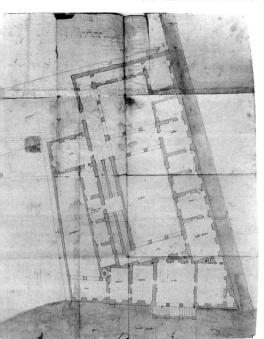

106

107

108

109

occupies a highly visible location on the Grand Canal, Sanmicheli's palace faces a minor *rio*, and consequently, there was no need to employ monumental orders made out of expensive Istrian stone on its exterior. In terms of style, its facade is clearly indebted to the palaces illustrated by Serlio in the *Fourth Book* (85). But Sanmicheli clearly surpasses his model in the sophisticated use of the *serliana* to link adjacent elements and the multiplicity of the readings it presents. Only the ground floor on the canal is rusticated, and the remaining stories are constructed of brick, with stone employed for window enframements, delicate string courses, and quoin blocks at the corners. Sanmicheli's mastery of Venice's characteristic rhythmic windows and their relationship to interior rooms allows him to obscure the actual location of spaces and floor levels. Is the central *salone* composed of three or five bays? Are the mezzanines intermediate stories, or are they individual floors in their own right? These are provocative visual questions with which Sanmicheli teases the observer.

Just how Sanmicheli accomplishes so much with minimal means is also related to the Palazzo Cornaro's use. For instance, the S. Polo building is less a grand family palace than a structure composed of two superimposed palatial apartments, the upper of which was rented for income. As a result of this shared occupancy, which was by no means unusual in Venice, there was no need for a grand staircase or even a courtyard. Instead of imposing foreign elements or ideal geometries on his plan, Sanmicheli accepts the irregular outlines of his site and moves the atrium to the rear of the palace to serve as its land entry. The migration of this entry to a non-axial location also allowed the creation of a second facade with superimposed logge on the Campo S. Polo, the largest open space of its kind in the city. For most Venetians, here was the most visible part of this unique palace. By contrast, the main facade upon which Sanmicheli lavished so much attention originally was visible only at some distance from a bridge over the Rio di S. Polo.

The Palazzo Grimani (begun circa 1556) was the most conspicuous palace designed by Sanmicheli (109). Its prominent site on the Grand Canal was visible from the *fondamente* near the commercial hub of the Rialto, thereby asserting the eminence of Girolamo Grimani, procurator and member of a family renowned for its collection of Greek and Roman art. No doubt the interests of Sanmicheli's patron in antiquity accounted for the recurrence of a

triumphal arch motif on the exterior and perhaps even for the barrel-vaulted entry hall modeled on the Palazzo Farnese in Rome. The
palace was barely begun at the time of Sanmicheli's death in 1559,
and there are lingering questions as to whether the third floor was
originally planned by the architect or a later addition by the client.
While critics often claim that Sanmicheli was taking issue with
Venetian design traditions, the evidence of the building itself shows
that he was demonstrating their continuing vitality.

  Though uncustomary in Sanmicheli's architecture, the Palazzo
Grimani's overt display of *romanità* is expressed within the confines
of Venetian practices. Apart from the imposing atrium, the plan follows the characteristic tripartite division as applied to the irregular
outlines of the site. The facade's deep cornices, boldly projecting
orders, and the rhythm of their disposition all owe their origin to
Codussi's Palazzo Loredan, just as the disproportionately tall lower
floor with a vaulted central opening and lower arched openings at its
side derives from similar configuration motifs on the Palazzo Lando.
A second *serliana* characterized by a multilayered relief and defined
by entablatures and archivolts is interwoven with the orders on all
three floors. On the ground floor, this arrangement specifically
recalls the arrangement of the Clock Tower (1496–99) on Piazza S.
Marco that serves as a triumphal entry into the *mercerie*, the network
of commercial thoroughfares connecting S. Marco with Rialto. The
effect of theatricality in the Palazzo Grimani is unprecedented in a
private structure, as if the entry as seen from the Grand Canal had
been transformed into a great street seen through the proscenium of
the palace's facade.

THEATRICALITY AND CHURCH DESIGN
~

During the course of the sixteenth century, a new attitude toward
church design emerged in Italy. As a consequence of the Sack of
Rome and the growing significance of new religious orders such the
Jesuits, church layouts were less likely to reflect the desire for central
plans favored by theoreticians than the need for workable interiors
for worship demanded by churchmen. Architects developed a range
of solutions that were, in one way or another, variations on the box-
type church interior first employed in the late quattrocento and later
applied by Antonio da Sangallo the Younger to S. Spirito in Sassia in

Rome (78). These solutions typically included in their plans separate spaces for chapels flanking the nave (and sometimes passageways connecting them), an independent chamber containing the main altar, and a retrochoir behind the main altar.

Accordingly, no churches embodying theatricality were built in cinquecento Venice before Palladio's S. Giorgio Maggiore (begun 1566) and the Redentore (begun 1577). The lack of ecclesiastical structures comparable in visual opulence to the Library or the Mint was due as much to local circumstances as it was to the new religiosity spreading across Italy. Venice had long exerted considerable control over the Church and its activities. Fearing the passage of great amounts of its limited urban area into ecclesiastical ownership, the Senate renewed a medieval law forbidding the construction of new churches. Thus, the kinds of ecclesiastical projects likely to be initiated were monastic and parish churches that had fallen into disrepair and had acquired sufficient funds from private donors for their reconstruction.

S. Francesco della Vigna (begun 1534), constructed for the Observant branch of the Franciscan order, exemplifies a characteristically Venetian response to monastic renewal in Italy (110). There can be no doubt that Sansovino's patrons demanded a structure as austere as the religious beliefs practiced by their order. Its overall sobriety (as well as its box-type nave flanked by chapels), Doric order, and pseudo-transepts are thought to derive from another Franciscan church, Cronaca's S. Salvatore al Monte (begun 1499) in Sansovino's native Florence. What is truly distinctive about this church, however, is the arrangement of its east end, an altar house covered by a domical vault followed by a deep, barrel-vaulted choir. While such an arrangement would have been considered unique in Rome or in Florence, parallels in Venice can be found in S. Giobbe (circa 1460–70), another church with a single nave followed by a domed altar house and a monk's choir. The visual consequences of this are significant. In place of the organic grouping of spaces around a prominent cupola (as in St. Peter's), one reads the interior as a horizontal flow of loosely connected spaces. Other cinquecento architects, most notably Sanmicheli and Palladio, were to exploit the visual definition of space in a theatrical manner.

The five-square plan, with four piers supporting a central dome and abutting four smaller domes in its corners, is employed in numerous Venetian parish churches. Originating in Byzantium and

190

110 Sansovino: Venice, S. Francesco della Vigna, begun 1534
111 Sanmicheli: Verona, Madonna della Campagna, begun 1559
112 Madonna della Campagna, interior

110

111

112

subsequently revived in late quattrocento Venice, the plan adapts well to the needs of small congregations with constrained urban sites and reflects the continuing impact of Byzantine culture in Venice after the fall of Constantinople in 1453. The sheer quantity of monuments built on variations of this theme is impressive, and it is surprising that Sansovino's three parish churches, all of which are small and centrally planned, were not designed along these lines. One project, the destroyed church of S. Geminiano at the narrow end of Piazza S. Marco, only involved the construction of a facade (begun 1557) for a five-square church that had been begun in 1505. Another, the reconstruction of S. Giuliano (begun 1566), replaced piers and domes with a simple, cubelike central space covered by a flat roof. Even S. Martino (begun circa 1540), the most impressive of the parish designs, omits piers and domes for reasons of cost.

The best illustration of the concept of theatricality as applied to ecclesiastical architecture is found in Sanmicheli's Madonna della Campagna (begun 1559). As in numerous other examples of votive churches, this central-plan structure was commissioned to house a miracle-working image on a site two miles distant from the city's walls (111–112). It is a truly stark building, originally in the country, but now, since the early 1950s, surrounded by rather dreadful public housing. From the exterior, the church appears ungainly; the external colonnade is diminutive in comparison to the domineering central cylinder and its cupola. But the interior and plan, composed of simple, contrasting geometric shapes, are on an altogether higher level of sophistication and beauty. An octagon is inscribed within the cylinder, with four chapels in the diagonal axes and three entries from cardinal points. In the fourth, an archway opens into a domed secondary space flanked by deep biapsidal tribunes and, at the rear, an even deeper space in which the altar is now located. The plan's clarity is matched by spatial and mathematical lucidity. Its principal dimensions are round figures based on interior dimensions, with the width of the octagon (50 Veronese feet) equal to half the diameter of the exterior colonnade (100 Veronese feet).

Closely related in design is Sanmicheli's earlier Pellegrini Chapel (begun 1527) in S. Bernardino in Verona (113). Within this tall cylinder, there is a vertically attenuated space (like an ancient tomb or a Northern Italian baptistery), and this cylinder of space is then invaded by a cruciform plan as marked by the altars and the shallow, vaulted entry hall. Verona is also notable for the rather quirky style of its antiquities, such as the Porta dei Borsari, and its most prominent features—the contrasting vertical and spiral fluting of its Corinthian columns—are employed to emphasize and differentiate its primary axes. It is as if the facade of Sanmicheli's contemporaneous design for the Palazzo Bevilacqua has trespassed upon the chapel's interior, but only to give it a neoclassical air associated with the eighteenth century rather than something typical of cinquecento Verona. What seems so remarkable is that some three decades later Sanmicheli would provide for another species of memorial structure; a design purged of nearly every kind of visual excess. But what exactly accounts for this change?

From the start, the Madonna della Campagna was intended to be understood as a combination of Early Christian and cinquecento architectural idioms. It cannot be a coincidence that the structure's exterior colonnade is made up of thirty columns, just as thirty columns surround the central drum of the mausoleum of S. Costanza (circa 350 A.D.) in Rome. It is also interesting to note that the semi-circular apses flanking the altar house find counterparts in the mausoleum's narthex. As in many Early Christian structures, it also exploits the potential of a double shell construction (for the central rotunda) in order to create an interplay of formal richness. But inserted into this shell is a design for a contemporary building that Sanmicheli would have known, Sangallo's project for the Madonna di Monte d'Oro in Montefiascone, seen in Uffizi, A 173. From this source comes the notion of a contrasting octagonal central hall with the circular altar area, albeit with a greater emphasis on the interrelationship of the parts in Sanmicheli's design. Along with Giulio's Cathedral in Mantua, the Madonna della Campagna represents an interest in the Christian architecture of the ancient era, though whether or not this was a conscious revival with ideological underpinnings is an open question.

The Madonna della Campagna has been recognized as "the only great cinquecento church to realize Alberti's ideal of a free-standing round temple." Yet, as a circular church, it is very sharply contrasted with the models which Leonardo had established and which had been followed by Bramante at St. Peter's. These examples and others are all apt to show a central dome surrounded by an accumulation of lesser domed spaces or apses. But, just if Michelangelo never fully abandoned this solution in his development of St. Peter's, Sanmicheli never seems to have considered it here. The dome now rises above a sort of shelf in the form of a colonnade. It and the drum form the building's identity to the exclusion of all other parts.

Attempts to assess the exterior of the Madonna della Campagna have all been colored by Vasari's assertion that the completed structure does not correspond to Sanmicheli's original project, a defect for which Vasari blames the deputies who oversaw the church's completion. A further complication is that no meaningful architectural drawings by Sanmicheli have survived. Scholars generally agree upon the clumsiness of the exterior and the lack of coordination between the spacing of the columns below and the blind arcade wrapping around the cylinder. Reconstructions typically propose that the Doric columns of the exterior colonnade would have been taller and that its shed roof would have risen to a point just underneath the blind arcade. It has also been suggested that the main altar was meant to have been placed directly under the minor dome, as indicated in Sangallo's drawing for the Montefiascone project.

There can be little doubt that the interior of the Madonna della Campagna is remarkable for its visual impact and subtlety. The central space of the church, its inscribed octagon, is surrounded by a blind arcade recalling the ambulatories around the central spaces of Early Christian and Medieval structures. Along the main axis, a recession of arches creates a calculated progression through discreet spaces and binds them together through the means of a scenic vista. It demonstrates Sanmicheli's full and deep understanding of how Venetian theatricality could be applied to buildings on the Terraferma, and it is one of the most impressive examples of spatial design in the cinquecento.

The ideas expressed at the Madonna della Campagna were later exploited in Venice by Palladio in the Redentore, Longhena in S. Maria della Salute (begun 1631), Scalfarotto in SS. Simeone e Giuda (1718–38), and by Juvarra in the Superga (1717–31) in Turin.

SANSOVINO AND SANMICHELI AS THE DESIGNERS OF VILLAS

Neither Sansovino nor Sanmicheli are normally associated with the design of villas either as pleasurable retreats or as working farms. This is misleading because Sansovino designed a villa—the Villa Garzoni at Pontecasale—that was as stunning in its austerity as his Venetian buildings were elaborate in their theatricality. Yet the Villa Garzoni has been dismissed by contemporary critics because of its lack of resonance on later architects, especially Palladio. Sanmicheli, on the other hand, designed several villas varying in size and type that merited mention in Vasari's *Lives of the Artists*.

The Venetian Republic, of course, held in its dominion some of the most extraordinary arable farmland on the Italian peninsula. The vast alluvial plain at the foot of the Alps had been intensively cultivated in previous centuries, and beyond its numerous small cities lay a landscape punctuated by agricultural structures. Most were small, unassuming structures adapted to the exigencies of farming. Occasionally these structures, with their thatched roofs and nearby barns, can be discerned in the distant backgrounds of altarpieces by Venetian painters and were recorded by Serlio for future publication in his *Sixth Book*. Less often there was also a second kind of structure that married forms from castles with conveniences (and pretension to style) commonly associated with urban residences. The intensive cultivation of this bountiful landscape was rendered necessary by the circumnavigation of Africa by the Portuguese, which which Venetians immediately knew would cause the economic ruin of their city.

But this new source of income from the investment in land was almost lost during the Wars of the League of Cambrai. Even though little territory was lost, land commanded higher and higher prices, and therefore reclamation became a necessity. Within a century the transformation had become nearly complete. In 1612 the English ambassador, Dudley Carleton, wrote that "... (the Venetians) here change their manners.... Their former course of life was merchandising: which is now quite left and they look to landward buying house and lands, furnishing themselves with coach and horses, and giving themselves the good time with more show and gallantry than was [their] want..." Six years later, the Spanish ambassador, Don Alonso della Cueva, remarked that the Venetians "...have for many years largely neglected maritime affairs and have applied themselves to huge purchases of land.... In this way they have so far expanded by purchases, acquisitions, usurpations, and confiscations that we can say three-quarters of the land in Paduan territory is now in the hand of Venetian nobles."

The Villa Garzoni at Pontecasale (begun circa. 1536) was Sansovino's first and only commission for a villa in the Veneto (114–115). While the structure's function as the center for the reclamation of a vast area of land by the Garzoni was progressive in economic terms, its architectural forms were retrospective and derived from both Venetian and central Italian buildings of the previous half-century. The scheme of a dominant central block with surrounding barchesse was hallowed by tradition in the Veneto, and superimposed loggias recalled castellated residences of the previous century. Yet the Villa Garzoni's exterior gives no hint that behind it lies a perfectly symmetrical, U-shaped structure with an unroofed loggia surrounding an open court. This arrangement has been compared to the diagrammatic plans of similar villas in Francesco di Giorgio's architectural treatise, which was known to Serlio and Palladio and disseminated throughout the Veneto in the form of copied drawings. Most of all, Sansovino's design exudes a Roman air as self-conscious as his structures on the Piazza S. Marco, but one that is characterized by reduction instead of embellishment. The sharply profiled Doric and Ionic columns are by comparison abstract and refined, and their effect is comparable to the courtyard of the Palazzo Farnese or Serlio's illustration of the exterior of the Theater of Marcellus. To be certain, Sansovino's choice of architectural grammar explains why even today the Villa Garzoni appears remote and solitary in the flat plains south of Padua.

Demonstrating Sanmicheli's achievement as a designer of villas is a daunting challenge to the architectural historian. Of the four examples that can be securely attributed to him, three have been destroyed or lack sufficient construction documenting his contribution. In three cases—the Villa Canossa at Grezzano, the renovations to the Bevilacqua Castle, and the Cornaro Villa at Piombino Dese—Sanmicheli designed villas for members of families for whom he was concurrently designing urban palaces in Verona and Venice. What is known about these commissions indicates that they were simple structures without much pretense to style and that they typically involved the integration of an earlier structure into the new design. The grandest and by far the most influential was the Villa La Soranza (commissioned circa 1537) at Treville di Castelfranco, which was decorated with splendid frescoes by Veronese and Zelotti (116). Like

114 Sansovino: Pontecasale, Villa Garzoni, begun circa 1536
115 Villa Garzoni, courtyard
116 Sanmicheli: Treville di Castelfranco, Villa La Soranza, begun circa 1537

114

115

116

the contemporary Villa Garzoni by Sansovino, it was composed of a central residential block separated by a short distance from two barchesse. Yet the visual effect of the ensemble was totally different—a symmetrical, tripartite composition focusing on the residential block, which was clearly the focal element in the design. In assessing Sanmicheli as an architectural planner, it must be noted that the layout of the residential block repeats a scheme invented by Peruzzi and later published by Serlio in the *Third Book*. If the design for the Villa La Soranza was not wholly original, Sanmicheli's success lies in his transformation of these foreign themes into a building that would be identified with the Veneto. Palladio understood these qualities best, drawing from it the inspiration for buildings as different as the Villa Godi in Lonedo and the Palazzo Chiericati in Vicenza.

199

Almost all of the villas designed by Sansovino and Sanmicheli were begun in the 1530s, a moment at which the development of the villa is characterized by a variety of solutions rather than the recognition of an identifiable architectural type. To be sure, Sansovino received no other commissions for villas, and Sanmicheli's only villa executed during the last two decades of his career never had such a profound effect on architects as La Soranza had on Palladio. There is a temptation to explain this phenomenon as a failure of the architects to provide a suitable style and scale for villas in the Veneto, but it should be avoided. Sansovino and Sanmicheli were simply too preoccupied with their other responsibilities in Venice and elsewhere to take on projects far from their customary centers of activity. Instead, their achievement was to pave the way along which others, most notably Palladio, were to follow.

We came upon Caprarola, a palace of Cardinal Farnese, which is greatly renowned in Italy. I have seen none in Italy that may be compared with it . . . The form is pentagonal, but to the eye it appears distinctly square. Inside however, it is perfectly round, with wide corridors going around it, all vaulted and painted on all sides... The location is barren and alpine. And the Cardinal has to draw all his water for the fountain from Viterbo, eight miles away.

MICHEL DE MONTAIGNE,
Travel Journal, 1581

9

BETWEEN FRANCE & ITALY:
VIGNOLA

117 Vignola: Bologna, Facciata dei Banchi, 1565–68
118 Rosso Fiorentino and others: Fontainebleau,
    Galerie François I, 1533–40
119 Gilles Le Breton: Fontainebleau, La Porte Dorée, 1528–40

~202

117

118

119

Vignola's Portico dei Banchi in Bologna (1565–68) is, sometimes, also known as the Facciata dei Banchi (117). And the emphasis on its vertical surface which it shares with Caprarola may have as much to say about the qualities of Vignola's achievement. An important aspect of Vignola's architecture is his orchestration of a flat surface with an equally flat apparatus of pilasters and strips so that even when he employs elements of robustness and depth, these have the quality of stretching through a sort of highly stretched membrane. In other words, their behavior is eruptive. And it may be said, with some plausibility, that, if his contemporary Palladio was (and remains) the great analyst of the plan, Vignola was the equally great protagonist of the elevation.

203

Jacopo Barozzi was born at Vignola outside Bologna in 1507, and received his initiatory training in the second city of the Papal States. This seems to have been related to hydraulics and perspective—to hydraulics because of the need to regulate rivers and canals in the extensive region of the Romagna, and to perspective, because this was a traditional preoccupation, already evinced by Serlio, of Bolognese artists. Among Vignola's earliest products are architectural perspectives, the interest in which he may have acquired from Peruzzi, who would become a significant influence on his later work. Yet this resulted in no independent projects of the architect, excepting a dovecote at the Villa Isolani at Minerbio. Given the lack of concrete evidence for Vignola's earliest endeavors, it might be best to pass on to the next stage in his career, that of his first residence in Rome from the late 1530s onward.

In the early 1540s, there had been established in Rome an association of humanists and clerical nobility devoted to the elucidation of Vitruvius, the deciphering of inscriptions, and the excavation of antiquities. In preparation for a definitive, annotated illustration of Vitruvius, Vignola was charged with measuring the antiquities of Rome. Nothing came of the project, though Vignola presumably acquired an intimate knowledge of Roman ruins and a working understanding of their relationship to Vitruvius's treatise. These events and Vasari's account of them suggest that as an architect Vignola was something of an autodidact, never in any master–pupil relationship like that of Peruzzi upon Serlio or Bramante-Raphael upon Giulio Romano. What is known of Vignola's personality suggests that he would have been disinclined toward such a servile relationship.

So, one might still think of Vignola in his early 30s as furthering his own education by intensive inspection of the more fashionable recent buildings such as Peruzzi's Palazzo Ossoli and Palazzo Massimo, Raphael's Palazzo Jacopo da Brescia and Palazzo Alberini, and Giulio's Palazzo Maccarani. What this diverse grouping shares is, in general, a preference for the use of pilasters on their exteriors and an incipient form of complex layers of architectural membering that would characterize Vignola's later work. With little or no work of his own to show, Vignola was appointed in March 1541, as architect of the basilica of S. Petronio in Bologna, a post that he would not take up for another two years.

FONTAINEBLEAU AND BOLOGNA

The reasons why Vignola did not immediately assume this important position further illuminate his early career. In Rome, Vignola worked in a variety of media—as a painter of furniture and banners, and as a designer and builder of theatrical scenery in addition to his architectural pursuits. More important was his experience in the preparation of plaster casts of ten ancient statues in the papal collections. For this task, he was selected by Francesco Primaticcio (1504/05–70), who had been commissioned by Francois I to make bronze copies of the ancient statues for fountains in the gardens of Fontainebleau. Primaticcio, a student of Giulio Romano and an executant of some of the stuccoes in the Palazzo del Te, was attracted to Vignola as a fellow worker in gesso. Italian *campanilismo* was also a further reason. Primaticcio, who was Vignola's senior by only two or three years, was also Bolognese by birth. Ultimately, Vignola was invited to serve the court of Francois at Fontainebleau, and in the summer of 1541, he left for France. In due course, he would also meet up with another émigré architect of Bolognese origin, Sebastiano Serlio.

Fontainebleau was born of Francois I's desire to create an art in France comparable to that of the Renaissance in Italy. For three decades, Italian architects and artists had participated in this wholesale transformation of a visual culture, and the decoration of the Galerie François I (1533–40) might be considered an explication of the genius of the endeavor (118). With its Michelangelo-style nudes, putti, cartouches, copious garlands and strapwork, the ensemble is at once a tribute to the power of the king and a sophisticated union of decorative sculpture and painting. While the project is customarily attributed to the older—and better-paid—painter Rosso Fiorentino (1495–1540), there can be no doubt that Primaticcio had a share in its design and execution. Primaticcio's own creation, the bedroom of the Duchesse d'Étampes (1541–43), is a luxurious chamber displaying the latest Italian repertory of forms—long, lissome figures, an emphasis on corners of the room, and a general feeling of sex on ice. It was in this environment that Vignola spent two years assisting in the completion of the casting operation and in an undefined architectural capacity, which may have involved providing clever *dal di sotto in su* perspectives. When the work was completed in 1543, Vignola returned to Bologna, almost certainly bored or frustrated that Fontainebleau had been little more than a peripheral figure in the most important artistic project in France.

$\widetilde{205}$

It might be fruitful to speculate on the influence of French Renaissance architecture on the impressionable young Vignola. Although his arrival coincides with one of the great periods of classical architecture in France, there were then few buildings that fully accepted the Italian idiom of architectural design. For example, there was little to see at Philibert de L'Orme's first major project, the chateau at St. Maur-lès-Fossés (begun 1541), which was among the very first to apply the Italian idea of a single order of pilasters to a French building whose plan was dominated by masses. Yet the experience would not have been a total loss because there Fontainebleau was itself an intermingling of French and Italian motifs. Vignola's soon-to-emerge preference for layers in low relief would have been confirmed by Gilles Le Breton's Porte Dorée (1528–40), where the vertical stacking of windows in the side bays anticipates the upper story of the facade of Caprarola (119). Similarly, Le Breton's staircase (begun 1531) in the Cour de l'Ovale—a double ramp bridging a main arch—also can be compared to Caprarola. If Italian sources can also be easily identified for these examples, Vignola's French sojourn helped to establish this taste for specific motifs.

Vignola's study of French architecture was not confined to classical structures. In all probability, he would have acquired some knowledge of the chateaux of the Loire valley, and he certainly would have wanted to see Paris. After Vignola returned to Bologna in 1543, the design that he presented for the facade of S. Petronio reflected his encounter with French Gothic architecture (120). To be

120 Vignola: Bologna, Scheme for facade of S. Petronio, 1544
121 Vignola: Bologna, Palazzo Bocchi, engraving of facade, begun 1545
122 Vignola: Scheme for Villa Cervini, 1540s

120

121

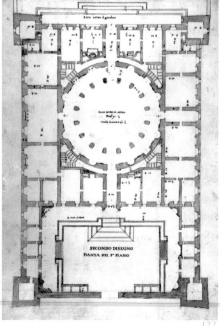

122

sure, the overall treatment of the exterior as a flat plane subdivided by pilasters and entablatures reflects Italian logic by corresponding to the main divisions of the church. Yet the source of some of Vignola's features is to be found in Paris. It is as if he had taken the gables, rose windows, and *rayonnant* tracery of the south facade of Notre Dame, and altered their sizes and redistributed them to harmonize with the facade's equilibrated division into a classical architectural grid. Unfortunately, in Bologna, it was almost a tradition to find an architect for this never-to-be-built facade, and there was outrage and controversy about any solution.

$\tilde{2}07$

Fortunately, there were other commissions at hand. The outlandish exterior of the Palazzo Bocchi (begun 1545) was Vignola's first conspicuously important project. Its patron, Achille Bocchi, a philosopher and professor of law at the University of Bologna, conceived of the structure as the home of a private academy. The design was modified as it was built and remains unfinished, but an engraving of 1545, shows what was Vignola's original intention (121). Planned as a structure five bays wide, its rusticated basement is separated from the rest of the structure by a string course with a biblical inscription in Hebrew and a quotation from Horace in Latin. In its central bay, a rusticated portal erupts from the building's block. Above it are both a first and second *piano nobile* and mezzanine, the lower of which employs windows from Giulio Romano's Roman house. A complicated cornice with brackets, animal heads, and windows separates the main floors from an attic level with a *serliana*; above this, for the purposes of profile, there are a temple front and figures at its sides. The result is a striking accumulation of novelties that investigate an entirely new expressive territory.

So far, no mention has been made of Vignola's skills as an architectural planner. Recently, a set of drawings has come to light that show his design for a fortified villa (122). The project, which was commissioned by Cardinal Marcello Cervini (later Pope Marcellus II) sometime in the later 1540s, was not particularly original. Its austere, unornamented exterior with corner towers looks back to various schemes illustrated in the treatises of Francesco di Giorgio, and its circular courtyard culminates a tradition originating in antiquity and culminating in the Villa Madama. What is intriguing is its particular combination of contrasting features—its fortified appearance and circular courtyard were to reappear at Caprarola, and the scheme is entered through a *cour d'honneur* typically found in French architecture and very infrequently in Italy. In spite of the breadth of Vignola's wide knowledge of planning techniques, the layout of the Villa Cervini lacks the effortless fluidity and refinement of his later efforts for the Farnese.

THE VILLA GIULIA
~

For all of his exposure to the French court, at home Vignola lost the support of the overseers of S. Petronio and left for Rome in late 1549 or early 1550. He soon entered into the service of Pope Julius III (1550–55). The new Pope had been a chamberlain to Julius II and had risen into prominence during the reign of Paul III, during which he was nominated as cardinal in 1536. With close connections to the two most illustrious pontiffs, Julius was politically and temperamentally their heir in the support of the arts and the advancement of his family through aggressive nepotism. In some ways, he was the last of the Renaissance popes, and he was also rumored to be a pedophile. Histories of the papacy repeatedly mention his infatuation with Innocenzo, a fifteen-year-old youth who was picked up in the streets of Parma. Subsequently, the youth was adopted by the Pope's brother, no doubt by papal order, and made a cardinal. Be this as it may, to a liberal judgment Julius III appears to have been a fairly relaxed humanist with a fondness for hunting and grand banquets. "Let virtuous delight be enjoyed by the virtuous" may well have been the attitude of his papacy.

Julius III suffered excruciatingly from gout, and he seems to have died from it. But despite his growing incapacity, he still presided over an important stylistic change—in both music and architecture—through his appointment of Palestrina as papal choirmaster and his support of Michelangelo as chief architect of St. Peter's. But what is most important is that for himself, he began the construction of a luxurious suburban residence and estate alongside the Via Flaminia, the Villa Giulia (1550–55). Julius III, known for being temperamental, querulous, and hard-to-please, must have been only too happy to select three architects to work on the job. At once, it is the first great piece of planning with which Vasari was connected. And not only was it Vignola's initial masterpiece, as well as Bartolomeo Ammannati's earliest important design, but just to make things more complicated, Michelangelo was the critic! The primary question resulting from this unusual relationship is "who did *what* and *where?*" All of the architects were about forty years old, and as yet, none of them had developed their personal style or constructed a major building on their own.

The Villa Giulia evoked the idyllic mood of a classical landscape that its grounds had once been. Composed of woods, groves, caves, and an elegant residence, it was the place where Julius III and his cronies could enjoy the pleasures of nature as well as its mischievous delights. The focal point was the Casino, garden-courtyard, and Nympheum, an enclosure whose axial arrangement followed the general line of an intimate valley (127). Apparently, the ensemble of landscape and buildings was conceived by Vasari, presumably working up the ideas of the Pope and Michelangelo. This arrangement allowed Vasari to serve as a coordinating architect while his colleagues took on specific tasks. Vignola completed the Casino according to his own designs and presumably offered advice on the hydraulics. Ammannati created the courtyard's enclosing walls and loggia. He also designed the Nympheum with the assistance of Vasari, whose role in this part of the project is uncertain. In the Villa Giulia, the worlds of Vasari, Vignola, and Ammannati impinge and overlap.

The Villa Giulia is the architectural conclusion to a leisurely progression that began at the Tiber. A concave public fountain was built along the Via Flaminia, and a nearby rusticated portal marked the beginning of the gentle ascent up the slope of the Monti Parioli. Set in a landscape of vineyards and gardens, Vignola's pseudo-palatial facade emerges as the rather incongruous conclusion to a bucolic excursion (123). Significantly, it gives no indication of the rich variety of spaces located behind. Immediately upon entering the villa, the distinctly axial arrangement of the garden-courtyard and its enclosing walls urge the visitor to move onward. From this follow abrupt changes in style. With greater theatricality, the walls of the garden-court were designed by a sculptor-architect, Ammannati, for the display of all kinds of ancient sculpture—statuary, portrait busts, reliefs—now long gone (125). The progress is momentarily broken, first by a few steps leading up to the Nympheum's entrance, and then by the triple-arched loggia within. At this point, the axis reemerges and divides into three directed views across and down below in the Nympheum. Multiple spaces now emerge as alternative conclusions

209

to the *passeggiata*—the waters of the Acqua Vergine in the fountain on the lowest level, the grotto behind the *serliana* on the main level of the sunken Nympheum, and the garden seen through the smaller loggia and aviary on the opposite side (126). What was physical has now become visual, and clarity has given way to ambiguity. Descending to the enclosure of the grotto-Nympheum, the profusion of ornament, the variety of architectural grammar, and the diversity of architectural scales create the effect of a sumptuous *salone* in the out-of-doors. No wonder the Nympheum was the heart of the design, embodying all of the sensory pleasure of the villa.

Immediately, the plan of the Villa Giulia calls to mind the two most ambitious projects of the early cinquecento, Bramante's Cortile del Belvedere and the Villa Madama. In fact, Vignola appears to have conceived of the villa initially as a grander ensemble with wings projecting from either side of the casino. But the scheme illustrated in a now-lost master plan was never completed, and as a consequence of this, the smaller project became more intense in its architectural impact. When compared to the Villa Madama, the Villa Giulia is a more intimate and neurotic theater, where the water of the Nympheum was perhaps intended to serve—ineffectively—as relief for the Pope's gout.

Beyond these immediate precedents there were other traditions from which Vignola may have drawn. Clearly, he may have been excited by his association with Serlio in France and his knowledge of Serlio's unpublished designs. The plan for the casino is similar in some ways to two plans by Serlio in his *Seventh Book*, and it is immensely curious that they never seem to have been published in conjunction with it (128). Mix these two together, a plan with an apse and a plan with a semi-circular gallery, and one finds something very close to Vignola's plan. If his specific knowledge of these drawings is hypothetical, it is certain that Vignola was intimately familiar with Serlio's architectural vocabulary and repertory of forms.

Vignola's vertical development of this plan is something very different from Serlio; sophisticated where he is elementary. The predominant impression of this entrance facade is one of vigorous coordination of contrasts. Two stories high, with its entrance elevation the casino presents a centralized, tripartite composition framed by rusticated pilasters below and more normative pilasters above. Within this framework, there are subtle infringements of its visual

123

124

125

FONTANA FATTA DA PAPA IVLIO TERZO IN ROMA NELLA VIA FLAMINIA PER ABBELLIMENTO DELLA SVA VIGNA

126

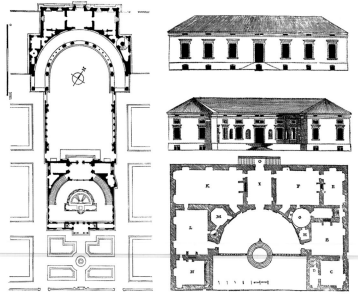

127   *128*

balance. Immediately, the observer senses a heightened visual tension in Vignola's employment of the Rustic-Tuscan order below and the Composite up top, the two extremes of the grammatical canon. Down below, the Casino presents itself as a fortified block in which five openings tend to appear as absence of mass, insured by both the robust scooping out of the niches on either side of the entrance door and the rusticated protuberances surrounding it. Up top, it becomes something more delicate in which seven openings appear as absence of plane—everything is more geometrical, angular, and reticent. The windows on the lower story show a flavor of Palazzo del Te, and those upstairs, belong to Vignola's repertory of window types. The theme of the aggressive entrance is derived from the Palazzo Bocchi; but the genealogy of the motif above it is not so easily stipulated. Altogether, the casino's exterior is a startling importation of Northern Italian motifs into Rome from Bologna and Mantua. To a mid-cinquecento sensibility, the results could not have been more startling; the Villa Giulia proclaims all of the shock of the new, while by comparison, the Palazzo Farnese is placid and reticent.

So from concealment outside, we proceed to disclosure. While the Casino's entrance facade is a matter of mass, or at least plane, its garden facade is an affair of nearly weightless surfaces, or almost-paper cutouts (124). Like the exterior, it is another tripartite composition (or is it *cinque-partite*?) but, this time, apsidal in form and theatrical in effect. It can be easily understood as a variant of the hemicycle of Trajan's markets or the interior of the Pantheon, but its more immediate antecedents are hard to come by. Utterly unlike anything Northern Italian, and too intelligent for Serlio, this manipulation of triumphal arches, complete or only partial, of intervening trabeated episodes, can only suggest the influence of an ideal Peruzzi—of a Peruzzi that as of yet has never been seen or heard of. Taken together, the two vertical surfaces, outside and in, might be construed as the public and private images which Julius III wished to convey. The entrance facade is austere, and the pontiff remote; but the garden facade is erudite, licentious, and in an interesting way—indeed—one can imagine Innocenzo lurking in the loggia.

Apart from the villa itself, one of the most astonishing structures on the estate is Vignola's highly concise and attractive church, or *tempietto*, of S. Andrea in Via Flaminia (1550–53). This small structure was especially important to the Pope, who constructed it to commemorate his escape when he was held hostage by German troops after the Sack of Rome. In conception, it is a recondite building full of wit—a severe rectangle from which rises an elegant oval drum. Yet for all of its clarity, the design is itself ambiguous if not contradictory. The origins of the design suggest alternative readings of it as either a mini-Pantheon or a Roman tomb similar to many found along the Via Appia and the Via Flaminia. It is both a structure conceived fully in three dimensions yet seen only in two; originally a wall along the Via Flaminia hid the rear portions of the church from public view. From certain points of view, the drum might be understood as circular. And on the interior, which is an elegant volume not unlike Brunelleschi's Pazzi Chapel, the drum and dome play only a minor role.

S. Andrea has, however, a character distinct from any ancient building. Its entrance front is emphasized by a pediment and six Corinthian pilasters, the outer ones being coupled and the intermediate bays being excavated by two niches crowned by fastidiously executed shells. These same characteristics are carried over into the interior where the floor is subdivided by paving and the walls by pilasters; the dome, in contrast, is placid and unarticulated. The side walls, like a facade, are now a series of superimposed planes that form an inverted Serlio motif (arches in the narrow side bays). The entablature is eliminated, reducing the pilasters to a sort of structural frame that has no particular suggestion of weight. Because there is no lantern, light seems to rise up into the dome rather than fall down from it. With a horizontal axis accommodating the needs of liturgy and a vertical axis emphasizing centrality, Vignola's solution stands at the head of a sequence of churches extending into the seventeenth century. Full of visual sophistication and erudition, S. Andrea is Vignola's first—and in many ways most compelling—statement about the relationship of a facade and the space it masks.

The Villa Giulia, a unique and highly complex statement of three major architects, is typical of the mid-century. While its intricate and rather spasmodic episodes may relate it to other contemporary gardens, in other ways, it is totally alien to the Italy of the Counter-Reformation; and, in this way, a characteristic that it shares with the Casino of Pius IV in the Vatican gardens. Although he was the uncle of S. Carlo Borromeo, Pope Pius IV (1559–65) was another belated High Renaissance personage, whose reign was sandwiched between popes of entirely different bias. Preceded by the terrible

Pope Paul IV (1555–59), and followed by the no less difficult Pope Pius V (1566–72), the papacy of Pius IV was part of an alternation between rigorist and casual popes, and, with all its humanist pseudo-archaeology, the Casino of Pius IV speaks to the departure of High Renaissance ideals no less than the Villa Giulia.

Burckhardt called the Casino of Pius IV "the most resting place for afternoon hours that modern architecture has produced." Designed by the Neapolitan antiquarian and architect Pirro Ligorio (circa 1510–1583), the Casino is an arrangement of villa (begun by Pope Paul IV), two gatehouses, and a loggia surrounding an oval courtyard on a secluded, sloping site in the Vatican gardens (129). As an architect Ligorio had one quality that assured his success in Rome: he created structures that his knowledge of ancient and modern buildings contributed to their completeness. There are reminiscences of an ancient nympheum and of Hadrian's Villa in the courtyard's oval shape; the profuse stucco decoration of the loggia gives it the look of an ancient sarcophagus. Yet the loggia's trabeated portico speaks to the generation of Peruzzi and its integration with the sunken fountain at its base recalls the Villa Giulia. Ligorio's approach is overtly eclectic, but it must also be said that the Casino's reclusive scale creates a environment befitting its purpose. It was everything the Villa Giulia was not: open to nature, intensely intimate, and utterly charming.

Pius IV as a builder sought to surpass the prodigality of the Florentine Medici, who were not his relations. Unlike many pontiffs, he initiated projects that were to change the urban topography of Rome, such as the Via Pia and its culmination gateway designed by Michelangelo, and the Borgo Pio, an extension of the Borgo. The individual buildings begun under his watchful eye included the restoration of numerous churches, the transformation of the Baths of Diocletian into S. Maria degli Angeli, and the refortification of the area around the Castel Sant' Angelo. His undertakings attracted the attention of agents and ambassadors for Mantua and Venice, who marveled at their cost and wondered if he would live long enough to complete them. Sadly, though, projects resulting from Pius IV's patronage have been overshadowed by those of Sixtus V and others. One reason is that they were not accessible to the public and many were completed by others, as in continuation of construction at St. Peter's, in the Cortile del Belvedere, and in many points within the

129 Pirro Ligorio: Rome, Vatican Gardens, Casino of Pius IV,
    courtyard and loggia, begun 1559
130 Vignola: Caprarola, Palazzo Farnese, begun 1559
131 Palazzo Farnese, plan

129

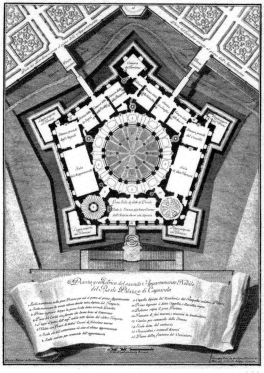

131

130

Vatican Palace. Still, the projects as a whole demonstrate a remarkably practical and comprehensive view of Roman life; his motto, as
stated in an inscription on the Porta di Castello, was probably: "Let
him who would preserve the city follow our example."

Julius III, with his gout and Innocenzo, and Pius IV, were intellectual kindred in an increasingly hostile world. With a serious frivo-
lity, they had made their choice; and, as a type, they were almost an
endangered species. Popes of this kind were not to recur, and following the example of his predecessor, the next Pope, Gregory XIII
(1572–85), established the model for the future. From this time
onward the Popes were no longer able to build pleasure pavilions for
themselves. For, though, it might be permitted to papal nephews
such as Scipione Borghese, Ludovico Ludovisi, and Camillo
Pamphili, for the pontiff himself, such indulgence was no longer
good public relations.

ARCHITECT TO THE FARNESE
~

The change in the papacy helped to inaugurate a new phase in
Vignola's career. After the death of Julius III, Vignola increasingly
began to find himself as the architectural satellite to Alessandro
Farnese (1520–89), "*il gran cardinale*." Hence, it will be useful to say a
few words about this incredibly important patron and prelate.

Cardinal Farnese was the grandson of an earlier Alessandro (b.
1468), who was created Cardinal in 1494, ordained as a Priest only in
1519, and finally became Pope, as Paul III (1534–49). By origin, the
Farnese were a *condottiere* family with extensive properties in the
plain around Viterbo and also to the west of the Lago di Bolsena. But
they were a minor family (possibly of Germanic beginnings), and
Paul III's rise to power is generally thought to have been the result of
producing his sister Giulia as a mistress for Pope Alexander VI. She
was the beautiful blonde in Pinturicchio's frescoes in the
Appartamento Borgia in the Vatican (known in Rome as the "Bride
of Christ"), and he, the future Paul III, as "Cardinal petticoat."

Paul III was a great Pope (after Julius II the greatest of the sixteenth century) and also a great nepotist. The family lands in the
Viterbese—Ronciglione, Nepi, Capranica, and Castro—were to be
stabilized and consolidated. In 1535, as a consequence of this strategy, he promoted his son, Pier Luigi, to be duke of Castro and Nepi.

Eight years later, in 1545, Pier Luigi became the duke of Parma and Piacenza, where—in Parma—Pier Luigi was assassinated in 1547. But Paul III's family ambitions extended further. In 1538, one grandson married Margaret of Austria, illegitimate daughter of Charles V; and, in 1552, after Paul III's death, this was to be followed by the marriage of another grandson to Diane de Valois, illegitimate daughter of Henri II of France!

So by the beginning of the 1550s, the Farnese were exceedingly well connected and related, if rather dubiously, to centers of great power in Vienna, Paris, and later, Madrid. The family had ceased to be the minor power from upper Lazio—almost, they had become a European power. And it has been said that, in 1914, every reigning Catholic prince in Europe was a descendant of Paul III! So much for Spain, Austria, Bavaria—so much for the fortitude of the Farnese and the forbearance of the Church.

Vignola's most spectacular building, the Palazzo Farnese at Caprarola, is the consummate statement of Cardinal Farnese's self-esteem (130-131). Caprarola was a fairly recent Farnese acquisition. Until 1464, it had belonged to the Anguillara, another family of northern Lazio. From them it had been taken, in a highly successful ten days of war, by Pope Paul II (1464–71), and, as a papal property, it had been sold by the duke of Urbino, the nephew of Julius II, to the future Paul III in 1504. At a convenient distance from Rome, and on the southern slopes of the Monti Cimini, its site must have made it from the beginning—with easy access, extended views, and a comfort-giving orientation—one of the most desirable items of Farnese real estate. So, as Caprarola prospered under the Farnese dispensation, the Farnese themselves began to think about a suitable residence.

But how did the concept of a five-sided and quasi-fortified palace-villa emerge? Admittedly, Serlio's *Sixth Book* has a project for such a building called a "Palace for Tyrant Prince." But, for the origins of the theme, one must think about the development of sixteenth-century fortification, where for the purposes of ballistics, a five-sided fortress was a favorite theme. And apart from the Fortezza da Basso in Florence, one might notice this type in Livorno, Turin, Parma—indeed in places all over the world—and, as a militarist stronghold, persisting even into the twentieth century, as the Pentagon in the District of Columbia.

We know almost nothing about the origins of the Farnese Palace at Caprarola. Prior to his elevation to the papacy, Alessandro senior commissioned the design of a *rocca*, or fortified country residence from Antonio da Sangallo the Younger. Some of the commission's inherent difficulties may be demonstrated in a drawing by Sangallo for a pentagonal palace or fortress within a pentagonal courtyard (Uffizi, A 775). Although the plan was admirably suited to the exigencies of warfare, it also resulted in awkwardly shaped rooms at the junction of its sides. In an attempt to resolve the problems of the pentagon, Sangallo introduces the circular courtyard—with obvious indebtedness to Raphael's Villa Madama—in a scheme for a *rocca*. Clever as the scheme may be, it cannot be identified with any certainty as a design for Caprarola. Peruzzi also proclaimed that the theme of the fortified palace had been a small building with bastions at the Castellina di Norcia and in two drawings for Caprarola. Sadly, Peruzzi's project for Caprarola itself is a rather inept plan showing little of his characteristic feeling for architectural circumstance (Uffizi, A 506). Parts of the *rocca's* moat and external walls had been built before construction was halted, and Farnese resources were redirected toward the construction of Castro.

In 1556, after Antonio da Sangallo had been dead for ten years, Cardinal Alessandro commissioned Vignola to transform the unfinished *rocca* into an elegant residence, one that was to be part palatial and part villa. With its plan almost determined, what does he do? By this time, Vignola can manipulate the general idea of the pentagon in terms of its section. And in terms of the courtyard, he makes two supremely important decisions—its plan is to be circular, and in the section, the walls of the courtyards are no longer to rise to the height of the walls of the pentagon. It is a strongly personal invention, conceived in theatrical terms that force the observer to be surprised and deceived. Thus, Vignola dislocates the section, creating at once the particular astringency from which Caprarola derives: what you see on the outside no longer concurs with what you find within.

As Montaigne already observed in the cinquecento, the contrast between the courtyard and the exterior is remarkable (132). The former is a refined restatement of Bramante's Palazzo Caprini; the latter is a brutal enlargement of Fontainebleau's Porte Dorée and Peruzzi's Villa Farnesina. There are unresolved difficulties of approach. The entrance facade of the palace, arrived at by that narrow, restricted street, is perhaps too much a *coup de théâtre*, too much an overt brilliance, and too many levels, with too many staircases. Vignola's exacting grammatical construction in the entrance facade is lost in the glamour of his sudden *coup de théâtre*—all the staircases and the ascending levels. And then, after this, there follows intimacy and the centralized tranquillity of the courtyard. In the 1550s, the arcades in Bramante's Cortile del Belvedere had been walled up, and it seems likely that Vignola was paying a private tribute to the earlier master. For a better understanding of Vignola's private rigor, it will be best to concern ourselves with the less dazzling elevations, which are accessible at eye level from the gardens. And therefore, to take a garden elevation and look at it (133).

There are two major stories, stipulated by the two major orders, Ionic and Corinthian; perhaps there is a general allegiance to the externals of Peruzzi's Villa Farnesina. However, the most extraordinary of things, though conducted with the most extreme discipline, seem to be going on. For everything seemed to be linked to two interwoven systems—one of the orders and another to a system of almost cardboard strips, which show a tendency to back up these orders or to lace them together. The various elements are inextricably connected, and simultaneously, denied by contrary systems of organization. Ornamental elements such as the arches and window heads have become as assertive as the entablature above.

In contrast to the aggressive horizontal emphasis of the lower floor, the upper floors emphasize vertical alignments. The stacking of windows—or voids—is the complement to the solid pilasters enframing them. There are no elements to contradict the pilasters or the molding strips, and the wall surface behind them appears to be unbroken. It is as if Vignola's penchant for contrast has been focused onto a single surface—a lower floor that demands to be seen frontally, as in one point perspective, while the upper floor is understood obliquely, with the implications of a *dal di sotto in su* perspective.

As in the Villa Giulia, Vignola approaches Caprarola's vertical surfaces with a Michelangelo-style sensibility and then proceeds to articulate their surface and depth. The wall has become a topic for an anatomical dissection, in which, as in an illustration by Vesalius, layers are gradually subtracted and cut away. The result is a building that is simultaneously both an opaque and visually impermeable

133 Palazzo Farnese, detail of garden elevation
134 Hubert Robert: *Capriccio of Interior Staircase, Palazzo Farnese, Caprarola*
135 P. de l'Orme (attr.), drawing of a spiral staircase

133

135

134

phenomenon and a lattice-like accumulation of wires and straps, as in a gigantic birdcage. This arrangement may owe something to Michelangelo's S. Lorenzo facade, something to Giulio Romano's Palazzo Maccarani, and something to the intricate happenings in Peruzzi's courtyard of the Palazzo Massimo.

The most striking feature of Caprarola's interior is its circular staircase (134), certainly the best of all specimens of its type. For it, there exists an illustrious pedigree, part of which is derived from tradition. In the Middle Ages, the spiral staircase was for the most part precipitous and inconvenient. However, after 1500, it begins to emancipate itself from its Gothic matrix and even to become external to the building which it serves. The most famous example of this type is the staircase at Blois, which Vignola must have almost certainly known. Vignola also would have been attracted to Chambord, which was based on the ideas of Leonardo. Although its famous double-spiral staircase resembles those in sketches by Leonardo, the origins of Chambord's stair are French and largely medieval. The dilemma posed by giving an Italianate appearance to a medieval French architectural type is best expressed in a drawing for a staircase attributed to Philibert de L'Orme (135). The stair it depicts has been explained as an attempt to correct Bramante's design for his famous stair in the Vatican, and this drawing is an exquisite indication of French intelligence and preciosity. Demonstrating a sophisticated classicism and invoking a medieval know-how in construction, one can feel in this drawing that almost every stone has been subjected to intense scrutiny.

To walk up Vignola's corkscrew at Caprarola is a completely different experience. The helix at Caprarola is based on Bramante's Vatican stair, but it exceeds it in every possible way. And it reduces poor Bramante to a primitive. Bramante's spiral ramp labors up through all the five orders of architecture as it makes its ascent. It doesn't stand on a basement-high pedestal, and for its consummation, there is no more to look at than the roof of a cottage. Vignola's staircase, on the other hand, is a triumphant affair, exceeding in splendor the rooms to which it leads. It is Doric all the way up, its aggressive spiral completes itself in the dome that caps its cylindrical void. With its assertive pedestal and its no-less assertive cornice, it makes of its cylinder a volume that is both two and one. With its vaulted ceiling, the staircase is a quasi-independent entity until it merges with the enclosing cylinder as it approaches the courtyard level of the house. It is also infinitely exciting in the window recesses, each with its little approach steps, adjacencies, and sources of illumination, which might be considered an early version of Louis Kahn's differentiation between service spaces and spaces served. In these ways, the Caprarola helix-corkscrew, with its strong internal logic, is the climax of the sequence introduced by Leonardo and Bramante, and it exceeds everything that was subsequently done with this motif. Subsequent spirals at the Palazzo Quirinale and at the Palazzo Barberini simply do not possess its authority and forcefulness. By comparison, they are more than a little garrulous, tedious, and bland.

Caprarola is but a small part of the greater topographical themes that constitute Fareneseland in northern Lazio. It is a territory to be examined, literally, at three levels. First, it is a great rolling land with distant presiding mountains—the Monti Cimini to the north and Monte Soratte to the east—and then, incised within it, it has intricate and secret little valleys, sometimes wholly private, sometimes admitting to the datum of the plateau; and, sometimes receiving the more remote mountain signals. It is the landscape of Nicholas Poussin; a landscape which achieves its clarity through the introduction of architecture. At Capranica, some fifteen kilometers from Caprarola, you know you are there—you have arrived within the full Farnese orbit. In English terms, Capranica is almost the estate village for Caprarola and the little church of S. Maria del Piano (1559–65), the visible anticipation of Vignola's *rocca* (136). Although the church is insufficiently documented, Capranica is so close to Caprarola and of such high quality that we are disposed to look upon it as an almost certain attribution.

The exterior of S. Maria del Piano is a variant on themes with which Vignola had already experimented in S. Andrea in Via Flaminia. It is an altogether more ambitious design that can be regarded as a slightly larger, more expansive brother, a *tempio* in relationship to a *tempietto*.

Without a dome, it is less complex and less crowded in detail than its predecessor. It is pilaster and Ionic rather than Corinthian, broad and flat rather than cramped. Notable in both buildings is the activity of the niches, which act to dilate and to give tension to an otherwise, ostensibly innocent vertical surface. Also notable is the slightly different pitch of the pediments, that of the temple front and that of the door; and the subtly destabilizing effect of the white panel precariously perched on the apex of the lower pediment cannot be overlooked. Apparently straightforward, it is a facade of multiple contrasts and ambiguities, a mask or disguise to what lies behind it; while the church in the Via Flaminia, offers an integrated conception of frontispiece and dome. For not a very large building, the S. Maria del Piano vibrates, almost trembles with intimations of monumentality, and it is pleasant to think of it as some kind of herald, or preliminary manifesto, of what will subsequently be discovered at Caprarola.

225

PIACENZA AND BOLOGNA
~

At about the same time Vignola designed two secular buildings—the Palazzo Farnese in Piacenza (1558–59) and the Facciata dei Banchi in Bologna (1565–68). If the palace derives its importance as an example of the failure of Farnese ambition, the Facciata is Vignola's most important contribution to urban building.

The Palazzo Farnese in Piacenza is more ambitious than it is impressive—and one can wonder why the Farnese ever felt they needed it (137). That the Farnese needed what they could not afford was, no doubt, the product of the desire to place their family on a level with the great families of Europe. Part fortress, part urban residence, and part suburban villa facing its extensive gardens, the main lines of the palace had been determined by Francesco Paciotto, an architect-engineer known primarily for fortification design. At Caprarola, Vignola demonstrated his skill in the creative adaptation of existing construction, but here work was abandoned due to the lack of funds. But from the incomplete mass of this palace, almost impossible to contemplate, there are certain details of the plan envisaged by Vignola that distinguish the Palazzo Farnese from other grand residences. The first and most important is the courtyard's semi-oval theater that suggests Vignola conceived of his design as a palace in the form of a theater, a suggestion already present in the Villa Giulia and taken up later in Palladio's Teatro Olimpico, Scamozzi's theater in Sabbioneta, and Aleotti's Teatro Farnese in Parma. Equally notable are its apsidal corners, first proposed for the Villa Cervini and which will recur in Borromini's Oratory in Rome in the seventeenth century.

136

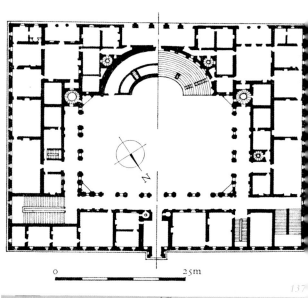

0   25m

137

138

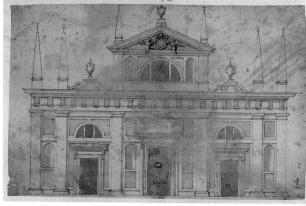

139

The Facciata dei Banchi (1565–68) is one of the great urbanistic achievements of the Renaissance, an endeavor equal to Sansovino's renovation of Piazza S. Marco or Michelangelo's Campidoglio (117). It has been widely assumed that its site on the Piazza Maggiore adjacent to S. Petronio was comprised of a number of buildings of different heights and widths, with shops and arcades down below and interrupted by the entry of two streets, making Vignola's design a refacing of the equivalent of Serlio's Comic Scene. But in reality, Vignola's ninety-six-meter-long uniform facade, as has been recently shown, enclosed a unified, late-Gothic portico in its lower stories and comprised new construction on the upper floors. By approximating the height of the arcade of the adjacent Palazzo del Podesta in the Banchi's lower story, Vignola gave a cohesion to the buildings on the square. But this visual unity was selective. The new stylistic identity that it gave to the Piazza Maggiore was emphatically triumphant and theatrical—as if a *scenae frons* had been constructed across the eastern side of the square. The perfect viewpoint for Vignola's design is found in the papal palace opposite it on the Piazza Maggiore, from which the papal governor (or even the Pope himself) could contemplate an emphatic Roman presence in the second papal capital.

227

Something has been said about the eruptive behavior of much of Vignola's detail, and in the individual bays of the Facciata dei Banchi, this is very apparent (138). The pilasters down below are equipped with the most profusely developed capitals, but they support only the most tenuous and abbreviated of entablatures. On the other hand, the upper level follows its own logic. Pilasters receive no trace of anything like a capital, and instead, merge into something like an entablature to become—backed up by another layer of relief—the framing of a series of panels. The most obvious trait that distinguished the facade as a whole is an obtrusive horizontal motion—that of the mezzanine and its supporting apparatus—that straps together the diverse parts of what is an ambiguous *parti*. But, also, the repetitive quality of the typical bay of this facade is mitigated by local manipulations. Minor but highly assertive motifs interweave the composition, of which the most notable are inverted *serliane*. In both the mezzanine and upper floors, the central window in the middle is not arched. As a consequence of its trabeation, it can

scarcely accommodate any central focus, and a result of this peripheral emphasis, there is the distribution of animation throughout the
entire vertical surface.

In its general design, the Facciata dei Banchi is a simplification
of the facades of Caprarola, and inspection of it may clarify remarks
already made about what Vignola was doing for Alessandro Farnese.
Above all, it is a palatial facade for a public structure. A drawing by
Vignola shows that he envisaged a structure with somewhat taller
and narrower proportions for the individual bays and clock towers
with coats of arms to designate the two streets that pass through it. At
the same time, there is overtly a whiff of the medieval in the disposition of its parts and attenuated proportions, suggested perhaps by the
necessity of incorporating Gothic vaulting. Yet its arrangement of
arcading and windows may recall bay rhythm, layering of surfaces,
and the interior elevations of churches Vignola may have seen in
France (Autun Cathedral, Cluny). But the executed design is nevertheless squarely in cinquecento Italian usage.

ROMAN CHURCHES
~

It may be best to move on to the topic of Vignola's churches in
Rome. Of these later works, there are four which, in a group,
include the S. Maria del Orto (1564–67); the facade project for S.
Maria in Traspontina (1566); the world–renowned Gesù (1568–75);
and the S. Anna dei Palafrenieri (begun 1565). Of the three designs
that were built, the first is primarily a facade attached to an existing
nave, and the last two are primarily internal volumes, with facades
either added to by others (as at Il Gesù) or left incomplete (as at
S. Anna dei Palafrenieri).

In S. Maria in Traspontina (139), Vignola conceives of the facade
as a rather public affair of architectural scrim. Above all it demonstrates a compulsive trabeation that results from its attachment to a
church with an excessively wide plan and low nave. To compensate for
this uncustomary horizontality, Vignola manipulates a wealth of
empirical detail into an architectural fugue. For example, the central
bay is emphasized by its greater width, concentration of ornament,
and larger thermal window and central portal. The architectural
counterpoint is even more subtle. The implication of an eruptive central force is held in check by secondary elements—niches, panels, and

urns on pedestals flanked by scrolls—that deflect the observer's attention to the lateral bays. Here, the elaborate skyline of urns and obelisks serves opposing aesthetic purposes—concentration and equilibration.

In S. Maria dell'Orto a similar—and in some ways less ingenious—arrangement creates a totally different kind of facade (140). There is again present that eruptive tendency which, though always held in check by the wall, seems to have been so natural to Vignola. But at S. Maria dell'Orto, eruption is signified by the way in which the main door and its framing break through the Bramantesque apparatus of the lower walls—derived from the Belvedere arcades—which it has been Vignola's affectation to adopt. There is also a further excitement in the obelisks, pinnacles, and other spiky stimulants, to which Vignola by now had developed an extreme addiction. Of these, S. Maria dell'Orto is equipped in abundance—five obelisks above the frontispiece, and six more, three on each side, to decorate the end walls of the aisles. This is almost intolerably wild, and can make one think not just about Rome but Bologna, too, about the unbuilt obelisks that could have contributed to the silhouette of and the pinnacles that decorate the roofline of the Gothic facade for S. Petronio. To paraphrase Vasari's comments in the *Lives of the Artists* on Giulio Romano, S. Maria dell'Orto is medievally modern and modernly medieval.

Vignola's last years were largely devoted to designs for Il Gesù, his most celebrated and influential religious structure. It is not surprising that this structure, which was the architectural culmination of the reform teaching of St. Ignatius of Loyola (1491–1556), founder of the Society of Jesus, soon became one of Alessandro's concerns. Initially, Vignola may have proposed an oval plan for Il Gesù, but the executed design drew on an established church type—the vaulted nave flanked by chapels—that originated in S. Andrea in Mantua (141–142). Although begun in 1470, Alberti's masterpiece was so very long in building (scarcely approaching anything like completion before 1565) that it might be regarded as a contemporary of Il Gesù. But what made Il Gesù so compelling and original is how Vignola adapted this arrangement to the needs of preaching to great numbers of the faithful in a church on a constrained urban site. The differences are immediately apparent. S. Andrea is a Latin cross, expanding easily into transepts comparable to the nave. But at the Gesù, the transepts become compressed without any great individuality and are almost

229

fully incorporated into the rectangular volume of the church. As a result, its spatial composition—a broad nave culminates in a domed crossing which is followed by a tall, semicircular apse—is simple but its overall effect is stunning and theatrical.

To approach the inside of the building and its internal elevations is to reveal Il Gesù's complicated history (143). Under Vignola's direction, the interior was completed up to the level of the main entablature, while the nave and cupola were subsequently built by Giacomo della Porta and raised higher than Vignola originally intended. Yet, with many differences, it is *still* an obvious descendent of Alberti's S. Andrea (26), but with important qualifications. To itemize the more glaring differences, the lighting of Alberti's nave is indirect and subdued—it derives from the side chapels—while that of Il Gesù is more brilliant—it is supplied by tall, generously sized windows cut out of the curve of the vault. Alberti's side chapels are rather open to the nave and Vignola's rather screened from it. Alberti's nave elevations show both pilasters and arcade rising to the same entablature and cornice, while Vignola posits a much more complex condition. Vignola's arches do not rise very high, and above them, he introduces a *coretto*, a sort of mezzanine which—slightly like the boxes of a theater—create conditions of secrecy and elaborate privacy. Alberti's cornice is reticent and discreet; Vignola's is more "pushy" and abrupt. Above this, at the springing of the vault, there is an attic that allows for a movement from outside to inside, asserting a horizontal emphasis in the equivalent to the lateral emphasis of the Facciata dei Banchi in Bologna.

The facade of Il Gesù demonstrates the stylistic conflict that broke the bond between Vignola and Cardinal Alessandro (144). As Heinrich Wölfflin observed in *Renaissance und Barock* (1888), Vignola's definitive design invokes a type exemplified by Antonio da Sangallo the Younger's S. Spirito in Sassia (begun 1539) or Guido Guidetti's S. Caterina dei Funari (1560–64), where Ignatius of Loyola previously established a school for poor girls. It clearly is, in fact, a descendent of these churches, but it must be seen to be one that is *very* highly qualified. Vignola's scheme is less festive, its reentrance is triplicated to become a cavernous triumphal arch, and the assertion of the nave as opposed to the flanking chapels is more aggressive. Much greater emphasis is placed on the variety of its orders, as shown by single pilasters, paired pilasters a three-quarter

140 Vignola: Rome, S. Maria dell'Orto, 1564–67
141 Vignola: Rome, Il Gesù, plan, begun 1568
142 Alberti: Mantua, San Andrea, plan, begun 1470
143 Vignola: Rome, Il Gesù, interior

140

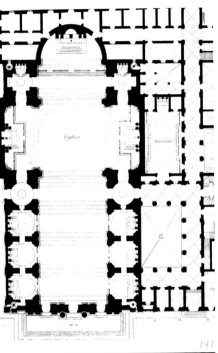

141

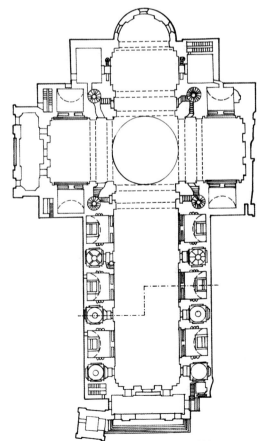

142

143

144 Vignola: Rome, Il Gesù, drawing of facade
by Giacinto Vignola after Jacopo Vignola, 1573
145 G. della Porta: Rome, Il Gesù, facade, begun 1571
146 Vignola: Rome, S. Anna dei Palafrenieri, begun 1565
147 S. Anna dei Palafrenieri, plan

144

145

146

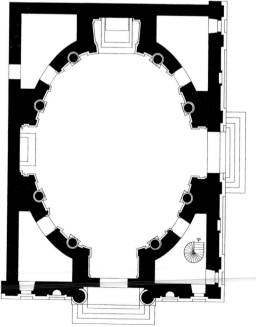

147

column placed in close proximity to each other. Arguably, the entrance triumphal arch motif is a miniature version of Alberti's entrance portico to S. Andrea at Mantua and this may be highly appropriate because, in many ways, the plans and the interiors of the two churches have so much in common. This was one of several schemes that Vignola prepared to please his patron. Yet the real reasons for their rejection still remain unclear, though issues of taste must have played a role.

233

The Gesù facade executed by della Porta (145) may therefore be introduced as a drastic commentary upon Vignola. With its greater verticality in proportion and clarity in its concentration upon its central area, della Porta has created an imposing exterior that would easily satisfy the most demanding patron. To accomplish this, he has broadened the frontispiece and somewhat raised its height. That is, in his lateral emphasis, he has not wished to reproduce the graceful curves of earlier churches such as S. Caterina dei Funari, which conceal the lean-to roofs and buttresses above the flanking chapels. Instead, della Porta has introduced a motif definitely more robust. This is the type of scroll or volute found on Alberti's facade of S. Maria Novella in Florence, and from 1479–83, in S. Agostino in Rome. Then further, with a succession of pediments around the main entrance—segmental, triangular, and segmental again—he has produced a triumphant conclusion.

Is this inferior to Vignola, or is it rather better? This is a question that cannot be answered. While Vignola's facade may be an index of his formal preoccupations, Giacomo della Porta produced an orchestration of the Church Belligerent which was to spread throughout the Counter-Reformation world, in one form or another, all the way from Mexico City to Macao.

In this decade, Vignola also embarked upon his most original central plan church, S. Anna dei Palafrenieri (146-147). The *palafrenieri* were the grooms of the papal horses, and, appropriately enough, the church for their confraternity is situated in an extension to the Borgo laid out by Pius IV. The history of this small church is complex and presents important questions of chronology and attribution. S. Anna was begun in 1565, but Vignola died in 1573 and within a few years work had been halted. By this time, construction had reached the level of the entablature on the exterior, and the supervision of the work had been entrusted to the architect's son, who had no reason to alter his father's designs. There were major renovations to the interior in the seventeenth century, and the facade and dome were not completed until the eighteenth century. Today, the church is located alongside the present main entrance to the Vatican, but in the cinquecento, it sat at the intersection of two streets serving different purposes—one leading to the private gate into the Cortile del Belvedere, and the other, a pilgrimage road leading to St. Peter's. Both functions were ultimately to affect Vignola's design.

The assertive novelty of Vignola's S. Anna contrasts with the subtle provocations of his earlier design for S. Andrea in Via Flaminia. The layout of S. Anna, which derives from the repertory of Peruzzi and Serlio, originally had entrances on both its short and long axes. This scheme may have been suggested by the different functions of the church's two altars—the long axis led to the confraternity's high altar, while the short one, led directly to an altar dedicated to S. Anna that was venerated primarily by pilgrims. Each axis, as such, addresses one of the church's dual functions. The church is equipped with an oval dome rising above a completely oval plan encased within a rectilinear shell. Thus, by extending its plan into the dome, S. Anna differs from S. Andrea where an elliptical dome exists in contradistinction to a rectangular plan. At S. Andrea, there is a dialectical distinction between a gridded floor and a dome, but at S. Anna, the pattern of the pavement is focused and centralized, as presumably Vignola would have done in the dome as well. At S. Anna, Vignola has paid a tribute to Michelangelo, if not to his more overt demonstration of columns engaged within the wall, as in the *ricetto* of the Laurentian Library, but at least to their more submerged presentation in the Palazzo dei Conservatori on the Campidoglio. Eventually, S. Anna's oval plan came to influence both Borromini (who drew and studied Vignola's church and adapted its interior in that of his masterpiece, S. Carlo alle Quattro Fontane) and Bernini (who tended to use the short axis as the main axis for the constrained sites of the initial chapel of the Collegio di Propaganda Fide and S. Andrea al Quirinale).

Nowhere are the differences between the essentially planar architecture of Vignola's earlier buildings and his later work more sharply drawn than in S. Anna. A crucial difference is found in the conception of Vignola's architectural expression, which has given way to an architecture of mass. S. Anna's most characteristic features—a domed interior inscribed within a rectangular volume and

234

its interrelated facades—suggest their origin in Sangallo the Younger's S. Maria di Loreto, an uncustomary source for Vignola. The alterations to the facade introduced by Alessandro Specchi in the eighteenth century—the recession of the center, the prominence of the flanking bell towers, and the projecting dominance of their cornices—diminish but do not destroy S. Anna's unsettling force. Is S. Anna, then, a not-to-be-expected work that serves as a premonition of all sorts of seventeenth-century goings on? We shall briefly return to this topic in the epilogue.

235

A blameless court—or a virtuous republic—may well prove less artistically stimulating than a tyranny.

MICHAEL LEVEY,
Painting at Court, 1971

10
~

ARCHITECTURE *at* COURT:
VASARI & AMMANNATI IN MEDICEAN TUSCANY

148 Vasari: *Duke Cosimo de'Medici and his Artists*, 1558
149 Tribolo: Florence, Medici Villa at Castello, 1537,
view by G. Utens showing garden, circa 1599

238

148

CASTELLO

149

Among the lavish decorations executed under Vasari's direction in the Palazzo Vecchio is an intimate portrait typically identified as *Duke Cosimo de'Medici and his Artists* (1558). It should be noted that in this case the term "artist" is used broadly. In this roundel, the second Duke of Tuscany is shown at the center of a composition surrounded by eleven individuals—sculptors, architects, engineers, and a financial administrator—who transformed his political ambitions into fountains, fortresses, and buildings (148). If the arrangement appears paternalistic with its focus on Duke Cosimo, it conveys the image of a ruler with strong ideas of his own. In keeping with his depictions in other frescoes in the same room, Duke Cosimo is represented as an active participant in the making of monuments, holding drafting tools in his left hand. This is, of course, precisely the myth that Vasari wanted to advance. Cosimo neither drew architectural plans nor did he issue any directives about the visual appearance of buildings. Yet, the numerous projects initiated during his twenty-seven-year reign ranged from the construction of new highways to the creation of grand residences for the ducal court. The professionals who surrounded him knew that state interests and ducal building policy were inseparable and that their task was to render the legitimacy of Cosimo's rule in bricks and mortar.

What constitutes a court and how did this institution make Florentine cinquecento architecture unique? In Medieval and Renaissance Europe, a court is commonly understood as the surroundings in which an established sovereign and his councilors and other members of his retinue attend to matters of state, culture, and the arts. In addition to its ruler, a court then requires loyal advisors and a specific physical environment in which their tasks are performed. While courts like those at Urbino or Mantua are renowned for enlightened patronage of the arts and a climate of intellectual splendor, the architectural vision of Cosimo I was essentially self-glorifying. The purpose of architecture was to propagate the concept of an enlightened and magnificent ruler and to further his political and dynastic ambitions.

Artistic novelty was not always the result. Detractors always smile at the uninspiring results and point to the obscure allegories of the Palazzo Vecchio's decorations and renovations, even if they were placed within a palace that had been cleverly renovated to serve a new political purpose. With only a few notable exceptions, the centralization of

power in Florence effectively strangled the patronage of public buildings elsewhere in Tuscany, and private architectural commissions usually came from members of the Medicean court. Over the course of
the following centuries, Florentine architecture was to vary little from
what had been built by Vasari, Ammannati, or Buontalenti. All the
same, it must be agreed that architecture at the court of Cosimo I
de'Medici became an instrument of statecraft, and that Cosimo's aesthetic and political programs culminated in the policies of his great-
great-grandson, Louis XIV of France.

EARLY PROJECTS
~

Medicean Tuscany was a kingdom in everything but name. It was
born of revenge when Pope Clement VII sought to place Florence
under Medicean control in retribution for the reestablishment of a
republican government. The Pope's timing was perfect. He had reconciled with Charles V after the Sack of Rome by Imperial troops in
1527, and the subsequent eleven-month siege of Florence brought the
city to capitulation in April 1530. With the assistance of an Imperial
patent, Alessandro de'Medici, who was presumably the Pope's illegitimate son, became the Duke of Tuscany and the first in a long line of
hereditary rulers who would govern Florence until the eighteenth
century. By 1532, the republican constitution had been dissolved. In
spite of the positive and sometimes even enlightened aspects of rule
by their Medicean overlords, the Florentine people would not live
under freedom for several centuries. Alessandro, whose authority was
now absolute, was murdered in 1537, by a distant relative.

Almost immediately after Cosimo I de'Medici was chosen to
succeed Alessandro, he began the embellishment of the Medici Villa
at Castello (1537). Located only a few miles to the west of Florence
on the site of an old Roman reservoir or *castellum*, the property was
an appropriate vehicle for proclaiming that the greatness of the new
ducal state was rooted in Florence's Roman past. As conceived by the
sculptor and garden architect Nicolò Tribolo, the site was
approached by a road that began at the Arno riverbank. Today, the
enlarged main palace (which dates from the 1590s) is not symmetrically related to the garden behind it, and it is likely that this was the
case when Tribolo prepared his plan.

The garden is composed of separate, self-contained spaces gently sloping upward to the north (149). Its principal part is composed of two terraces set within a walled enclosure. In the first, a U-shaped arrangement of rectangular compartments planted with herbs, grasses, small trees, and topiary surrounds two fountains—the first depicts Hercules and Antaeus, an allusion to Duke Cosimo and the triumph of virtue over evil, while a circular labyrinth of cypress trees surrounds the second, in which Florence is personified by the goddess Venus. The walls on either side were to contain niches with twelve figures symbolizing virtues associated with the Medici family, and above them, portrait busts of Medici who embodied these ideals. A low wall separates this sector from a narrow enclosure suitable for exhibiting orange trees and the retaining wall into which the grotto was placed. The second terrace, which was reached by stairs in the retaining wall, was a trapezoidal *bosco* containing a fishpond and a loggia at its highest point.

Tribolo died in 1550, and four years later, Giorgio Vasari was appointed to supervise the completion of the garden. During Vasari's stewardship, three significant changes were made to Tribolo's design—the construction of an island in the fishpond, the design of a new garden just to the east of the palace, and most significantly, radical changes to Tribolo's design for the Grotto. Just how much of the Grotto Tribolo may have been built before his death is uncertain. Two drawings indicate that he envisaged a rectangular interior with architectural membering, framing figures of Pan and Neptune, as if Brunelleschi's Old Sacristy in S. Lorenzo had suddenly been transformed into a manmade cave. Vasari, on the other hand, changed the Grotto's proportion and altered its plan by adding three barrel-vaulted recesses. Seeking to recall the kinds of geological formations found in Rome and Umbria, he dissolved the Grotto's architecture into stalactites and shells on nearly every available surface. Instead of employing figures from classical mythology, Vasari placed an assortment of sculpted wild and tame animals above the fountain basins in each recess. Tribolo's sober Grotto of the Elements had become Vasari's playful and exuberant Grotto of the Animals.

The arrangement was unique in both design and content. Approaching the garden from the palace below, the visitor's experience was formed by the garden's component parts. Proceeding along the main axis that experience would have stressed water in various guises in the fountains and the grottos, arriving at its symbolic source, the Apennines, only at the end of an elaborate journey through architectural and natural spaces varying in light, shadow, and color. By contrast, the return stressed the entirety of the garden, and through symbolism, the Tuscany of Cosimo I. For example, the passage of water in the garden echoed the hydrology of the Arno basin. The menagerie of animals in the Grotto displayed a peaceful co-existence with their neighbors, precisely the myth that Cosimo wished to convey to the more powerful states surrounding his own. From the unbuilt loggia, Cosimo could have seen an extraordinary panorama encompassing several cities under his dominion, although something similar can still be seen from the terrace above the Grotto.

Another prominent figure in the *Duke Cosimo de' Medici and his Artists* is Battista del Tasso (1500–55), who holds a model of the Loggia of the Mercato Nuovo (1546–51). This under-appreciated project was the first public structure built during Cosimo's reign and the only independent architectural commission executed by Tasso. In concept, the building is simple, its twelve open bays being composed of domical vaults supported by Corinthian columns; piers at its four corners contain niches elaborated by Michelangelo-style detail. The building type, of course, is traditional, and Tasso's interpretation draws its open plan from the original layout of Orsanmichele and its overall appearance from the Rucellai Loggia. In the *Lives*, architects trained as wood-carvers and other artisans were often subject to vituperative criticism, and Vasari delights in pointing out defects of architectural grammar that occur when column capitals meet the corner piers. Vasari also criticized Tasso's additions to the Palazzo Vecchio as lacking proportion, something that Vasari thought he later corrected. Although many of Vasari's points are well taken, he failed to mention neither Tasso's vigorous rusticated entry to the Palazzo Vecchio on the Via de Leoni (1550–52) nor the slender Doric columns on the Terrace of Saturn (1551–55), which were later adopted for the ground floor of the Uffizi. As a consequence of inheriting the position of Cosimo I's favored architect after Tasso's death, Vasari opened up a new and vital period in Florentine architectural history.

ARCHITECTS AT COURT —
GIORGIO VASARI AND BARTOLOMEO AMMANNATI
~

The physical setting of life at Cosimo I's court is largely the creation of Giorgio Vasari (1511–74) and Bartolomeo Ammannati (1511–92). Although Vasari's organizational skills gave him a dominant role in conceptualizing and executing the vast Medicean artistic program, the roles played by Ammannati and him and were in fact complementary. With training as a sculptor and a greater command of technical matters, Ammannati took on projects such as the Neptune fountain and the reconstruction of the Ponte S. Trinita. On the other hand, Vasari's success as a painter and inexhaustible knowledge of Italian art and architecture allowed him to define the public face of the Medicean regime in the Palazzo Vecchio, the Uffizi, and the Florentine church renovations. Although their architectural commissions followed separate paths, Ammannati sometimes criticized Vasari's work and may have designed parts of some of his projects. If the courtly style of architecture was a cross between the austerity of Vasari and the exaggerated relief of Ammannati, it served to glorify only one dominant figure, Cosimo I himself.

Of the two, Vasari was perhaps better suited to the necessities of art at court. Well-educated, deferential to those of higher rank, and hard working, he exhibited many traits of behavior described by Castiglione in *The Courtier*, the famous sixteenth-century handbook of courtly life. Trained as a painter in his native Arezzo and later in Florence, Vasari became an influential painter through the completion of commissions that took him to Bologna, Venice, Naples, and Rome. Possessing a remarkable memory for both facts and images, his first-hand knowledge of art and architecture since Giotto was unparalleled.

Vasari's circle of friends included Pietro Aretino, Paolo Giovio, and his frequent collaborator Vincenzo Borghini, to name three of the most important *literati* of his day. Vasari evidently saw himself as their equal in literary qualifications, and it was a gathering of individuals such as these in Rome that convinced him to write the *Lives of the Artists*. Originally published in 1550 (with a dedication to Julius III) and then reissued in a greatly expanded second edition in 1568 (now dedicated to Duke Cosimo I), the *Lives* became necessary reading for cultivated artists through its establishment of a pervasive model for understanding Renaissance art. Combining oral history, personal experience, and just plain workshop gossip in a compelling series of biographies, the work is Vasari's greatest contribution to the definition and understanding of Renaissance culture.

Vasari's architectural education was leisurely and largely self-taught. Never having apprenticed to an architect in the tradition of the Sangallo family, his initial experiences with architecture were typical for a painter—knowledge of wall construction for frescoes, floor construction for ceiling decoration, architectural backgrounds for paintings and theatrical productions, and the like. By 1555, the date of his appointment to the court of Cosimo I, Vasari had been involved in several architectural projects as either an independent designer or as a collaborating architect. The first project was for his own house in Arezzo and the next three were for Julius III—an unexecuted plan for a villa outside Monte San Savino, the Del Monte Chapel in S. Pietro in Montorio (with Ammannati), and the Villa Giulia (with Vignola, Ammannati, and the advice of Michelangelo).

Vasari's own ideas about architecture, though necessarily brief and never presented systematically, are worth noting. He seems to have been familiar with the major architectural printed books: first Vitruvius and Serlio (1537 on) and later Bartoli's translation of Alberti (1551); Vignola's treatise on the orders (1562); and finally, Palladio's *Quattro libri* (1570), of which he had advanced, pre-publication knowledge. As a theorist and critic in the *Lives*, Vasari claims that architecture is the "most universal, necessary and useful of the arts," a clever variation on the famous Vitruvian triad. Its principles are embodied in *disegno*, the universal basis for all the arts that is rooted in the intellect. In fact, Vasari employs architectural terminology (*regola, ordine, misura*) as standards for painting and sculpture. Nevertheless, Vasari still remained true to the craftsman tradition, as indicated by his indictments against the purely theoretical approach to architectural design he found in Alberti.

Ammannati's initial training could not have been more different. He was born in Settignano, the small town near Florence where he received his initial instruction in stone cutting and carving. He later worked in the shop of the sculptor Baccio Bandinelli and became familiar with Michelangelo's sculpture, which would continue to serve him as a touchstone for his entire career. But the political climate was uncertain, and the ambitious young sculptor sought to gain his education and establish his career elsewhere. Sometime around 1529, Ammannati left Tuscany for Venice, and although Ammannati left Northern Italy on several occasions to execute sculptural commissions in Florence, and Venice, the Veneto became his artistic center and the focus of his professional career for almost two decades. During these decades, Ammannati would have seen Sansovino's buildings change the appearance around Piazza S. Marco, and in the early 1540s, he was a member of Sansovino's workshop for the Library. No other architect in Rome or Florence would have had such a familiarity with the most important works in Northern Italy, which would include the early works of Sanmicheli and Palladio.

Ammannati was a sculptor with a considerable intellect. In 1550, he married Laura Battiferri (1523–89), a poet renowned for her culture and deep religiosity. Shortly after their wedding (which took place at the Santa Casa in Loreto), the couple took up residence in Rome, where Ammannati immersed himself in the study of ancient sculpture. At the same time, his training as a sculptor and his technical knowledge of fountains led to his collaboration with Vasari on the Del Monte Chapel and the Villa Giulia. With the possible exception of a trip around 1558, to gather ideas for the Uffizi and the Palazzo Pitti, Ammannati was never to return to the Veneto again. Over the course of the next three decades the couple's circle of friends was to include *literati* and artists like Annibale Caro, Benedetto Varchi, Agnolo Bronzino, and Benvenuto Cellini.

Ammannati's religiosity, however, differed markedly from that of Vasari, who tended to see religious questions in aesthetic terms. Perhaps through the influence of his wife, Ammannati clearly espoused Counter-Reformation dogma. Ammannati's close friendship with the Florentine Jesuits not only accounted for the commission to design their church, S. Giovannino, and their adjacent collegiate structure, it also led to Ammannati naming them as the major beneficiary of his will. Ammannati also loaned a considerable sum of money to the Jesuits for the construction of the Collegio Romano, a structure designed by the architect Valeriano in a style that clearly echoed that of its primary financial contributor. Late in life, he denounced the nude figure in painting and sculpture as lustful.

Ammannati also differs from Vasari in his clear and systematic architectural thinking. Already in the 1540s, he may have begun to prepare a comprehensive treatise that would illustrate the major design challenges faced by architects of his day. All that remains today are a series of building plans in the Uffizi. Apart from a couple of phrases, the text that would have accompanied the illustrations is lost. Yet its remains are sufficient to delineate Ammannati's architectural theory. Its scope was clearly comprehensive, including both grand buildings such as cathedrals and ruler's palaces and the more humble designs for markets, mills, and a public school. Paradoxically, it only includes one contemporary building—the Palazzo Farnese—yet the additional drawings known to have existed may have included others. It is an open question as to how Ammannati would have treated his own work in this publication.

Almost certainly this enterprising project was inspired in part by Serlio, whom he probably met during his early years in Venice, and perhaps even by Palladio, who by the 1540s, may have begun to acquire material for the *Quattro Libri*. As the author of a treatise-in-progress, Ammannati took an interest in other publications. His ownership of books by Serlio, Cataneo, and Alberti is documented, and there is no reason to think that he failed to acquire those by Vignola and Palladio as well. Unfortunately, Ammannati was in no rush to publish his treatise, and nothing had appeared by the time of his death. Had Ammannati completed this treatise, it would have been recognized as the most important architectural publication of the Medicean Era.

THE SOVEREIGN'S COURT
~

Just what, in architectural terms, constitutes a sovereign's court? Normally this is taken to mean the place where the ruler and his advisors conduct matters of state. In Italy, princely courts were centered on large, sprawling palaces that were comprised of heterogeneous structures. Typically, such palaces, as those in Mantua and Ferrara, evolved over centuries and encompassed several changes in building style; the Palazzo Ducale in Urbino is unique for its concentrated period of construction and consistency of design. The court in Florence, by contrast, was composed of three structures different in form and use—the Palazzo Vecchio, the Uffizi, and the Palazzo Pitti—that were united by a private passageway, the Corridoio. Notable for the dispersal of its ceremonial, residential, and governmental structures throughout the city on different sides of the Arno, Cosimo's newly constituted court changed the political topography of Florence with scarcely any alteration to its urban form. The creation of a palace fit for the ruler of a quasi-royal state was apparently one of Cosimo I's first concerns. In 1540, he transferred his official residence from the Palazzo Medici to Florence's former communal palace, the Palazzo dei Priori, which later was known as the Palazzo della Signoria, Palazzo Ducale, and eventually, the Palazzo Vecchio. With this act, Cosimo I made manifest his rule over Florence and set the stage for the permanent autocracy that was Medicean Florence. Prior to Vasari's arrival in Florence in 1555, the first projects were decorations or tapestries that involved scarcely any change to the structural fabric of the palace. Yet a major transformation of the republican communal palace was necessary not only because of its new symbolism but also the need for both ceremonial chambers and domestic space in a structure composed of only a few large volumes.

247

In renovating the Palazzo Vecchio, Vasari left the exterior unchanged but transformed the interior to satisfy the needs of a completely different kind of palace (150). The pathway from the western entrance on the Piazza della Signoria to Tasso's recently built portal on the Via dei Leoni (1550–52) became the spine along which main architectural features were located. The courtyard underwent a radical transformation in 1565, as a complement to the temporary architecture constructed for a Medici wedding; the richly ornamented architecture would have exuded a similarly festive air. Each of the nine columns was enclosed in a different arrangement of stylized foliation both recalling the Romanesque architecture of Tuscany and contributing to the myth of Medicean greatness through their allusions to King Solomon and the Temple of Jerusalem.

The courtyard became virtually an atrium preceding the monumental staircases located further along the visitor's path. Here, Vasari replaced a series of independent stairs with an integrated system composed of a single grand staircase with two sets of flights around a light well. In practical terms, this symmetrical arrangement provided access to the Salone dei Cinquecento; an additional flight in the northern arm led to chambers at the front of the palace. The new stairs were easy to ascend, well-lit, and full of visual drama due to their alternation of inclined barrel vaults and a changing sequence of rising and descending ramps. With this arrangement, the practice of courtly ceremony now had spatial and architectural logic, and new clarity and grandeur enhanced the palace's system of circulation. Thus purely architectural considerations led to the adoption of double-ramped staircases similar to those employed by Mauro Codussi in his *scuole* in Venice. Yet Vasari gave the stairs a suggestive monumentality inspired by ancient staircases such as those on the Quirinal that were regularly drawn by cinquecento architects, a key consideration in his desire to create a residence worthy of all rulers of all times. Sadly, Vasari's aim fell short of the mark in the Salone dei Cinquecento, where his paintings of the achievements and apotheosis of Cosimo I hide the technical ingenuity involved in raising the height of the ceiling (by about 7 meters) and illuminating Florence's most important hall of state. In the Palazzo Vecchio, Vasari's architectural achievement only reveals itself after close study.

The Uffizi (begun 1559), Vasari's most significant and lasting contribution to Florence, was the first monumental landmark of Cosimo I's autocracy (151). In concept and design, a building that was meant to be seen in conjunction with the Palazzo Vecchio, the Uffizi contained on its ground floor the administrative offices for eight magistracies and five guilds; upper floors contained additional offices, the court theater, studios for artists and artisans, and the nucleus of the Medicean art collection. Its U-shaped form can be read as both a frame for the Palazzo Vecchio and as an extension of ducal power to the Arno, and further, to all of Cosimo I's dominion of Tuscany. It both mirrored the autocratic power of the duke and was a primary agent of his survival. In a state obsessed with centralized administration and the consolidation of its legal systems, the Uffizi stood for the idea of the absolutist ruler. Although the Uffizi was a building with few direct precedents and no real progeny, it nevertheless anticipates Louis XIV and Napoleon, who saw architecture as an integral part of the political culture of their states.

In concept, the Uffizi is a pair of architectural facades that incorporates a church, monumental stairways, a riverfront loggia, and the Florentine Mint into a single building (152). The Uffizi's unforgettable effect is due to its construction along the street alignment created by Cosimo in 1546 that extended to the Arno. Ample evidence indicates that there were several earlier projects for this site. In size, they ranged from a modest proposal by Francesco Sangallo to build shops (or government offices) along its eastern

150 Vasari: Florence, Palazzo Vecchio, axonometric drawing showing
    staircase system and major interior spaces
151 Vasari: Florence, Uffizi, begun 1559

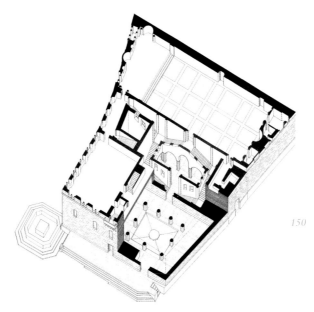

150

151

152 Uffizi, plan
153 Uffizi, view looking north

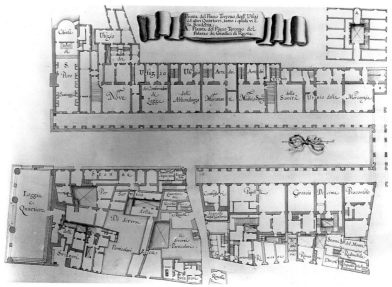

152

153

flank to grandiose schemes for governmental palaces by Ammannati and Vasari that required the destruction of buildings as far to the west as the Ponte Vecchio.

Restraint, if not outright austerity, is the quality that permeates this eclectic exterior. Rudiments of the Uffizi's architectural vocabulary are found in the elevation of Bramante's Cortile del Belvedere, Peruzzi's sketches for the Palazzo Massimo, and the windows of Raphael's Palazzo Pandolfini. The riverfront loggia recalls the garden facade of the Palazzo del Te. When seen from the Palazzo Vecchio, the statues of famous Tuscans intended for the ground floor niches and the representation of Cosimo underneath the focal *serliana* of the riverfront loggia give the ensemble the appearance of a *salone* open to the air, as if the main hall of the Palazzo Vecchio had been transposed out-of-doors. Yet when seen from the Arno, the slight realignment of the existing street brings Brunelleschi's Cupola, the Palazzo Vecchio, Michelangelo's *David*, and the Uffizi together into a single view, as if Vasari's *Lives of the Artists* had now come to life (153). Such a dramatic arrangement of Florentine history merits comparison with epics of modern cinema.

Although there is no proof, Vasari sought to make the Uffizi an urban building comparable in stature to Michelangelo's Campidoglio, Sansovino's Library, or Palladio's Basilica. Vasari, of course, was familiar with all of these examples. But the question of why a building with such a distinctive character was not appreciated is difficult to answer. The unique circumstances behind its design do not lend themselves to generalization in the way that Palladio's villas embodied universal principles of design. The failure to publish the Uffizi in a timely fashion through a treatise or engravings also contributed to its recession into the past. Perhaps the most important factor contributing to the Uffizi's lack of critical recognition was that Florentine art was a spent force by the end of the cinquecento. Significantly, it was the admiration of architects and artists rather than historians that contributed to the revival of interest in Vasari's seminal creation. In the nineteenth century, the French architect and theoretician Viollet-le-Duc admired the Uffizi for its simplicity and dramatic siting, and in our own time, its capacity to merge with its urban context has been held in high esteem.

Not surprisingly it was another painter who best understood Vasari's pictorial approach to architectural settings. In the early twentieth century, John Singer Sargent's *Study of Architecture, Florence* (1910) depicted the riverfront loggia as a frame for a *capriccio* looking out to a garden and fountain (154). More than any modern photograph, this fanciful combination of forms taken from the Uffizi and the Boboli Gardens captures the spirit of Vasari's visual link between central Florence and its surrounding countryside.

Meanwhile, Cosimo I's wife, Eleonora di Toledo, had acquired the Palazzo Pitti in 1549, from the heirs of its original builder. After a decade of marriage, she had given birth to eight Medici children, and it seems understandable that she would seek a new residence with spaces more appropriate to family life than civic ceremony. From the outset, it appears that the new palace was to be linked axially with the hippodrome-shaped garden on the hillside above. Initially the project was under Vasari's supervision, but Ammannati began work in earnest in 1560, when Vasari was preoccupied with the Uffizi. Among palatial Italian residences the Palazzo Pitti was notable as a hybrid structure. It retained the monumental, rusticated facade of the old palace to which were added two wings that created the appearance of a grandiose, U-shaped villa, a conceit appropriate for the garden setting of its rear facade.

In the three-story courtyard, Ammannati was motivated by Serlio's theory of decorum that judged rustication suitable for gates, fortified buildings, and country dwellings (155). Other architects—most notably Sansovino and Sanmicheli—followed this dictum, but here, Ammannati did so according to the circumstances of his building. In the context of the Palazzo Pitti, both the *bugnati* and the banded rustication in the courtyard were justified by their sympathy with the massive blocks of stone on the exterior facade of the palace. Such an approach was not unique, and Ammannati certainly had seen how it had been employed by Peruzzi in the *Presentation of the Virgin* in S. Maria della Pace (82) and Sansovino on the facade of the Venetian Mint (102).

Even more important was how the rustication evoked the pastoral (if not primitive) character of a site that opened onto a grand garden. From both the palace and the garden, the sloping sides of the hippodrome and the wings of the courtyard appear as extensions of each other. As in the Villa Giulia, both palace and axis follow an axis determined by the landscape, and the rough-hewn stone in the courtyard is the perfect complement to the natural forms in the

154 John Singer Sargent: *Study of Architecture, Florence*, circa 1910
155 Ammannati: Florence, Palazzo Pitti addition, courtyard, begun 1560

154

155

wooded garden. Ammannati's great achievement is, then, the creation of an extraordinary unity between palace and garden.

The tripartite arrangement of the palace also addressed the complex requirements of courtly life. The central (original) wing of the palace housed ceremonial rooms, including the grand-ducal throne. The new additions, on the other hand, were almost entirely residential. The eastern wing was a small palace modeled on the rear wing at Poggio a Caiano. It contained the family apartments, which were a cluster of rooms surrounding a central hall with a private staircase that incorporated the family chapel. The western wing was a totally different kind of layout that recalled the Palazzo Ducale in Urbino. Its apartments clustered about a large hall adjacent to the palace's main staircase, creating a suite that was often used for housing visiting dignitaries. Although the use of palatial rooms was always in flux and the evidence for this description is drawn on seventeenth-century records, the distinctive plans for both wings suggest that Ammannati foresaw different uses for them.

Up until 1565, the three buildings that constituted Cosimo I's court evolved as three separate commissions. Each project was a different kind of architectural challenge, and there is no evidence to indicate they were conceived according to any master plan. What brought them together was the construction of Vasari's Corridoio (1565), the private passageway linking the Palazzo Vecchio with the Palazzo Pitti.

The Corridoio was not a building in the common sense of the word because it was composed of all the buildings along its oblique, winding course. It has three major sections. The first is a tract made up of passageways through other structures, from the Palazzo Vecchio across the top of the Uffizi and through houses adjacent to the Uffizi's western wing. Only in the second part is there any visible construction, such as aqueduct-like arches along the Arno and the hallway over the eastern side of the Ponte Vecchio. The final tract is more heterogeneous, passing around a medieval tower, running across the facade of S. Felicita, and following the course of an old alley to the gardens adjacent to the Palazzo Pitti. Despite its bold concept and great length, its construction—Vasari claims it took only five months—was facilitated by privatizing existing rights of way and passing through or around private structures. As Charles

Dickens put it in *Pictures from Italy*, "Above [the Ponte Vecchio], the Gallery of the Grand Duke crosses the river. It was built to connect the two separate palaces by a secret passage, and it takes its jealous course among the streets and houses with true despotism; going where it wishes, and spurning every obstacle, which goes before it."

The precedents for private urban passageways are numerous and are frequently Roman in origin. The ancient example closest in concept to the Corridoio was Nero's Domus Transitoria, the mile-long triple portico connecting the Palatine with the Gardens of Maecenas on the Esquiline. A similar passageway built by Pope Paul III once connected the Palazzo Venezia with a small villa that once stood on the northern slope of the Capitoline Hill. But the example that Cosimo I and Vasari had in mind was the Passetto, the passageway from the Vatican to the Castel Sant'Angelo that was incorporated into the walls surrounding the Borgo. The Passetto must have been known to all the Medici because Pope Clement VII, the cousin of Leo X, used it in his attempt to evade capture during the Sack of Rome in 1527. During a visit to Rome in 1560, Cosimo I may have had an opportunity to use the Passetto, and at the time of his death, it was openly acknowledged as the inspiration for the Corridoio. To those visitors who attended festivities celebrating the wedding of Cosimo I's heir, Prince Francesco de'Medici, and Joanna of Austria, the Corridoio would have been understood as an architectural emblem of Medicean status and prestige.

With the construction of the Corridoio, the transformation of Florence into a princely court was now complete. The sovereign's district was both within and above the city that he ruled. What were originally separate projects became a *palatium*—the residence of a ruler whose authority derives from an emulation of Imperial Rome. Cosimo I was fond of flattery by reference to antiquity; he is often depicted in the guise of an ancient emperor, and his projects for renovating the Palazzo Vecchio have been interpreted as a metaphorical "Forum" for Florence. If Cosimo I's project had little effect on the form of Florence, it brought about drastic changes to civic life and identity. Most important of these was the eventual transferal of the center of courtly life to the Palazzo Pitti and its surrounding area. The Palazzo Vecchio was sapped of significance because it no longer had claim to rulership. The era of modern tourism was around the corner.

255

COURT AND THE CITY
~

Life at court was never confined to the sovereign's residence. In exceptional instances, such as the baptisms and weddings of Medicean heirs, the city's appearance was radically changed by temporary constructions whose Imperial Roman form and iconography exalted the Medici. More frequently, ambassadors and other dignitaries would be accompanied to the Palazzo Vecchio or the Palazzo Pitti with pomp befitting their status. Florentines could see symbols of grand ducal aspiration and achievement everywhere, though not all were accessible on a regular basis. The triumvirate of courtly buildings established an administrative district primarily for members of the court; the Uffizi was the only structure the activities of which had a direct impact on the citizenry.

If the sovereign remained aloof and distant from his subjects, the likeness and symbols of his rule were to be found nearly everywhere. Just as the Medici coat of arms was frequently attached to a courtier's palaces as a badge of affiliation, portrait busts of sovereigns appeared on public and private buildings throughout Florence. In time, twenty-five structures openly displayed adulatory images of one or more of the first three Medici grand-dukes. Statuary in visible, public locations often showed the sovereign in the guise of a hero. Giambologna, the Flemish-born sculptor who served the Medicean court for nearly five decades, provided memorial effigies of Cosimo for the Uffizi's riverfront loggia (1585) and the Piazza della Signoria (1587–95) as well as a monument to Ferdinando I (1601–8) in Piazza della SS. ma Annunziata. Elsewhere in Tuscany, Pietro Francavilla provided uninspired statues of Cosimo I for the Piazza dei Cavallieri in Pisa and Ferdinando I for a site opposite the Duomo of Arezzo. On both a local and international level, the city had become the stage for statecraft.

The most visible public demonstration of Medicean dogma evolved through several separate projects, all of which were executed by Bartolomeo Ammannati. On September 13, 1557, the Ponte Santa Trinita was destroyed in a calamitous flood that also destroyed part of the nearby Ponte alla Carraia. Work on the Ponte Santa Trinita (1565–78), which connected the center of Florence with the roads leading southward to Siena and Rome, was not begun until the next decade (156). There is evidence to suggest that the three elliptical arches that form the bridge may have been suggested by Michelangelo, but the structure that stands today is the result of Ammannati's execution of this bold project.

While the bridge was under construction, Pius IV presented Cosimo I a granite column that had come from the Baths of Caracalla in Rome. As an obvious extension of his responsibilities on the nearby Ponte S. Trinita, Ammannati oversaw the erection of the column in the Piazza S. Trinita in a position that accented its visibility from the bridge, the Via Tornabuoni, and the Via delle Terme. At first, a statue of Cosimo I was proposed for the column, only to be exchanged for figures of Justice by Ammannati and later by Tadda (1581). Ammannati also erected a column surmounted by a figure of Peace (1572) in Piazza S. Felice, which stands at the southern end of Via Maggio in Oltrarno. Ammannati also proposed the erection of a third column supporting a figure of religion in front of S. Marco. When taken together, the bridge, the two completed columns, and their statuary created a new triumphal entryway to the Duomo that extolled Cosimo I's victory in the Sienese War and the supposed magnanimity of his rule. The message must have been a bitter pill for the Sienese to swallow.

The construction boom caused by Cosimo I's building program found its counterpart in the palaces built or remodeled by his courtiers, who tended to be either Spaniards in service of Eleonora or members of the lesser Florentine nobility. As courtiers to the duke, their residences had to be deferential in their general sobriety to his residence and palaces of older Florentine families. In several instances, existing construction limited new work to the creation of a new facade, whose system of design and individual elements—elaborate arched entries and rusticated window frames—derive from fourteenth- and fifteenth-century prototypes. All of the most significant projects for this new class of patrons were designed by Ammannati.

In recognition of two decades of service at court, Cosimo I paid the expenses for the residence of his Spanish *maggiordomo* Ramirez da Montalvo (begun 1568). Located in the densely packed center southeast of the Duomo, the palace is actually an amalgamation of several different structures with irregular layouts (157). Existing construction did not permit the location of the main entry along the facade's central axis, but Ammannati nevertheless overcame this difficulty by emphasizing its impact on the surrounding area. In regularizing its

257

156 Ammannati: Florence, Ponte Santa Trinita, 1565–78
157 Ammannati: Florence, Palazzo Ramirez da Montalvo, begun 1568
158 Ammannati: Florence, Palazzo Grifoni, 1557–74

156

157

158

distribution of five bays, the central window on the *piano nobile* dominates the vista up the Via dei Giraldi. The culminating element is an elaborately framed cartouche that contains the Medici coat of arms, and window frames were surrounded by *sgraffito* decoration illustrating themes selected by Vincenzo Borghini and executed from designs provided by Giorgio Vasari. Even in projects for Cosimo I, collaboration at such an exalted level rarely occurred.

259

The Palazzo Grifoni (1557–74) posed the greatest challenge to Ammannati's great skill as a designer of palatial residences (158). The corner site on the Piazza della SS. ma Annunziata acquired by Ugolino Grifoni, the secretary to Cosimo I and Eleonora, demanded a layout with three distinct elements—a primary facade facing the Via dei Servi, an imposing secondary facade facing the square, and a garden on the open space at its rear. Although this combination of elements can be found in Michelozzo's Medici Palace, Ammannati sought in his design to emulate the Palazzo Farnese in Rome. Its most unique feature is its brick exterior that departs from local tradition, where exterior masonry walls were coated with stucco. The result is a warm contrast of its rose-colored brick and tan stone, a rich chromatic appearance never repeated in other Florentine palaces.

Ammannati solved the problem of siting the Palazzo Grifoni by treating each of the five-bay facades as a variant on the exterior of the Palazzo Farnese. On the Via dei Servi side, Ammannati created an architectural frontispiece composed of three parts: an arched, rusticated portal superimposed over Doric trabeation; an attic zone with Medicean emblems; and an Ionic *serliana*. The side facing the square is slightly longer, and the same elements reappear with the exception of a rusticated panel below the *serliana* and arched doorway that communicate with the garden loggia. Even more impressive are the facade's many subtle details—the kneeling windows set squarely upon the benches, their Michelangelo-style enframement, and string courses carved in sharp relief. In the exterior of this palace can be seen the tendency to exaggerate otherwise trivial details, an attitude that would characterize Florentine palace facades for the next two centuries.

Although Cosimo I saw religion as an extension of his political activities, he initiated no new church construction. Florence underwent a boom in church construction that lasted from the thirteenth to the fifteenth centuries, and understandably, the most significant ecclesiastical commissions were the modernization of Florence's two great monastic churches. The renovations made by Vasari to S. Maria Novella (begun 1565) and S. Croce (begun 1566), echoed the three-fold desire of Catholic Reformers—visual unity, direct involvement of the laity in the Mass, and accessibility of sacred images (159). In both churches, the rood screens that divided the nave into two separate zones were destroyed, and the choir was moved to a position behind the high altar. The naves of both churches were whitewashed, and new aedicular chapels based on the Pantheon for S. Croce and the Laurentian Library for Santa Maria were placed in the side aisles. The new altars also served as the architectural frames for the cycle of new altarpieces executed by Vasari and members of the Accademia del Disegno. Although the unobstructed and unified church interior was by now commonplace in Italy, it did not escape criticism. To monks, the open interior meant sacrificing their central role in the Eucharist, and to individuals, it meant participation in group prayer instead of private devotions. But to Cosimo I, who provided immediate motivation for the project as well as some of the funds for its execution, the renovations served to portray him as the faithful Christian prince, a quality necessary for the title of Grand Duke that he and his progeny were awarded by Pius V in December 1569.

The religious orders, by comparison, played a minor role in the development of ecclesiastical architecture in sixteenth-century Florence. This is due to a combination of several factors—the lack of a clear division between church and state in the era of Cosimo I, the existence of many capacious churches dating back to the Middle Ages, and the late arrival of the reforming orders. The peregrinations of the Jesuits, who arrived in Florence in 1551, are a clear example of this circumstance. Their first quarters were in a private residence near S. Spirito, and later after 1557, in the small church of S. Giovanni Evangelista that had been consigned to them by Cosimo I. Neither the reconstruction of their church, which came to be known as S. Giovannino, nor the construction of the Florentine Jesuit college adjacent to it, can be considered Medicean propaganda, although both were executed to designs made by Ammannati. Although for S. Giovannino initial designs date to 1572, the structure's construction began only in the decade following Cosimo I's death. Nor is the style of its elegant interior particularly Florentine. Its box-like interior and implied transept originate in Sansovino's

159 Florence, S. Croce, interior after renovations by Vasari, begun 1566

S. Francesco della Vigna in Venice, and its rhythmic integration of chapel and confessionals reveals the new functions of Counter-Reformation churches as much as it echoes the upper level of Bramante's Cortile del Belvedere from which it is derived. Ammannati employed a variant of this scheme in his last major commission, S. Maria in Grado (1592) in Arezzo.

COURT AND STATE
~

At the funeral of Cosimo I in 1574, orators compared the deceased grand-duke's activity as a builder with the emperors of ancient Rome. The comparison was a fitting one; Cosimo's projects could be found throughout his entire state, in any town, city, fortress, pathway, or street, as one speaker suggested. Their scope was similarly broad, ranging in use from palaces to the repair of bridges and canals. Yet there was a clear hierarchy in the distribution of his projects across Tuscany. The structures redolent of ceremony and symbolism were most likely to be found in Florence, while those elsewhere in his dominion were usually less visible and responded to different necessities, often that of defense.

The immediate challenge that Cosimo I faced upon election was the consolidation of his powers and the defense of his territorial boundaries. Although relations with the Papal States, which bordered Tuscany to the north, south, and east, were cordial, they also depended on the whims of individual popes. One of Cosimo's preoccupations throughout his reign was defending Tuscany's long western border along the Tyrrhenian Sea from the incursions of both North African pirates and other states wary of Cosimo's growing power. Recognizing the potential role of Elba as a staging point for attacks along the Italian coast, Cosimo ordered the construction of Cosmopolis (begun 1547, now Portoferraio) to serve as a fortified naval base for ships. Another of his projects was the refortification of numerous smaller cities, among them Pisa, Pistoia, Arezzo, and Cortona. There were also new fortress towns such as Eliopolis (1564, now Terra del Sole) and Sasso di Simone (1566) constructed in strategic locations along Tuscany's eastern boundary. All of these urbanistic endeavors were conceived in terms of military defense and bear no relationship to the ideal cities of Renaissance Humanists.

To turn to Medicean building outside Florence can often lead to disappointment. Another major urban project under Vasari's supervision involved the transformation of Pisa's medieval civic center on the Piazza di Sette Vie into the Piazza dei Cavallieri (begun 1562). The complex served as the headquarters for Cosimo's knightly order of mercenaries, the Cavallieri di Santo Stefano, and the buildings included a conventual palace, a church, and a multipurpose structure fashioned out of two older buildings (160). The complex as a whole perpetuated the myth of Pisa's recovery of her long lost sea power—now in the service of Cosimo I. This is conveyed by marked parallels with Michelangelo's Palazzo dei Senatori and the undeniable elegance of the conventual palace's thin *sgraffito*-laden facade. But the overall effect of the buildings on this irregular triangular square is an overwhelming lack of harmony, in part due to Vasari's self-imposed financial restrictions. Ultimately, the absence of a clear precedent for such a medieval institution forced Vasari to give precedent to concept over form in this project.

263

Cosimo I did not live to see how his expansionist maritime policies were fulfilled in the construction of a new city addition to Livorno (161). The town's importance lay in the fact that it offered a site for a large harbor; the harbor of nearby Pisa, some 25 kilometers to the north, which had been silted up for centuries. Early in the sixteenth century, the town was given a new fortress designed by Antonio da Sangallo the Elder, and later, Cosimo I began construction of the breakwaters that were to form the new harbor. Presumably this would have included a base for the Cavallieri di Santo Stefano, who were established in Portoferraio for lack of suitable facilities on the Tuscan coast. In 1576, two years after Cosimo's death, plans for the new port city were prepared by Bernardo Buontalenti (1531–1608), the Medicean jack-of-all-trades whose tasks ranged from fortifications to the design of gardens, fireworks, and jewelry. The challenge that he faced was the creation of a port city that would be linked by canal to Pisa, which was still Tuscany's maritime center. In its layout, the old town was incorporated into larger city in the shape of an irregular pentagon, no doubt inspired by the Fortezza da Basso in Florence. Within its walls, the regular layout of its generously sized blocks and straight streets contrasted markedly with the old town. For more than a decade, economic

160 Vasari: Pisa, Piazza dei Cavallieri, renovations begun 1562
161 Buontalenti: Livorno, begun 1576
162 Vasari: Arezzo, Loggia, view from Piazza Grande

160

161

162

stagnation did not permit its realization, and in 1590, the construction of the new city was begun according to a different plan. The transformation was largely completed in the next century, and according to John Evelyn, the arrangement of the cathedral on a piazza surrounded by porticoes had suggested to Inigo Jones the design of Covent Garden.

Of all Tuscan cities, Arezzo was the one that acquired a reputation of disloyalty to its Florentine overlords. At the same time, the city owed its economic prosperity to rich agricultural land and ease of communication with Florence, Siena, and the Tiber valley to the south. In order to maintain its domination over the Aretines, Florence systematically destroyed many of Arezzo's medieval monuments, including both the Palazzo del Comune and the Duomo Vecchio. The completion of its fortress also brought considerable damage to structures located just to the north of the main public square, the precipitously sloping, trapezoidal-shaped Piazza Grande. The devastated site must have provided an eerie backdrop to two buildings that escaped ritual desecration—the stunning Romanesque apse of the Pieve (begun 1185), the collegiate church of the Aretines, and the adjacent facade of the Palazzo della Misericordia (begun late fourteenth century).

The clearest evidence for the union of statecraft and stagecraft can be seen in Vasari's Loggia in Arezzo (1570–96). Here, Vasari developed a coherent urban strategy within a specific historical context similar to what he had achieved at the Uffizi and lost in Pisa. As a native of Arezzo, Vasari was keenly attuned to the desires and needs of other Aretines. He must have been saddened by the squalor surrounding the Piazza Grande and recognized the opportunity to redesign the center of his native city. Although the Loggia's patron was the Confraternity of the Misericordia, it is not improbable that Vasari himself initiated the project by suggesting the Loggia's construction.

The Loggia is an imposing structure 126 meters long that separates the Piazza Grande from the destroyed structures to the north (162). Following Vitruvius and Italian tradition, the twenty bays facing the square contain shops with mezzanine chambers above. There are marked parallels of the austere facade's A–B–A rhythms with the adjacent Palazzo della Misericordia. It is arguable that in the Loggia Vasari showed a remarkable sympathy for medieval architecture, which he considered in the *Lives* to be "monstrous and barbarous." The tall, narrow proportions of the individual bays echo the medieval houses flanking the remainder of the square, which was rehabilitated during the Mussolini Era. Taking advantage of the sloping site, Vasari placed a stair in the eleventh bay that leads to higher ground at the rear, where the building takes on an anonymous appearance. It is at this level where one finds access to the governmental offices in its western half and the five row houses overlooking the square.

Neither style nor Medicean patronage can show how the Loggia was an example of courtly architecture. Although the Confraternity of the Misericordia promoted the seven works of mercy, it provided social services consistent with Medicean policy and was accountable to the grand-duke. The Loggia also contained the Monte di Pietà, the chancellery, and the customs office, creating a grand-ducal administrative center in Arezzo. At the same time, the row houses were rented by civil administrators and members of the nobility who frequently held administrative positions. The Loggia was, then, an aristocratic district contained within a single building. In the seventeenth century, "plebs," or simple ordinary citizens, were prohibited from passing underneath the Loggia's portico, making the structure the exclusive domain of the Medicean state and its aristocratic supporters. Just as Matteo Villani observed at the end of the fourteenth century, the loggia as a building type signified tyranny instead of freedom.

Even more so than the Uffizi, the Loggia illustrates the dilemma faced by architects who had to reconcile their own innovative designs with social and political considerations that are now considered objectionable. In both buildings, Vasari imparts a classical resonance to his designs without any overt reference to antiquity, and in the case of the Loggia, without any element of classical architectural grammar whatsoever. Implicitly if not explicitly, the Loggia is a demonstration of Vasari's unique pictorial approach to design. What gives his buildings their identity and form is determined by their dialogue—sometimes conducted in a totally different architectural language—with one or more additional structures. In the cases of the Uffizi and the Loggia, the dialogue is conducted with adjacent structures, and it is no surprise that Vasari's buildings look best when seen from a viewpoint illustrating this architectural conversation. Time has softened the contrasts envisaged by Vasari, and today the Loggia serves to link two different kinds of public space—a verdant park on the site of the old fortress above and the public piazza below.

The novelty of Cosimo's court lies in how patronage traditions drawn from Florence's past were enlisted in establishing the future of Medicean Tuscany. No doubt the achievements of his ancestors Cosimo the Elder and Lorenzo the Magnificent weighed heavily on his shoulders. It is true, of course, that there were other courts in Italy, like the papal court in Rome, and even sub-courts within the papal context, like those of wealthy Roman cardinals. In contrast to these examples, Cosimo's hereditary title permitted building during a long, unbroken period of rule, so unlike popes who were elected at an advanced age and often ruled for only a few years. As a consequence, Cosimo was able to initiate large projects such as the Uffizi and the Palazzo Pitti addition, which would be completed by his heirs. At the same time, he also held a *de iure* authority of rulership, giving his projects a sense of authority that surpassed that of other patrons whom he appeared to emulate, like that of the earlier Medici and the Farnese in Rome. Just what Cosimo thought about the many architectural projects he initiated remains a mystery, and surviving evidence suggests that he appreciated them for utilitarian rather than aesthetic or symbolic qualities.

Another novelty involves the range of the artistic and architectural projects initiated by Cosimo I. In earlier Renaissance courts, like those of the Este at Ferrara or the Gonzaga at Mantua, the artistic production was rich and aristocratic, and accessibility to it was limited to family members and their courtiers. Even the revolutionary- and epoch-making projects such as Michelangelo's Sistine ceiling and Raphael's Stanze fall largely within the established conventions of private art. Cosimo I, on the other hand, broke decisively with this tradition by initiating projects such as the decorations of the Palazzo Vecchio, which were largely meant to be seen by visiting dignitaries, and by constructing a range of public buildings that were meant to impress the public as a whole. As a result, the court was now externalized to include Florence, other Tuscan cities, and the entire state.

267

Ferrara! in thy wide and grass grown streets,
Whose symmetry was not for solitude,
There seems as 'twere a curse upon the seats
Of former sovereigns, and the antique brood
Of Este, which for many an age made good
Its strength within thy walls...

LORD BYRON,
Childe Harold's Pilgrimage, Canto IV

11
~
THE CITY

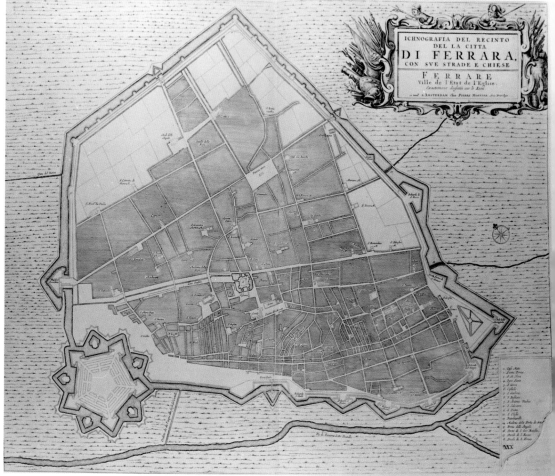

The Ferrara evoked by Byron at first seems as distant from other sixteenth-century Italian cities as from the urban centers of our own
times (163). Yet his observations cannot be dismissed outright
because they suggest several important issues in cinquecento urbanism—broad, straight streets; a variety of regular formal arrangements;
patrons and the influence of antiquity; and the impact of military
architecture on city designs. As in any great poetic statement, allusions are plentiful. Questions of what constitutes a public or private
space arise when the name of Ferrara's rulers, the Este family, is
recalled. Even the mention of "grass-sown streets" poses the question
of a reciprocal relationship between nature and gardens on the one
hand and cities on the other. To many historians, the last question is
considered perplexing because patterns of influence between different art forms are difficult to establish.

   The vast addition to Ferrara begun under Ercole I d'Este (reg.
1471–1505) in the 1490s embodied all of these features. Its new walls
and moats enclosed land that had previously been occupied by
Venetian troops during their siege of Ferrara in 1482–83, and consequently, its northern *borghi* and the Este retreat, the Villa Belfiore,
were suitably defended. Its broad and straight streets structured a city
that was not a theorist's abstract diagram but an organic link to
Ferrara's medieval core, with its major north-south arteries following
preexisting routes of communication. It has even been suggested that
the purpose of the addition was to provide courtiers and members of
the ducal bureaucracy with sites for impressive residences befitting
their status, an opportunity not to be found in the older sectors of
the city. The Piazza Nuova, a vast rectangular open area that forms
the heart of the scheme, was likely intended to serve as a market, and
its adjacent areas included both impressive palaces along major thoroughfares and more modest forms of housing elsewhere in the addition. The result was effectively a city within a city, an endeavor whose
scale and scope was rarely attempted in the cinquecento. To understand the significance of this accomplishment, we must turn to individual discussions of the typical elements of cinquecento urbanism.

WALLS, BASTIONS, AND GATES
~

In Ferrara, as in any other Italian city, a city's walls and gates were as
often symbols of its greatness as they were of its primary means of

defense. Fortifications were often the most expensive building projects undertaken by any city or state, and completed projects were visited by travelers and closely studied by architects. Military architecture was regularly included in most architectural treatises. In fact, the number of books on fortificatiions surpasses architectural publications with claims to omni competence. If the production of fortifications was once considered within the purview of artists, as it had been for Giotto and Michelangelo, by the end of the sixteenth century, it was a field dominated by specialists. As in the practice of civil or religious architecture, the qualifications for practicing military architecture were numerous. Military service was a logical means of professional training, as it had been in Roman antiquity. Demonstrated expertise in the design of fortifications did not disqualify talented architects such as Buontalenti from taking on civil commissions or designing temporary structures for public ceremony. Similarly, both princes such as Cosimo I and gifted amateurs such as Giovanni de'Medici, were knowledgeable in the arts of war and fortifications despite their lack of practical experience on the battlefield.

Renaissance fortifications were also largely a process of refortification, or the replacement of tall curtain walls and square towers that were the legacy of medieval techniques of warfare. The need for a radical change in form was itself the result of the advent of the cannon, which rendered old systems of defense obsolete. Both Vitruvian theory and medieval practice no longer mattered because city walls could be breached in a matter of hours by the repeated impact of the iron cannonball. At first, the efforts of Francesco di Giorgio and others to resist the impact of enemy fire led to the adoption of energetic polygonal or circular forms for the shapes of towers or bastions at Mondovi or Rocca S. Leo in the Duchy of Urbino. Handsome as their abstract forms were, such arrangements could not exploit flanking fire from artillery embrasures because curved shapes invariably created a blind area at the base of the bastion under attack. The eventual adoption of the triangular (or V-shaped) bastion meant that it could be easily defended by flanking batteries, and the low trajectory of a cannon shot was countered by low walls with reinforced earthen ramparts. The laws of ballistics had now become primary determinants of urban form.

The walls built by Luca Paciotto for Lucca (begun 1561) illustrate both the potentials and problems of this new defensive system

(164). Even to this day, it is one of the few cities where the entire enceinte remains intact. If the ideal conception of a fortified town suggests geometry, symmetry, and regular spacing of bastions, its application is a flexible response to the circumstances of the existing city. Lucca's trace of over 4 kilometers circumscribes the irregular polygon formed by the plan of its Roman grid and post-classical additions. The spacing, size, and form of its eleven bastions vary considerably and several take on asymmetrical shapes in response to the length of walls that they defend. But Lucca's relatively flat site had no topographical feature that would expose an enemy attack, and a glacis composed of zigzag earthworks was cut into the landscape surrounding the walls. The immense cost of refashioning the city's periphery proved to be a sound investment; the design increased the vulnerability of attackers and ensured Lucca's independence down to the nineteenth century.

Not all cities were willing to undertake the modernization of their walls. The prohibitive financial cost of fortification projects was an obvious reason, but it was not the only one. Social cost was another factor because walls, like modern superhighways, required vast amounts of open land on both the city's inner and outer sides if it were to function effectively. Most of all, refortification imposed on one city by its overlord was seen as a fatal blow to civic identity. For example, Bologna rejected defensive projects three times during the sixteenth century—the reconstruction of the Castello of Julius II, the refortification schemes of Sangallo the Younger for Clement VII, and rehabilitation of papal defenses during the papacy of Pius IV. For reasons of ideology and politics, complete reconstruction of Bologna's medieval walls was considered by the residents as distrustful of their independence, and partial fortification or remedial repairs satisfied neither party to the dispute. As Machiavelli had noted earlier in the century, urban walls are unnecessary when there is political cohesion among the citizenry.

The increasing professionalization of military architecture tended to limit the participation of civil architects in fortification projects. A notable exception is Baldassare Peruzzi, whose experience as the Architect to the Republic of Siena reveals an expressive response to the new demands of warfare. Although military architecture was a field in which Peruzzi had no previous experience, his solutions cannot be considered incompetent or old-fashioned.

164 Paciotto: Lucca, city walls, begun 1561
165 Peruzzi: Siena, Porta San Viene bastion
166 A da Sangallo the Younger: Florence, Fortezza da Basso, 1534–36

164

165

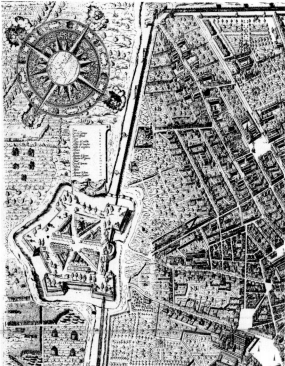

166

274

Unlike Florence and other cities, where a single fortress was the primary means of protection from attack, the five bastions built by Peruzzi to flank city gates created a reciprocal, self-supporting defensive network. What makes Peruzzi's fortification designs so impressive is how his solutions create organic and rational connections to the surrounding landscape. For example, the projecting plan of the Porta San Viene bastion is an expressive variation on a common, early sixteenth-century type. Three superimposed casemates give it an uncustomary, almost medieval, emphasis on height (165). By virtue of a position on high ground at the end of a valley, the lines of fire embrace the low ground in front of a bastion whose eminence is due to illusionistic devices. Perhaps the most compelling view of this construction is from within, where its vaults recall the unfinished appearance of St. Peter's as Peruzzi knew it. Warfare was thus ennobled through medieval and classical decoration, and the Porta San Viene's picturesque siting seems to look back to an earlier era.

Antonio da Sangallo the Younger, on the other hand, approached military architecture with a ruthless efficiency. Constructed shortly after the Siege of Florence (1529–30), the Fortezza da Basso (1534–36) is his fully developed response to changes in firepower (166). Located on a flat site along the northwestern periphery of Florence's walls, the fortress employs a pentagonal plan with five projecting bastions. Its striking exterior walls are complemented by well-planned facilities for its defenders that included open parade ground, barracks, warehouses, and stables. The purpose of this grandiose construction, already the largest structure in Florence, was less to defend the city than to prop up the reign of its dissolute and sexually voracious ruler, Duke Alessandro de'Medici. To Florentines, the fortress was clearly understood as a loss of liberty, because their fate was now to be decided by the emperor.

Sangallo's most ambitious military project was an aborted scheme to completely refortify the Aurelian walls of Rome. In 1534, the Turkish fleet, anchored just beyond Ostia, posed a major threat to the security of Rome itself. Eventually, the Turks departed to raid the Tuscan coastline, but the recognition of the weaknesses of Rome's defenses prompted Pope Paul III to consider the reconstruction of the city's northern and southern fronts. Sangallo and the pope's military consultants proposed the construction of eighteen new bastions and a new internal wall linking the two fronts along the line dividing

275

the hills of Rome from the Campo Marzio. The scheme was obviously expensive in financial terms, and only parts along the southern flank were built before the project was abandoned.

The most impressive part that remains is also Sangallo's greatest achievement in the field of military architecture. The bastion at Porta Ardeatina (1535–40) was a veritable machine for the delivery of firepower (167). Because of the doubling of its crossfire from two levels of gun positions, the bastion was in effect a small fortress. Its unornamented exterior masked a sophisticated arrangement of vaulted shafts and chambers that included provisions for detecting enemy attempts to mine underneath the fortress. The scheme continued to exert a major influence on military architecture through numerous references to it in the treatises of Scamozzi and others. No doubt part of its power was due to the combination of conceptual boldness and visual sobriety that characterizes all of Sangallo's architecture. There is a striking similarity in the bastion's meticulous brickwork, sharp edges of its protective escarpment, and the blunt curves of its upper embrasures to the understated elegance of the Palazzo Farnese, the only other building of comparable power by Sangallo.

Sangallo's career as an urban planner is closely tied to his work as a military architect. The refortification of Nepi (1537), a fortress town north of Rome, brought with it the opportunity to lay out new streets, begin construction of a new communal palace, and provide designs for several small residences. The replanning of Castro (1537–45) was altogether more complex on account of its function as a center for the duchy ruled by Pier Luigi Farnese, son of Paul III. The project has been incorrectly interpreted as an ideal Renaissance city, whose geometric form and social structure Castro resembles in no way whatsoever. In reality, the scope of the work is closer to Pienza or Urbino, where a series of related individual projects changed an old town into a modern courtly city. Its heart was the Piazza Maggiore, which was dominated by a thirteen-bay loggia behind which were the ducal palace and another official residence. Other projects included a new Mint building, the rehabilitation of other governmental structures, and commissions for residences of courtiers. However, Pier Luigi, who was given the title of Duke of Parma and Piacenza in 1545, lost interest in the endeavor and construction eventually came to a halt. Castro never received its fortifications, and its new gates were built to modified designs. In 1649,

167 A. da Sangallo the Younger: Rome, Porta Ardeatina bastion, 1535–40
168 Sanmicheli:Verona, Porta Nuova, outer face, 1533–40
169 Sanmicheli:Verona, Porta San Zeno, outer face, 1542

167

168

169

papal armies razed the town at the conclusion of a war with the Farnese, and nowadays, nothing remains of the splendid new appearance Sangallo began to give to a decrepit old town.

Michele Sanmicheli's fortified architecture shows the same concerns for material, structure, and grammar that characterize his civil works. When Vasari described Sanmicheli as having "fortified and embellished" his native city, he used words that were both accurate and that sum up Sanmicheli's achievement in light of sixteenth-century cities in general. Although Sanmicheli traveled to Crete, Cyprus, and Corfu as the foremost military architect of Venice, he left his greatest mark on his native city. If the concept of theatricality embraces fortifications, then those built by Sanmicheli in Verona protected Venetian territory from invasion by land, rendering possible the opulence and retardation so characteristic of sixteenth-century Venice.

Sanmicheli's city gates were a direct result of the growth and expansion of Verona. From prehistoric times, Verona had been an important crossing of the Adige River and an intersection of trade routes. Surrounded by the Adige on three sides, the Roman *castrum* laid out during the reign of Augustus is still recognizable to this day. The first major extension was a twelfth-century addition to the south that brought the Roman amphitheater within Verona's walls. But the most significant addition occurred under Scaliger domination in the thirteenth and fourteenth centuries when a vast area of open fields, religious institutions, and suburban settlements that grew up around them were incorporated into the city. In the sixteenth century, with Verona now securely under Venetian control, the fortress built by the Visconti at the southeast corner of the Scaliger addition was demolished, its fortified walls were realigned, and new bastions and gates were constructed under Sanmicheli's supervision.

Common to all gateways is the striking use of rustication to evoke a sense of strength and power, as Serlio was to suggest in his *Fourth Book* on architecture. Sanmicheli's handling of rustication is, in fact, so compelling that it is commonly understood as a hallmark of his architectural style. Throughout the project, his responsibilities included the layout or refurbishing of the streets in the Scaliger addition and preeminent among these were those passages connecting the new gates and the historic center of Verona. Consequently, each of the three gates represented a particular solution to different problems in fortification and urban design.

278

The Porta Nuova (1533–40), the first of three gates to be constructed, was in reality a disguised artillery emplacement composed of two low towers at its sides. Its massive construction contains a vaulted, atrium-like entry related to those found in palatial residences. On the outer facade, layers of drafted rustication culminate in an aedicule supported by coupled pilasters and columns (168); the inner facade retains the Doric aedicule while it treats the rustication as a form of enframement for openings and panels. The gate opens on to the Corso Porta Nuova, a street that in Sanmicheli's time was the primary artery linking the countryside with Verona's market square, the Piazza dell'Erbe. The most consequential event along the route was the Piazza Bra, the site of the Roman amphitheater whose rustication surrounding its arches Sanmicheli adapted for the Porta Nuova. During the Middle Ages, the area around the amphitheater had been abandoned, but by the sixteenth century its northwest side became a favorite site for residences of the nobility. With the addition of the Porta Nuova, the street took on the characteristics of a triumphant passageway, even if no ceremonial entries ever followed the thoroughfare.

By contrast, the brick and stone block of his second gateway, the Porta San Zeno (1542), may appear inadequate because its purpose was primarily commercial (169). Giving access to the main road to Milan, it is small in size yet its narrow width gives the impression of considerable height. Like the walls themselves, the gate is constructed out of brick with rustication only used at its corners and around its portals. Although this gate may have been executed without Sanmicheli's supervision, its incised and subtle details—such as the pilasters emerging from behind the corner quoins, the contrast between classical moldings and the supporting rusticated enframement of the side portals, and the larger arched portal opening to the city on the inner elevation—attest to its designer's originality in manipulating architectural grammar.

The setting for the Porta Palio (circa 1555) offered even more potential for splendid display. Unlike the Porta Nuova, it never was meant to serve as an emplacement for artillery. As a result, its interior arrangement was more open, containing a vaulted hall modeled on the *frigidarium* of a Roman bath, which in turn opens onto a five-bay portico. What makes the Porta Palio so extraordinary in terms of its architectural grammar is how the linearity of the outer facade, built

279

up in two layers of elegantly drafted rustication, and a third composed of a fluted Doric order, contrasts so violently with the gigantism of the oversized rustication on the inner facade. Practical concerns such as accessibility to Castelvecchio, the seat of the guards and the city's military depot, explain the Porta Palio's strategic position, but its primary role was visual and symbolic. Of Sanmicheli's gates, this is the most elaborate, and its heightened sense of triumphancy can also be explained by its urban circumstances.

It is not surprising that Sanmicheli, an architect by profession, conceived of his gateways as urban ornaments. The Porta Palio opens to an extension of the *cardo* of Roman Verona, offering justification of why it can be read more clearly than the Porta Nuova as a classical triumphal arch. The formal progression along the thoroughfare passes a representative selection of Verona's history as embodied in its monuments—the imposing medieval bulk of Castelvecchio, the contrasting facades of Sanmicheli's Palazzo Canossa and Palazzo Bevilacqua, the elaborate display of the late-Roman Porta dei Borsari, and culminating site of the ancient forum—and even the present day Piazza dell'Erbe. If the presence of these monuments along the same route is accidental, it is Sanmicheli's attentive development of the Porta Palio's exteriors that binds separate structures into a single experience.

On the other hand, military engineers thought of the city as a mechanism of supplying and defending its bastions. The ideal form of shifting troops and artillery was a polygonal plan whose spoke-like arrangement of straight radial streets connected bastions on opposite sides of the enceinte. In the quattrocento, Francesco di Giorgio had proposed similar layouts in his treatise, and a modified version of this scheme was put into practice by Girolamo Marini, a Bolognese engineer for Francis I at Villefranche-sur-Meuse (1544). Its plan—eight streets emanating from a central *place-des-armes* and set within a rectangular enclosure—was the first realization of this type of city. Constructed diagrams of this sort, however, could hardly be built as part of the refortification of an existing city; military towns were normally on flat land at the frontiers of a political domain.

The conflict between civil and military interests in urban design can be seen in Palmanova (begun 1593), the only radial-plan city built in Italy. Responding to the threat of Turkish attack on its eastern frontier, Venice initially sought to build a polygonal fortress with twelve powerful bastions, which were later reduced to nine because of their cost. Numerous plans for the reduced version have survived, and among them, is one that fulfills the military ideal with radial streets leading from a nonagonal central piazza to bastions on its nine-sided circumference. But to civic-mined Venetians such as Marcantonio Barbaro, supervisor of the project and patron of Andrea Palladio, the scheme must have seemed overly militaristic. Eventually, the plan was altered to accommodate a staggered system of radial streets, of which six led to central points on the sides of the hexagonal main piazza (170). The changes produced a compromised plan and thus could not satisfy either party to the dispute. Military engineers were appalled how Palmanova's complex pattern of streets, not all of which led directly to the main piazza, left six bastions isolated from distant parts of the city. Likewise, citizens must have felt constrained in their wedge-like quarters, which were separated by the six radial master streets. Palmanova saw battle only against Austria in the war of Gradisca (1615–17), and its subsequent refortification deterred further aggression. The increasing range of artillery increased the distance separating defenders and aggressors, and consequently, seventeenth-century fortification practice emphasized the need for a clear field of fire provided by the glacis. To Vauban and his generation, the radial plan was a remnant of an earlier age of warfare, and Palmanova's singularity had become history.

THE STREET
~

The cinquecento street served many purposes. It was always an element of circulation, but often it was much more. In metaphorical terms, streets were elongated public squares, spaces that had their own integrity and identity. Streets could be an index of status and power, as in the many *strade di palazzi* found in Italy. Within individual streets, the observer could see vistas terminating in major buildings (such as the Palazzo Farnese) or symbolic objects (as obelisks in the streets begun by Sixtus V). More rarely, a street such as the Strada Nuova in Genoa demonstrated a coherent aesthetic vision, and in the case of the Uffizi, it became a building in its own right. Most of all, streets are inseparable from the historical development of their cities.

To theorists like Alberti, the street was primarily an element in the defensive infrastructure of a city or town. In his *De re aedificatoria*,

170 Palmanova, begun 1593; plan as built, circa 1695
171 Rome, Via Giulia and Via della Lungara,
detail of large plan by Cartaro, 1576

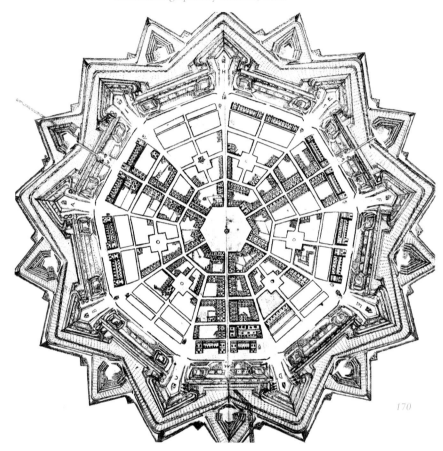

170

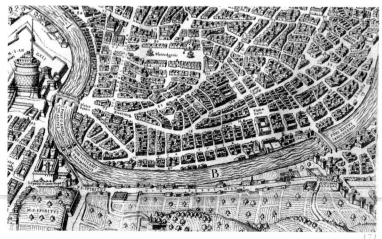

171

Alberti claimed that military roads outside a city were to be clear, straight, and without any impediment to an army on the march. Yet within the city, he considered indirect thoroughfares safer, implicitly endorsing T-shaped intersections where streets focus on building facades at the end of their vista. At the same time, he considered this arrangement, which gave prominence to houses directly facing streets, to be aesthetically superior to openness, which was disagreeable and unhealthy. Using Alberti's criteria, it can be argued that now a street could be considered a defined space in its own right, just as were *piazze*. Although Alberti's treatise was first published in Latin (1485), its subsequent translations were published in Italian (Venice, 1546; Florence, 1550), which gave his ideas new relevance to cinquecento architects.

In practice, the situation was different. Truly few cinquecento streets were created or evolved in Florence because its urban infrastructure had been determined in the late Middle Ages. Both the original *castrum* plan, dating back to Florence's foundations in the middle of the first century B.C., and the centuriation of the landscape surrounding it left a permanent imprint on subsequent growth. When the city began its spectacular growth in the eleventh and twelfth centuries, a first (1173–75) and second (1284–1333) set of city walls incorporated properties whose alignment with the Arno contrasted with the cardinal orientation of the narrow streets built over the old *castrum.* New streets such as the Via dei Servi were laid out in the new additions to the city, and structures such as the Palazzo Medici and the Palazzo Rucellai creatively adapted the often irregular alignments caused by the intersection of divergent systems of orientation. In the densely populated core, modifications were localized and often linked to the creation of monumental public spaces. The desire for regularity and monumental focus is best illustrated by streets that were given repetitive rusticated facades (Via dei Calzaiuoli, Via S. Reparata) or were widened (Via dei Calzaiuoli, Via delle Farine) as components of the restructuring of the area around the Duomo or the Palazzo Vecchio. The urban structure of trecento Florence remained remarkably resilient and survived with scarcely any alteration through the grand-ducal era.

Developments in Rome were another matter. In the Middle Ages, Rome did not prosper like Florence and Siena because its economy was dependent upon tourism and the vagaries of individual popes. It is significant that during the papal exile at Avignon (1308–77) and the Great Schism (1378–1417) was when Florence's physical image and spatial topography were being created. In the early quattrocento, Rome was little more than a desolate village of approximately 13,000 that had suffered from neglect and the lack of central authority. Before the city could be rebuilt, mounds of debris and other impediments to movement had to be removed. To relieve Rome from this profuse disorder, Martin V revived the ancient office of the *maestri di strada*. The immediate need to restore the city's infrastructure is underscored by the offices's powers to pave streets and squares, prevent encroachments upon public space, and maintain and repair the city's walls. Health and criminality were also concerns, and Sixtus IV ordered that the city's numerous porticoes be walled up. Once Rome's physical survival was assured by law, the transformation of the city's structure could proceed by design.

The most remarkable urban project of quattrocento Rome was the proposal in a biography of Nicholas V (1446–55) to rebuild the Borgo. Details of the project are sketchy and open to contradictory interpretation, but its main features are clear. New squares were to be created in front of St. Peter's and the Castel Sant'Angelo, and they were to be linked by three streets that were to be flanked by continuous porticoes on each side. Underneath the colonnades were to be shops of various trades segregated by class and status, with those on the central street reserved for the most prestigious trades. The arrangement clearly recalled the *piazze* and the streets of Bologna and Florence, which were familiar to both the pope and his preeminent artistic advisor, Leon Battista Alberti. Unfortunately, no explanation is given for why the project was never realized, and it has been proposed that it was purely a theoretical exercise, a form of architectural rhetoric. Nevertheless, it posed issues that were faced in one way or another by Bramante, Bernini, and Mussolini in their designs for St. Peter's and the Borgo.

Only in the sixteenth century are found the beginnings of impressive streets and squares that characterize Rome. In preparation for the jubilee of 1500, Alexander VI began the construction of the Via Alessandrina, the first straight street to be laid out in Rome since antiquity. Running from the Castel Sant'Angelo to the main entrance of the Vatican, the Via Alessandrina followed the path of one of the streets already proposed by Nicholas V. Its purpose was less to direct pilgrims than to provide an impressive thoroughfare for official visitors to the Pope. From the Vatican, Alexander VI wanted a street made up of fine palaces, and he was willing to use all means at his disposal to achieve this. Plans called for the demolition of all houses along the route, and if property owners did not build new residences to a predetermined height, the plots were to be sold to others who would obey the restrictions. Although the project was never completed in Alexander VI's lifetime, the street became the setting for three of Rome's most impressive cinquecento palaces—the Palazzo Giraud-Castellesi (after 1499), which has been attributed to Antonio da Sangallo the Elder; Bramante's Palazzo Caprini; and Raphael's Palazzo Jacopo da Brescia.

The desire to build new monumental streets was shared by Julius II, but with different emphases and different results. The Via Giulia and the Via della Lungara (171), the two streets laid out by Bramante for Julius II, have already been introduced in our discussion of Leo X. Both streets bypassed the core of medieval Rome by following parallel courses on opposite sides of the Tiber. Precisely where and how the Via Giulia could have begun is open to debate, but its course along the Tiber to Ponte Sisto is straight and direct. Conceived as a street of grand palaces, the Via Giulia was to have been dominated by the imposing bulk of the Palazzo dei Tribunali. The Via della Lungara was its counterpart, a setting for elegant suburban villas such as Baldassare Peruzzi's Villa Farnesina. Because neither street was completed as envisaged by Julius and Bramante, we can only imagine how they would have looked in three dimensions. During the papacy of Leo X, the Via Giulia's lot sizes were reduced, and the residential structures eventually built along the street were diverse in size and type. Because of its proximity to the site of S. Giovanni dei Fiorentini, the street became the favored residential area for Florentines in Rome.

The urban setting of the Via Giulia was to have been dominated by the imposing bulk of the Palazzo di Tribunali (172). Like the Castel Capuano in Naples and the Uffizi in Florence, the palace was meant to centralize the administration of the city, in this case, four law courts that exercised civil power in the name of the Church. In function, it was similar to the medieval communal palace, and the inclusion of an impressive courtyard and a church suggested similarities with a Roman cardinal's palace. The towered exterior of this vast quadrangular structure (1508) was derived from urban fortresses such as the Sforza in Milan, and opposite its facade, a vast square would have extended to the quattrocento palace once occupied by Rodrigo Borgia. During Julius's papacy, this structure served as the papal chancellery and was occupied by the Pope's nephew, Cardinal Sisto della Rovere. There was a double message to the triumphal street and its most important building—its medievalizing exterior alluded to Julius's absolute domination over the government of Rome, while the piazza expressed the victory of this ambitious pope over his adversaries, the Borgia. Like most of the proposals of Julius II, this one also came to naught. All that remains of the palace are a few courses here and there of some of the most grandiose rustication to have been built in the cinquecento.

Although papal attempts to revise Roman urban growth were ambitious, several smaller developments employed a modest radial arrangement of streets and these in turn stimulated other projects. In Italian design parlance this web-like pattern is known as a *trivium*, a three-pronged intersection that originated in the layout of new streets early in the sixteenth century. Neither created by accident nor informed by aesthetics, the *trivium* was primarily a solution to con-centrate traffic approaching bridges and main roadways and to allow direct access to different parts of the city.

The *trivium* became the primary means for structuring two parts of Rome: a larger vicinity in the outlying area of Piazza del Popolo and a smaller one in the more densely populated area opposite the Ponte Sant'Angelo. The *trivium* that evolved around the Piazza del Popolo was more visible and ultimately played a greater role in the history of architecture (173). Prior to the Cinquecento there was no easy way of reaching the Vatican from the piazza, located just beyond the northern entrance to the city. Connections with other parts of the city were difficult at best. The Via del Corso, the successor to the ancient Via Lata, provided access to the Campidoglio and the Piazza Venezia. But it was far from an impressive visual prospect, passing through land still largely undeveloped and along a narrow path cut in half by a Roman archway. As part of his proposal to create a Medicean center for Rome, Leo X opened the Via di Ripetta, Rome's fourth straight street constructed in less than two decades. In part the street was a project inherited from Julius II, who had begun the northern stretch of its path. Almost immediately connections

287

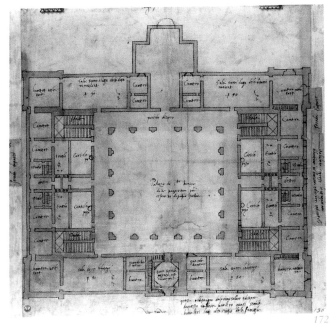

172

173

with both the area around the Pantheon and the Vatican were improved, and at this time the construction of the piazza's third prong, the present day Via del Babuino, may have been contemplated. Eventually Paul III constructed it, and his name for the new thoroughfare, Via Paolina Trionfaria (of the three ways), suggests the aesthetic roots of its origins.

The other important *trivium* around the Via dei Banchi was a short but strategic medieval street that emanated from the Ponte Sant'Angelo and connected the Vatican with the rest of Rome. By the sixteenth century the area surrounding it had become the location of offices for banking firms (hence the name "Banchi"), and impressive new residences such as Raphael's Palazzo Alberini (begun 1514–15) and Sansovino's Palazzo Gaddi (begun circa 1520) were constructed on the Via dei Banchi. Only a few blocks away were the site of S. Giovanni dei Fiorentini and the Via Giulia (which was still inaccessible at its northern end). In order to remedy their isolation, Paul III opened a street (the present-day Via Paola) from the bridge to the church. Soon afterwards the same pontiff created another street (the Via di Panico) that radiated from the piazza at almost the same angle. The creation of the second thoroughfare, however, must have been motivated by aesthetic and formal considerations; it disappeared in the jumble of streets around the old baronial fortress of the Cenci and Orsini clans, the Palazzo di Monte Giordano and, as a result, only marginally improved communication with the rest of the city by providing a short cut to the Via dei Coronari and the Piazza Navona. The piazza that resulted was no more than an irregular polygon framed by nondescript structures, and no one mourned its loss when it was destroyed in the nineteenth century during the construction of the Tiber's new riverbank.

In terms of future developments, the creation of the trident on the Piazza del Popolo was an inspired if somewhat lucky choice. Its form and suitability for urban communication suggest the plans of both the garden of the Villa Montalto and the streets laid out by Sixtus V. The Via del Babuino, in particular, provided access to the district around the Piazza di Spagna that rapidly became the foreigner's quarter in Rome. Later in the sixteenth century, it also provided a link with the new network of streets in the *disabitato*, although this connection was not direct and was recognized only in the eighteenth century by the construction of the Spanish Steps.

Most of all, the fact that the piazza's three streets do not meet at the same center created the irregular sites for the two splendidly domed churches built from designs by Rainaldi, Bernini, and Carlo Fontana in the seventeenth century. In one form or another, this was to reappear in innumerable cities, among them the Paris of Henri IV, the Versailles of Louis XIV, the St. Petersburg of the czars, and the Washington of L'Enfant.

STRADE DI PALAZZI
~

A street of a palatial residence differs from other thoroughfares because external circumstances often dictated the necessity for patrician families to live together. Districts composed of noble families and their associates could be found in many cities—quarters dominated by the Medici and the Doria developed around their palaces in Florence and Genoa respectively—and in several cities *strade di palazzi* can be identified in addition to those in Rome already discussed. The most famous—and exceptional—is the Grand Canal in Venice, where palaces face onto a water-borne street. The Via Maggio in Florence, already a palatial street in the cinquecento, became a favored address for members of Cosimo I's court because of its proximity to the Palazzo Pitti. Many palaces faced each other across the Strada degli Angeli (now Corso Ercole I d'Este), the main thoroughfare in the addition to Ferrara, but the desire for variety in style and siting and extreme width (16 meters) compromised the unity of the ensemble.

A far more formally complex and political manifestation of the straight street was the Via Toledo (1536/37–43), the most important street in Naples. Begun by Don Pedro de Toledo, the Spanish viceroy, it was the spine of the city's westward expansion from which extended other streets roughly perpendicular to it. Following in part the outline of the city's Aragonese walls, the street connected the city's administrative center near the harbor with the Porta Reale and a royal palace erected at the foot of Capodimonte. In terms of its inhabitants, the street formed a residential quarter largely occupied not by the older nobility but provincial families of means who had come to seek fame and wealth at the Viceregal court. The attraction of the city created a building boom out of which emerged the need for additional building sites. But the main aim of the Via Toledo was consolidation of the Viceregal dominance over the Neapolitans. Its southern stretch paralleled the dense checkerboard plan of the Quartieri Spagnoli, which originally served as military housing. Because most of its palaces have been replaced by later construction, it is difficult to visualize how the Via Toledo's new class of residents was concentrated in a privileged area.

The most remarkable and visually stimulating contribution to cinquecento urbanism, if squares such as the Campidoglio and Piazza San Marco are exceptions, was the Strada Nuova (begun 1550) in Genoa (174). In its own time, the Strada Nuova was recognized by Vasari as "the most magnificent street in Italy, and the richest in palaces." The great Flemish painter Rubens published a collection of measured drawings of its palaces (Antwerp, 1622) that portrayed them as models for the residences of wealthy European merchants. The Strada Nuova inspired other streets built in Genoa, and even in the eighteenth century, it was considered the most magnificent street in Europe.

What accounts for such high praise? Almost certainly it is the way in which the street plan, the sections of its flanking palaces, and the urban space of its street are inseparable from each other. The project was initiated by a decree permitting construction of a street composed of patrician palaces just inside a new set of walls begun in 1537. It represented a radical change in the social topography of Genoa, where members of its aristocracy lived in crowded quarters near the harbor. Almost certainly, the design was provided by the architect Galeazzo Alessi (circa 1512–72), who had constructed a new street in the center of his native city, Perugia. Although work on the street continued for the remainder of the century and its palaces were designed by other architects after Alessi's departure for Milan, the Strada Nuova demonstrates the tenacious survival of Alessi's original ideas.

The Strada Nuova was not a street in the typical sense of the term because it was a space with its own integrity, originally being enclosed on one end by a garden wall and a set of steps at the other. Unlike other urban spaces created by a single master plan, the design of the Strada Nuova emphasizes relationships between buildings. This is best seen in the first three blocks where palaces are built on plots equal in dimension, and each is flanked by a narrow alleyway. Scholars have assumed that the width, height, and locations of the

174

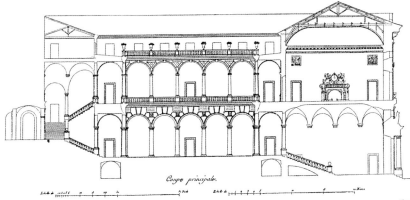

Coupe principale.

main entries were prescribed by Alessi's plan, leaving individual architects free to design distinctive facades and plans for each palace. The relationships posed by Alessi also must have assumed stylistic consistency rather than the repetition of forms. Alessi himself was the architect of only one of the palaces—significantly the first, the Palazzo Palavicino (1558), which shows the architect's characteristically eclectic combination of the ornamental effect of Raphael, the facade scheme of Sangallo the Younger, and details taken from Michelangelo. Even though none of the other palaces closely resembles that of Alessi, they all contribute to the pervasive common appearance for all the facades on the Strada Nuova.

Nature is the hidden determinant of the Strada Nuova's design. The construction of a street parallel to the contours of Genoa's steep hillside site meant that there would be two distinct kinds of palaces—those on the southern side facing the old city had to be built on platforms, while most of those on the northern side had to accommodate changes in level. In doing so, movement through the disproportionately large vestibules, up a straight flight of steps into the long courtyards, and up a second flight to the *piano nobile* creates the kind of dynamic movement through a palace that Le Corbusier would call in the twentieth century a *promenade architecturale*. In the gigantic Palazzo Doria-Tursi (begun 1568), originally built by Rocco Lurago on an oversized lot, the branching flights at the end of the courtyard create a cascading section that is without precedent in cinquecento palaces (175). A half-century later, the same idea would be treated with greater drama by Bartolomeo Bianco (before 1590–1657) in the Jesuit University on Genoa's Via Balbi, where columnar screens and terraced gardens created the structure's panoramic internal vista.

THE PIAZZA
~

The piazza is one of the glories of Italian life. Ever since Roman antiquity, it has been a focus of a city's commerce, government, or religion. It is customarily the physical setting for important civic buildings, palaces, and churches. By form and definition, it is public domain, a place of passage, rest, or assembly for citizens as individual and groups. As we have seen in Venice, public squares were the nuclei of insular parishes, the measure of the city's urban growth. Yet, as in

almost all spatial matters, what constitutes the public realm is difficult to define. Typically, public spaces are created by a corporate
body—like the procurators of St. Mark's who oversaw the administration of the Piazza San Marco—as a vehicle for the expression of
its own values and financial gain. Under special circumstances, the
piazza can become a semi-public appendage to a private residence, as
in the square opposite the Palazzo Farnese in Rome. When ghettoes
were created for the Jews of Venice, Rome, and Florence, what was
once public space—*piazze* or streets—was transformed into a place
of enforced residence with its own rules.

The recovery of the architecture of antiquity offered little that
was new or useful in terms of the knowledge of ancient urbanism.
For Vitruvius, knowledge of ancient Greek and Roman fora was limited to a comparison of their proportions and an indication of the
form and function of surrounding structures with their ground-floor
porticoes. Building upon Vitruvius, Alberti sought to extend the discussion to the proportions of buildings opening onto the square and
the desirability of erecting archways where squares intersect with
roadways. Ancient illusions of this sort were maintained in
Sansovino's Library (97), Vignola's Facciata dei Banchi (117), and
particularly, in the Piazza Ducale in Vigevano (16). The concept of
the ancient forum had little impact on urbanism in Rome; the dense
texture of its medieval fabric simply did not permit extensive
renewal. It is significant that Michelangelo's scheme to rebuild the
Campidoglio sought to display a more essential kind of *romanità* that
acknowledged no debt to archaeology.

Understandably, the message of enlightened rule was conveyed
in the numerous squares built or rehabilitated in northern Italy.
Surprisingly, little is known about the impressive square (now known
as the Piazza dei Martiri) that Alberto III Pio created opposite the
castello of Carpi, the Emilian city that he ruled until its transfer to the
Este family in 1525 (176). Neither the architect nor the exact date of
construction is known for the 210-meter arcade composed of fifty-
two bays that runs from the Portico del Grano to the new cathedral
begun by Peruzzi in 1514. What is so striking and so impressive
about this square is that its dimensions conceal numerous irregularities in its design. The most visible of these anomalies involve the
facade's lack of alignment with adjacent construction and the nine
bays that depart from the modular layout. But the arcade is neither

unsystematic nor disorderly, because in all likelihood, it was attached to a heterogeneous group of existing buildings. In fact the dialogue between the *castello* and the arcade seems to have transformed a medieval fortress town into a humanized city through the addition of a grand court of honor outside the castle of a Renaissance prince.

Piazze, on the other hand, played a minor role in the design of Sabbioneta, the only truly ideal city of the cinquecento (177–178). In the 1550s, the transformation of a modest *castello* town into a courtly center evoking the splendor of Rome was begun by Vespasiano Gonzaga, a soldier and *condottiere*, who was related to the famous family that ruled Mantua. The plan involved constructing a new courtly center within an irregular pentagonal enclosure, one side of which contained the old *rocca*. The framework of the new settlement was a modified grid plan where intentional breaks in direction were introduced along the path connecting the two main gates into the city. Although this arrangement has been interpreted as an example of Mannerist distortion on the scale of a city, it is more likely that its designers, Domenico Giunti and Girolamo Cataneo, were following Alberti's dictum on the desirability of indirect paths of circulation. But Sabbioneta's distinctive pattern of streets did not translate easily into an exceptional city. Emphasis was given to buildings and the topographic analogies they suggested, as both its palace and casino were Sabbioneta's counterparts to the Palazzo Ducale and the Palazzo del Te in Mantua. As in other ducal centers, life at court occurs within its palaces and other private structures; whatever public space remains is just an unbuilt portion of the grid plan. Sabbioneta's active disengagement from the realities of urban life is exemplified by Scamozzi's theater (1588–90), which contained fresco decoration alluding to ancient and modern Rome and was linked to the ducal palace by a private passageway. Even when walking the streets of Sabbioneta today, the observer feels somehow transposed into the world of the Tragic Scene, from Serlio's *Second Book*. Literally and metaphorically, the world of Sabbioneta was just a stage.

Sabbioneta was just one member of a family of small towns that were renewed and embellished by the Gonzaga during the last two decades of the sixteenth century. The towns were the children of familial competition. All were commissioned by Giulio Cesare Gonzaga, who clearly sought to surpass the achievements of his cousin Vespasiano in Sabbioneta. The towns demonstrated recogniz-

176 Carpi, piazza
177 Sabbioneta, piazza
178 Sabbioneta, begun 1550s, plan

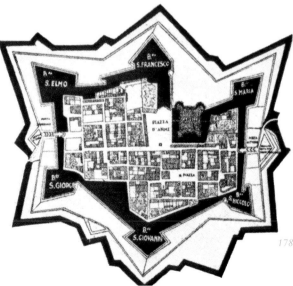

179 Isola Dovarese, piazza, view of central portion, 1587–90
180 Aleotti: Gualtieri, Piazza Bentivoglio, 1594,
view towards Via Vittorio Emmanuele

179

180

able family traits. Following the example of Carpi, the squares were typically laid out in front of castles as a continuing assurance of civil order. Their rigid rectangular layout was the formal and emotional complement to the interminable flatness of the terrain along the north bank of the Po River. Yet versatility was not constrained by the grid plan. In Pomponesco (1583–93), there is a progressive expansion of street and square that creates a grand axis leading from the river to the site of a destroyed hexagonal castle. The fragment of a new square facing the Gonzaga castle in Isola Dovarese (1587–90) was even more sophisticated in its evocation of ancient fora as understood by Vitruvius and Alberti. Parts of a continuous portico run along two of its sides, and a triumphal arch spans the street entering the square along its principal approach (179). Something similar can be seen in the tiny agricultural hamlets of Rivarolo Montovano and S. Martino dell'Argine.

If the strength of these towns is unbridled ambition, both political and intellectual, their main defect is architectural. Lacking a Scamozzi or a true Mantuan heir to Giulio Romano as their architect, the Gonzaga towns were, on one level, charming provincial endeavors. But on another level, they were models for the city as it was to become. Just across the Po from Pomponesco, the Bentivoglio began the enlargement of Gualtieri (1594) as the capital of their marquisate (180). The focal point was a square piazza opposite the castle, an open space that was part a market square and part a ceremonial *place des armes*. But what distinguishes it from its Gonzaga forerunners was the attainment of a high level of sophistication by its designer, the Parma architect G. B. Aleotti. Three streets enter the square at the center of each adjacent side, creating a T-shaped pattern of circulation through the space. A prominent clock tower spans the principal entry opposite the castle, and the town's collegiate church, S. Maria della Neve, is attached to the southern arm of the continuous arcade. The effect of the square depends, of course, to a great degree on the elevations of its arcades and the sense of enclosure that they convey. Here, Aleotti's model was Vignola's Portico dei Banchi in nearby Bologna (117), only now surrounding three sides of the square and shorn of the rich relief found on its model. Nevertheless, this conception of a square as a *piazza salone* rather than an accumulation of buildings, finds its parallels in Vigevano, the Piazza San Marco, and a handful of other examples.

The type of square created by the Gonzaga and further refined in Gualtieri may have had an impact on urbanism elsewhere in Europe. No doubt these examples were in the mind of Charles de Gonzague, Prince of Nevers and Duke of Mantua, when he founded Charleville (1606–20). The first residence city in France, it was certainly derived in equal measure from Henri IV's Place Royale (later Place des Voges) as it was from the earlier Italian towns. If the influence of the Gonzaga towns was not wide, it was at least profound.

SIXTUS V AND ROME
~

Few popes have left such a permanent mark on Rome as Sixtus V (1585–90). The basic outlines of his replanning of Rome are well-known (181). Its central core consists of streets that congregate on the S. Maria Maggiore, while others were planned to connect peripheral monuments, such as the Colosseum and S. Giovanni in Laterano. Ostensibly, the purpose of the streets was to permit access for pilgrims to the Holy City's basilicas, the primary destination for the pilgrims' sacred journeys. In particular, the area near S. Maria Maggiore and the pope's own Villa Montalto, sought to repopulate the *disabitato*, the evocative sixteenth-century phrase for the vast greenbelt of *vigne* and the ruins that overlook the populous quarters near the Tiber. By reconstructing the Acqua Alessandrina, later renamed the Acqua Felice in honor of the Pope, Rome was now provided with a new supply of water that culminated in a fountain in the form of a triumphal arch (1587–88) designed by Fontana. The repopulation of the *disabitato* was further encouraged by tax abatements, pardons of criminal penalties, and the granting of citizenship to foreigners. Sixtus V was as ruthless as a ruler as he was energetic as a builder. Within a short time, he had reorganized the administration of the Papal States, replenished its treasury, and had cut into the lawlessness and brigandage commonly found throughout Rome and the Campagna. Executions were such a common sight in the piazza adjoining Ponte Sant'Angelo that Romans claimed there were more heads on the bridge than melons in the market.

An important milestone in Renaissance urbanism was reached in Sixtus V's papacy when the distinctions between the layout of streets and gardens became blurred. Already in the 1570s Cardinal

Felice Peretti, the future Pope, had begun to purchase several *vigne* on the Esquiline near the basilica of S. Maria Maggiore with the intention of constructing a large casino from designs by Domenico Fontana (182). After his election, however, the small retreat was expanded into a grandiose estate covering more than 160 acres. The focal point was the block-like casino whose massing—a hipped roof culminating in a prominent belvedere—derived from vernacular rustic farm buildings.

299

What made this unpretentious structure important was the manner in which its harmonious setting mixed elements from garden and urban design. Originally, a triangular-shaped piazza separated the casino and the Porta Viminale, the main entrance to the estate. Subsequently, this area was transformed, presumably to Fontana's plan, into three radial alleys, of which the central one led to the casino and the two remaining proceeded to *giardini segreti* at either side of the casino. Like the earlier *trivia* composed of urban streets, those in the garden of the Villa Montalto permitted direct access to different parts of the garden. This is illustrated by its appearance in fragmentary form and irregular geometric settings elsewhere in the garden, near the iron gates at the southern and eastern periphery of the garden. In fact, the estate came to have three distinct forms of considerable significance for the history of urbanism—as a garden whose design disregarded distinctions between city and country; as magnet for the development of a market and trade fair to be held on the adjacent open area near S. Maria degli Angeli; and as a demonstration, on a smaller scale, of the techniques and ideas employed in his new system of straight thoroughfares that remade the face of Rome.

But what was initially functional became artistically and ideologically desirable once the visual potential of the *trivium* arrangement was recognized. Although the most dramatic examples are normally associated with the Baroque era, Sixtus V and Fontana introduced this arrangement and its most characteristic effects to the scale of the city. The new thoroughfares sought to create a system of circulation that bypassed Rome's medieval core, thereby permitting pilgrims easy access to churches and religious sites at the city's periphery. The problem of providing dramatic focal points to the long vistas created by the new streets was solved by the placement of obelisks adjacent to major pilgrimage churches, first at St. Peter's

300

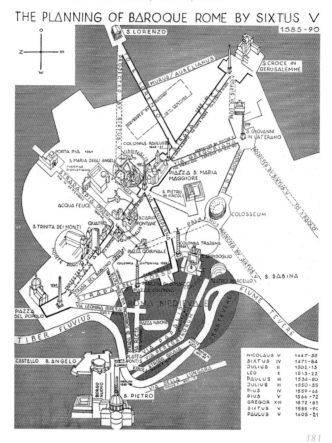

THE PLANNING OF BAROQUE ROME BY SIXTUS V
1585-90

NICOLAUS V	1447-55
SIXTUS IV	1471-84
JULIUS II	1502-13
LEO X	1513-22
PAULUS III	1534-50
JULIUS III	1550-55
PIUS IV	1559-66
PIUS V	1566-72
GREGOR XIII	1572-85
SIXTUS V	1585-9C
PAULUS V	1605-21

181

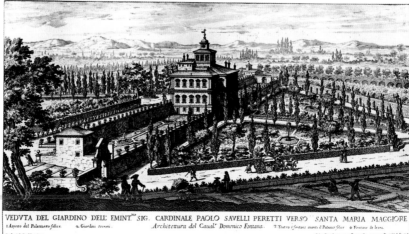

VEDVTA DEL GIARDINO DELL' EMINT.ᵐᵒ SIG. CARDINALE PAOLO SAVELLI PERETTI VERSO SANTA MARIA MAGGIORE
Architettura del Caual.ʳ Domenico Fontana.

182

(1586), and subsequently, at S. Maria Maggiore (1586), the Lateran (1588), and the Piazza del Popolo (1588). As a result of these transformations to the city's fabric, a religious geography was created for the Eternal City that exists to this day. Yet the obelisks were more than forms marking space, they were physical symbols of the triumphal church. Just as popes of the early Christian era usurped antiquity to create attributes of authority, Sixtus V reconsecrated ancient ruins to serve modern, Christian purposes. Rome, in effect, became a shrine.

The myth of Sixtus V as a great builder masks the fact that very little of what he did was original or new. The most stunning visual feature of his new streets—the use of obelisks as symbolic markers and the terminal features of an urban vista—was, it seems, suggested by the columns erected by Ammannati for Cosimo I in Florence. Nor were the new streets free of existing constraints, although they typically cut across virgin land. The framework for the renewal of the *disabitato* had been anticipated by earlier papal projects, especially by the construction of the Via Pia by Pius IV and the Via Merulana by Gregory XIII. Strictly speaking, Sixtus V created a coordinated network of streets that incorporated earlier projects rather than an entirely new system. Even the Acqua Felice has its origins in an initiative begun by private citizens under the previous pope to bring water at their own expense to their properties on the Quirinal. Most of all, there was never a master plan in the sense of one created by Baron Hausmann or even Le Corbusier. Each project was an independent initiative with little connection to others other than a common convergence at a specified monument. The Pope's unpredictable and piecemeal course of proposals was the antithesis of overall planning.

The notoriously uneven topography of the *disabitato* posed challenges all its own. The fashioning of the Villa Montalto and piazza around S. Maria degli Angeli required the grading of large areas of open land, and whatever soil or construction material that was left over was used to level the terrain for the new streets. But topography could be altered, less to enhance the long vistas of the streets than to ease the passage of carriages through vast open areas. Fontana himself noted that Sixtus V had stretched streets from one end of the city to the other, not heeding the hills and valleys which they have to cross, but cutting at one spot here and filling at another to create level roadways. Sometimes insurmountable site difficulties prevented the completion of a street, as the escarpment of the Pincio near S. Trinita de Monti prevented the extension of the Via Sistina to the Piazza del Popolo. In another case, the Forum of Trajan prevented the completion of the Via Panisperna from reaching its intended goal, the Column of Trajan.

It is a misconception to think of Sixtus V as the first modern planner, as Siegfried Giedion did in *Space, Time and Architecture*. Rather, his vision of papal patronage was motivated by the traditional concept of advancing the spiritual and temporal power of the Church. Unlike other popes of his era, he had little interest in antiquity unless it could be adapted to new and usually Christian purposes. Again, the examples are well known. The Colosseum was to have been converted into a wool factory and housing for its workers. The Septizodium, the scenic fountain below the south side of the Palatine, was ruthlessly dismembered and its remains were interred in several Sistine projects. The columns of Trajan and Marcus Aurelius became pedestals for statues of Saints Peter (1587) and Paul (1588) respectively. The entire medieval papal palace adjacent to the Lateran was destroyed for a new, uninspired residence by Fontana (1585–89), excepting the Scala Santa (1586–89), which, according to medieval tradition, was the staircase mounted by Christ in the Praetorium of Pontius Pilate. Sixtus V's opinions of the architecture of his century are unknown, but they must have been similar to those he held of antiquity. During his reign, the cupola of St. Peter's was completed but the stunning perspective of Bramante's Cortile del Belvedere was irrevocably lost when Fontana constructed the Vatican Library (1585–89) across its second level.

Architecture and nature, in service to the Pope and the Church, is a central theme in the architecture and urban planning of Sixtus V. The motivations behind his building and administration were remarkably clear and consistent, as befitting an elderly pontiff with only a few years to rule. The view of the papacy Sixtus V espoused was absolutist, emphasizing the authority of the Pope over that of the College of Cardinals. It should come then as no surprise that these forms were given even more powerful meanings at Versailles under Louis XIV.

THE GHETTO
~

The spatial organization of an Italian city resembles a richly textured mosaic composed of distinct elements. Unlike an abstract diagram, to which it is often compared, the city is a kind of urban mosaic where each *tessera* represents a space, structure, or neighborhood that retains both its identity qualities and interacts with other *tesserae* that surround it. Of all Italian neighborhoods, the one most often overlooked is the ghetto, the place of enforced residence of Italian Jews. In this context, "ghetto" refers to the neighborhood where Jews were required by law to live, as opposed to places of voluntary residence, where they once had dwelled for their convenience or protection. Like those cities whose juridical and physical identity was defined by walls, ghettoes had a legal and spatial definition that was circumscribed by their enclosure.

The first ghettoes were created in a period of general European intolerance toward Jews. In 1516, the Venetian Republic ordered all of the Jews in Venice to live in an enclosed area at the periphery of the city, a location far from their residences in the commercial district around the Rialto. Although there is debate on the derivation of the word "ghetto," it is commonly thought to have derived from the Italian word for an iron foundry that once existed on the site of the Venetian ghetto. For nearly a half-century, the earliest coercive Jewish settlement in Italy remained the only one. The Roman ghetto, on the other hand, is commonly understood as the most influential. Official endorsement of Jewish segregation came in 1555, when Paul IV issued a papal bull establishing restrictions on Jews in the Papal States. In due course, the Florentine ghetto was established in 1571, Padua in 1603, Mantua in 1612, and Ferrara in 1627. At the time of their dissolution after the Napoleonic invasions, there were nearly sixty ghettoes in Italy, about a third of which were founded during the eighteenth century.

The Venetian ghetto is the earliest, the best known, and one of the very few that retains something of its original appearance (183). It consists of three contiguous sectors. The first is the Ghetto Nuovo which was established in 1516, to segregate a Jewish population that was predominantly Germanic in origin. Built a half-century earlier as a grouping of two-story houses rented to artisans by the De Brolo family, the insular property proved to be insufficiently small. Situated across a canal just to the west, a second enclosure confusingly known as the Ghetto Vecchio was created for Levantine Jewish merchants who could not find accommodations in the existing ghetto. It is precisely these two areas that have defined the ghetto's visual identity as a series of towering, astylar structures composed of cramped apartments at the periphery of their insular sites. The third addition, the Ghetto Nuovissimo, was altogether different. Laid out in 1633, as a purely residential district without shops, an open space, or a synagogue, its stylistically homogeneous and palatial apartments were occupied by Sephardic Jews whose assistance was sought in reviving Venice's economy after the plague of 1630. As such, the Venetian ghetto comprised three discrete areas differing in size, appearance, and ethnicity of the population.

Although most Italian ghettoes were fashioned out of existing structures by anonymous builders, the Roman ghetto involved the interventions of two architects with name recognition. The original enclosure created by Paul IV was largely the work of Sallustio Peruzzi, son of Baldassare Peruzzi, the architect of the Palazzo Massimo. Shortly thereafter, his appointment of two new streets were opened in the area surrounding the ghetto. Cutting diagonally through two blocks, the first connected the Piazza di Pescaria with the Ponte di Quattro Capi and the Tiber. The second street linked the Piazza dei Judei—the square in front of the ghetto's main entrance—with the Tiber. Both of these streets, the walls built along their rights of way, and the three gates constructed under Paul IV, are clearly delineated in a circa 1556 plan by Bartolomeo de' Rocchi (184), which also shows a proposal for an adjacent walled precinct that was never carried out.

A smaller but no less significant addition was carried out under Sixtus V. The revision of the ghetto's edge along the Tiber, the provision for additional housing, and the construction of two new gateways were an integral part of Sixtus's renewal of Rome, representing on a smaller scale the concerns for communication and pragmatism that characterized his other projects. As expected, these works were executed under the supervision of Domenico Fontana. What was unusual about the working relationship, however, was that Fontana was paid for his efforts with concessions involving property within

183 Venice, Ghetto, exterior view
184 Rome, Ghetto Plan by Bartolomeo de' Rocchi, circa 1555
185 Florence, Ghetto, detail of plan of Florence by Bonsignori, 1584

183

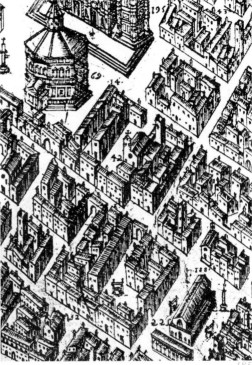

185

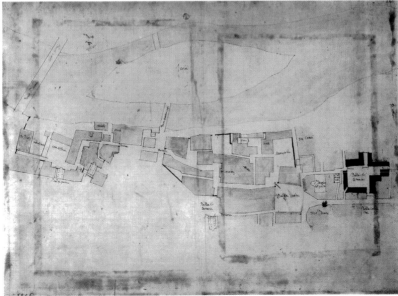

184

the ghetto. Of these, the most important are first, the title to unbuilt sites within the ghetto still in papal ownership; second, the nomination of Fontana and his heirs in perpetuity as keepers of the new gates; and third, an annual payment of two scudi by the Jewish community (also in perpetuity) relative to the two gates. No other architect benefited financially from the confinement of the Italian Jews.

The Florentine ghetto was created in 1571, by Cosimo I de'Medici in repayment for the title of Grand-Duke conferred on him two years earlier by Pius V. In comparison to other ghettoes, the Florentine ghetto was fashioned out of the medieval fabric of central Florence (185). Like the Venetian ghetto, its form was visibly insular—nearly a single block bounded by streets and the Mercato Vecchio on three sides and existing structures on the fourth. As one might expect, the layout was completely internalized. Two entries provided access to the enclosure, one passing through existing structures on the south face toward the market square and the other on the east face. At the center of the complex, a small piazza once belonging to the Della Tosa family served as the ghetto's only square. Within it, was the enclave's single source of water, the ghetto fountain. Although later documents refer to this space as a *cortile*, the complex can never be understood as a *palazzo*. Around the ghetto's "courtyard" were shops and entries providing access to the stairways and apartments on the ghetto's several floors. Because the shops on the ghetto's external boundaries remained, the entries to old residences at the periphery of the site were modified, thus requiring new entrances and inner corridors passing through bearing walls and adjacent rooms.

The Florentine ghetto was truly exceptional for the bewildering complexity of the overall layout. The course of circulation within the complex was never direct and often led to a discontinuous stairwell that began on one of the upper floors. To reach one of its apartments in the tower overlooking the Mercato Vecchio, one entered through a portal on the western side of the central courtyard. After rising two stories, one continued along a tortuous hallway to a common room, from which two stairs ascend to different groups of apartments on upper floors. From this intermediate level, another stair led to the apartments in the tower overlooking the Mercato Vecchio. Two stories higher, one found the entrance to the five-room unit that is spread out over three stories and connected by a wooden stair. The units were subject to continuous modification by the tenants, thereby making it impossible to define a single plan type for ghetto dwellings.

Although the layout resembles no other apartment unit, the size of its rooms and their irregular arrangement are characteristic of the ghetto as a whole. Much the same could be said for their rents, which varied according to the number of rooms and their location, with the amount for similar units decreasing approximately every two floors as one ascends through the building. The Jewish community was responsible for the rent of every apartment, whether or not it was occupied. The rental rolls also indicate that certain individuals paid for the rents of more than one unit. As in Venice, a right to control domestic space was maintained by subletting units to other ghetto inhabitants according to the Jewish doctrine of *cascod*, or the right to continuous possession of property owned by others.

No single city is emblematic of the cinquecento. As a physical artifact, the city has been proven to be impervious to notions of style; it resists the easy classification afforded to other forms of art. Factors of previous inhabitation, topography, and politics impose on urban settlements a dimension of time foreign to most painting, sculpture, and architecture. As is well-known, most cities are composed of buildings of one or more epochs that are laid down upon a physical infrastructure created in the past. Rome, of course, is instructional in its layers of history and in the incomplete projects of its rulers, the popes. But it, too, is exceptional, like any other Italian city that prospered in the cinquecento. We know the individuals who drew up the plans of new or nearly new cities such as Ferrara, Palmanova, Sabbioneta, and the Gonzaga towns near Mantua, but their creations can only be measured by comparison to other cities and not to other projects by the same individual.

It is understandable why historians now see cities as the result of an "urban process" rather than as the product of a single mind. But the temptation to understand cities exclusively in these terms is just as misleading in its avoidance of the interactions between individuals and their interests that lies at the core of the "urban process." Cities don't just grow; they are created through the bewildering multiplicity of actions taken by individuals for reasons ranging from form and appearance to a plethora of social, political, and economic considerations. It is then diversity rather than uniformity that characterizes the urban endeavors in this chapter, and this variety is further enhanced by the solutions created by designs for structures in an urban environment. We have sought not just to define historical problems but also to evaluate physical solutions to architectural and urban projects. The identity of the city is greater than the sum of its parts.

This is why the mind and all the senses are engaged in the cinquecento city.

186 Carlo Maderno: Rome, S. Susanna, facade, 1597–1603

EPILOGUE
~

Shatter the "schools"… as well as the "School of Vignola," I beseech you.

LE CORBUSIER,
letter to modern architects in Johannesburg, September 23, 1936

In exploring such well-established architectural territory as the cinquecento, it seems important to differentiate what was truly new from what was just conventional. Bramante's revolutionary application of new ideas regarding mass, space, and the role of antiquity determined the direction of architectural development for the remainder of the century; even the singular achievement of Michelangelo is unthinkable without Bramante's Roman work. It is important to note that these revolutionary ideas were initiated by a generation of architects who were trained or worked as painters (Bramante, Raphael, Giulio Romano, Serlio), continued by another generation of painter-trained-architects (Vasari and Vignola), and expanded upon by a new kind of practitioner (Sangallo the Younger, Sanmicheli, and Palladio).

Surveying cinquecento architecture today, it is all too easy to accept the kind of inevitable stylistic development that was first postulated by Vasari and continued by architectural historians of the twentieth century. But a study of building types demonstrates how little some aspects of design changed. Domestic architecture in Rome, Florence, and Venice was conditioned as much by factors of technique and tradition as it was by issues of style, which were expressed primarily on a building's exterior. In religious architecture, the necessity for visibility of the Eucharist and audibility of the preacher accounted for the new open interiors of box-type churches, which were a profoundly characteristic church form. Even the restructuring of Rome accomplished by Sixtus V was revolutionary in content rather than form, because it integrated streets begun by earlier pontiffs and employed planning devices established in the beginning of the cinquecento. Only in the field of fortifications, where form was conditioned by the laws of ballistics rather than the laws of architecture, can one find achievements such as Sangallo's Porta Ardeatina or the walls of cities such as Lucca that are independent of the language of antiquity. But there were exceptions; by virtue of their location and function, Sanmicheli's Porta Nuova and Porta Palio, for example, married the triumphal gateways of antiquity with modern military techniques.

A key factor in sustaining such outdated concepts of cinquecento architecture has been the ambivalence of modern architects. Although Frank Lloyd Wright spent much of 1910 in Italy, he seems to have left without gaining an appreciation of architecture after 1500. This was reinforced by his residency in Florence and Fiesole, where medieval and early Renaissance buildings were seen as a standard against which all others were to be measured. Having read Ruskin and Vasari, he had come to the conclusion that the arts of the cinquecento were merely an afterglow of the previous four centuries. Quite understandably, by contrast, he reacted innately toward the Italian landscape and its integration with buildings rather than to specific architects.

Walter Gropius, too, had read Vasari but drew different conclusions. Although typically portrayed as indifferent toward architectural history, Gropius showed a strong appreciation toward the Gothic in his writings. He approbated the Gothic cathedral as the collective representation of medieval *volk*, itself a premonition of his view of the architect as a collaborator among artists and the coordinator of economic, social, and technical challenges involved in the creation of a building. Not surprisingly, when Gropius mentioned Brunelleschi's cupola of Florence Cathedral in *The Scope of Total Architecture*, he admired a quattrocento construction deeply indebted to the communal identity of the Middle Ages rather than one associated with artistic freedom, a concept which Gropius apparently distrusted. To Gropius, Brunelleschi's cupola must have been more than just the collective achievement of Florentines; it was a supreme historical example of architecture as ennobled building.

Le Corbusier, of course, did not share Gropius's mythic faith in practical objectivity. Of all the major figures of modernism, Le Corbusier was the architect with both the deepest appreciation of architectural history and the most complex relationship to its achievements. Nothing if not ambitious in his writings, he sought to identify universal lessons to be derived from the architecture of Rome, and he studied vernacular structures wherever he traveled. Late in his career, for example, he demonstrated his deep sympathy for the city of Venice in his unbuilt scheme for its new hospital, a microcosm of everything he admired in Venetian urban structure. But Le Corbusier could be maddeningly selective about the Italian buildings he admired most. During his 1907 trip to Tuscany, he drew Santa Croce and the Palazzo Vecchio but left no record of having studied the Uffizi or the Pazzi Chapel. Le Corbusier returned to

Italy again in October 1911 at the end of his "Voyage d'Orient." This time his focus was broader, including studies of the Villa d'Este in Tivoli and Michelangelo at St. Peter's and on the Campidoglio. The mathematical and compositional systems associated with Palladio and later expressed in the Villa Stein at Garches would have been learned from books rather than a direct study of the monuments. In the end, the Middle Ages were his standard of achievement and Baedeker his guide to them.

It was all too easy for architects such as Le Corbusier to demonize cinquecento architects whose achievements could not be understood in modernist terms. Vignola was singled out for special criticism, most likely because of how his immensely successful treatise on orders—the *Regola delli cinque ordini d'architettura* (1562)—represented everything that Corbusier sought to achieve in his "Five Points of a New Architecture." What eluded Le Corbusier and others of his generation was an appreciation for the shift of architectural taste that began toward the middle of the cinquecento, and especially for the buildings representing these changes. All in all, Modernist reaction to cinquecento architecture was predictable and conservative.

All of this would not seem familiar to the last generation of cinquecento architects. Once more, Vignola's eruptive facades play a major role in the reevaluation of the ecclesiastical facade that culminated in Carlo Maderno's S. Susanna (1597-1603), where the ongoing re-evaluation of the ecclesiastical facade culminates in a major masterpiece (186). In his magisterial *Art and Architecture in Italy 1600-1750*, Rudolf Wittkower identified what he saw as its governing principles: a progressive concentration of bays, order, and decoration toward the center; a coordination of bays and their orders with three layers of wall; and the gradual elimination of the wall surfaces as the bays increase toward the center. Here, Wittkower seems to argue that S. Susanna is a first exposition of Baroque strategies and principles, the moment which decisively celebrates the end of a cinquecento ancient regime, now sterile and incompetent.

From the perspective of the Roman Baroque, this seems like an unassailable fact. But Vignola's churches, of course, were no less revolutionary or sophisticated. Il Gesù was Cardinal Alessandro Farnese's claim to spiritual and temporal immortality, a claim however based as much on the creative powers of his architect as on the power of the

Jesuit order. Therefore, it is not so paradoxical that Vignola's most persistently faithful patron, Cardinal Farnese, should have withdrawn his support at the moment when Vignola's inventive skill was at its peak. Until further documentation is discovered, the reasons for Vignola's dismissal must remain an open question. Could this have been because Alessandro, satiated and happy with what had been provided for him at Caprarola, felt no longer able to accept the subversive threat of another anthology of novelties? Was Cardinal Farnese guilty of the same fundamental misunderstanding of Vignola as Le Corbusier was to demonstrate three-and-one-half centuries later?

If S. Susanna stands at the beginning of a tradition culminating in the work of Borromini, it also represents the culmination of an equally long development stretching back to the quattrocento. Its lineage is long and honorable. Its forerunners are Alberti's facade for S. Maria Novella in Florence, Sangallo the Younger's facade of S. Spirito in Rome, and, of course, those both planned and built by Vignola. From the viewpoint of conventional facade types it was also the final flowering of the cinquecento version of what was essentially a quattrocento composition. And while Maderno's facade is the most dramatic and experimental example of his generally conservative architectural style, it illustrates even more strongly the constraints on style posed by types and modalities. The facade of S. Susanna was the product of an eclectic architectural culture which, like the cinquecento, was a conflation of retrospection and a search for novelty. In character and conception, it was, finally, the product of an architect's search for both authority in precedent and subversion in execution.

Something must be written about the publications consulted in the preparation of this book, and how in the last thirty years a profusion of scholarship has significantly altered our knowledge of cinquecento architecture. New documentation has clarified issues of authorship, concepts of building typology have been expanded and refined, and the history of individual projects has been augmented through the study of drawings and other forms of architectural representation. It is now as common for scholars to address the social context of an architect's career as it was to employ stylistic paradigms a generation ago. Most importantly, some of these new ideas have been brought to the attention of the general public through important exhibitions in Italy, Canada, and the United States.

Very little of this scholarly dynamism can be felt in the general studies of cinquecento architecture. For many their first introductions to the subject were Bates Lowry's *Renaissance Architecture* (New York, 1961) and Peter Murray's *Architecture of the Italian Renaissance* (London and New York, 1963). However the books were, in some ways, premature, having been written just before the outpouring of much new material. Of the two books, that of Lowry is more insightful, but it is also constrained by the brevity of its text. Murray provides a lively account of two centuries of Italian architecture, but its text is descriptive rather than analytical, and fails to address key issues such as cities, gardens, and fortifications, and never was updated.

Leonardo Benevolo's *Storia dell'Architettura del Rinascimento* (2 vols., Bari, 1968; 2nd ed. 1972, translated as the *Architecture of the Renaissance*, London and Boulder, 1978) is an altogether more ambitious endeavor. Benevolo employs an elastic concept of the Renaissance, covering developments in architecture and urbanism down to 1750, in both Europe and the New World. If the book is often rambling and unfocused, it nevertheless has an excellent chapter on urban changes in the 16th century.

The volume covering cinquecento architecture in the Pelican History of Art—Ludwig Heydenreich's and Wolfgang Lotz's *Architecture in Italy 1400–1600* (Harmondsworth and Baltimore, 1972)—had most of the virtues and some of the drawbacks of this important series. Lotz's chapters on the cinquecento are examples of brevity and clarity, often containing nuggets of insight taken up by a younger generation of scholars. Yet the structure of the book represented the views of an earlier generation, stressing biography and geography as the main criteria for its organization. Like Murray, there was no common acceptance of building types, gardens or urbanism as subjects in their own right. Recently the book has been republished as two separate volumes—Ludwig Heydenreich, *Architecture in Italy 1400–1500*, rev. by Paul Davies (London and New Haven, 1995) and Wolfgang Lotz, *Architecture in Italy 1500–1600*, rev. by Deborah Howard (London and New Haven, 1995) without significant alteration of their text or inclusion of new material. For the moment Heydenreich and Lotz remain the standard surveys, if somewhat out dated. The Milanese publisher Electa has begun to publish a multi-volume series, *Storia dell' architettura italiana*, that constitutes an encyclopedic survey of Italian architecture from the fifteenth to the twentieth centuries. Its answer to Heydenreich has already appeared—Francesco Paolo Fiore (ed.), *Storia dell'architettura italiana. Il quattrocento* (Milan, 1998). Two volumes covering the cinquecento are in preparation, of which the second, Claudia Conforti and Richard Tuttle (eds.), *Storia dell'architettura italiana. Il secondo cinquecento* (Milan, 2001), appeared as this book was going to press.

Subsequent publications are decidedly uneven in quality. On the one hand, the republication of some Lotz's most significant articles—*Studies in Italian Renaissance Architecture* (Cambridge, MA and London, 1977)—is a mini-survey in its own right. Yet on the other hand, Peter Murray's *Renaissance Architecture* (New York, 1978) now covers all of Europe without significantly advancing beyond his earlier book. Murray was also the editor of Jacob Burckhardt's *The Architecture of the Italian Renaissance* (London, 1985), a compilation of brief chapterlets that were to form part of a larger book covering all arts during the Renaissance. Ironically this nineteenth-century publication addressed many questions avoided by scholars in the twentieth century, though its discussion of cinquecento examples is skimpy. Peter Thornton's *The Italian Renaissance Interior 1400–1600* (New York, 1991) is more specialized and uses paintings as its primary form of evidence, but also contains much useful information about daily life for the architectural historian. The title of David Thomson's *Renaissance Architecture: Patrons, Critics, and Luxury* (Manchester and New York, 1993) is misleading because it addresses only the display of personal status in domestic architecture, mainly in northern Europe.

Building upon the success of previous exhibitions devoted to the architecture of Palladio (London, 1975), Raphael (Rome, 1984), Giulio Romano (Mantua, 1989), and Francesco di Giorgio Martini (Siena, 1993), an international team of scholars under the direction of Henry A. Millon and Vittorio Magnago Lampugnani organized an ambitious exhibition devoted to the representation of Renaissance architecture in drawings, wooden models, and other forms (Venice, 1994). The exhibition's catalog—H.A.Millon and V.M.Lampugnani (eds.), *The Renaissance from Brunelleschi to Michelangelo: The Representation of Architecture* (Milan, 1994)—is, like the show itself, daunting in its immensity and awkward to use. But many of its thirteen introductory essays revisit old problems in the light of current scholarship, and the over 400 entries contain a mine of new information. As a publication it is *sui generis*; as a reference source for scholarship up to the mid 1990s it is unsurpassed

317

CHAPTER 1

Quotations from Vasari's *Lives*: G.Vasari, *Lives of the Most Eminent Painters, Sculptors, and Architects*, trans. Mrs. Jonathan Foster, 5 vols. (London, 1850).

For Bramante in general: A. Bruschi, *Bramante architetto* (Rome and Bari, 1969), abridged English edition *Bramante* (London, 1977). The proceedings of the 1970 Bramante congress were published as *Studi Bramanteschi* (Rome, 1974).

For the perspective panels: R. Krautheimer, "The Panels in Urbino, Baltimore, and Berlin Reconsidered," in H.A. Millon and V.M. Lampugnani (eds.), *The Renaissance from Brunelleschi to Michelangelo: The Representation of Architecture*.

For Bramante in Milan: Heydenreich, *Architecture in Italy 1400–1500*; L. Giordano "Milano e l'Italia nord-occidentale," in *Storia dell'architettura italiana. Il quattrocento*.

For Leonardo: S.J. Freedberg, *Painting of the High Renaissance in Rome and Florence*, 2 vols. (Cambridge MA, 1961), chapter 1; C. Pedretti, *Leonardo architetto* (Milan, 1978).

CHAPTER 2

For the Cancelleria: C.L. Frommel, "Roma," in *Storia dell'architettura italiana. Il quattrocento*.

For St. Peter's: C. L. Frommel, "St. Peter's: The Early History," and "The Endless construction of St. Peter's" in *The Renaissance from Brunelleschi to Michelangelo: The Representation of Architecture*; C.Thoenes, *Sostegno e adornamento. Saggi sull'architettura del rinascimento: disegno, ordini, magnificenza* (Milan, 1998) contains several important studies on St. Peter's in the eras of Bramante and Sangallo the Younger.

For other projects by Bramante: J.S. Ackerman, *The Cortile del Belvedere* (Vatican City, 1954); C.L.Frommel, "Bramante's Nympheum in Genazzano," *Römisches Jahrbuch für Kunstgeschichte*, 12: 1969, 137–60.

For the Tempietto: E. Rosenthal, "The Antecedents of Bramante's Tempietto," *Journal of the Society of Architectural Historians*, 23: 1964, 55– ; H. Günther, Bramantes Hofprojekt um der Tempietto und seine Darstellung in Serlios dritten Buch," in *Studi Bramanteschi*, 483–501; D. Howard, "Bramante's Tempietto: Spanish Royal Patronage in Rome," *Apollo*, 137: October 1992, 211–17.

CHAPTER 3   For Raphael in general: R. Jones and N. Penny, *Raphael* (London and New Haven, 1993); C.L. Frommel et al., *Raffaello architetto* (Milan, 1984).

For Raphael's paintings and his painted architecture: S. J. Freedberg, *Painting of the High Renaissance in Rome and Florence*, chapters 3 and 5; C.L. Frommel, "Architettura dipinta," in *Raffaello architetto*; R.E. Lieberman, "The Architectural Background," in M. Hall, *Raphael's School of Athens* (Cambridge UK, 1997).

For urban projects: M. Tafuri, "'Roma instaurata.' Strategie urbane e politiche nella Roma del primo Cinquecento," in Frommel et al., *Raffaello architetto*; C.L. Frommel, "Papal Policy the Planning of Rome during the Renaissance," in T.K. Rabb and J. Brown, *Art and History. Images and their Meaning* (Cambridge UK, 1988).

For St. Peter's: C.L.Frommel, "San Pietro. Storia della sua construzione," in *Raffaello architetto*; C.L. Frommel, "The Endless Construction of St. Peter's" in *The Renaissance from Brunelleschi to Michelangelo: The Representation of Architecture*.

For the Villa Madama: C.L.Frommel, "Die architektonische Planung der Villa Madama," *Römisches Jahrbuch für Kunstgeschichte*, 15: 1975, 61–87; D. R. Coffin, *The Villa in the Life of Renaissance Rome*, (Princeton, 1979); J.Shearman, "A Functional Interpretation of the Villa Madama," *Römisches Jahrbuch für Kunstgeschichte*, 20: 1983, 313–327; C.L. Frommel,"Villa Madama," in *Raffaello architetto*; S. Eiche, "A New Look at Three Drawings for the Villa Madama and Related Images," *Mitteilungen des Kunsthistoriches Institutes in Florenz*, 36: 1992, 275–86; S.Eiche, "Villa Madama," in H.A. Millon and V.M. Lampugnani (eds.), *The Renaissance from Brunelleschi to Michelangelo: The Representation of Architecture*.

CHAPTER 4   For Giulio Romano in general: F. Hartt, *Giulio Romano*, 2 vols. (New Haven, 1958); *Giulio Romano* (Milan, 1989; English trans. of selections on architecture published as M.Tafuri, ed., *Giulio Romano* (Cambridge UK, 1998).

For Mantua: D. Chambers and J. Martineau, *Splendours of the Gonzaga* (London and Milan, 1982).

For the Palazzo del Te: K.W. Forster and R.J. Tuttle, "The Palazzo del Te," *Journal of the Society of Architectural Historians*, 30: 1971, 267–293; E. Verheyen, *The Palazzo del Te in Mantua: Images of Love and Politics* (Baltimore and London, 1977).

For the House of Giulio Romano: K.W. Forster and R.J. Tuttle, "The Casa Pippi: Giulio Romano's House in Mantua," *Architectura*, 1973, 104–30; B. Magnusson, "A Drawing for the Facade of Giulio Romano's House in Mantua," *Journal of the Society of Architectural Historians*, 47: 1988, 179–184.

CHAPTER 5   For Roman palaces in general: C.L.Frommel, *Der Römische Palastbau der Hochrenaissance*, 3 vols (Tübingen, 1973).

For the Palazzo Farnese: L. Salerno, "Palazzo Farnese," in L. Salerno (et al.), *Via Giulia. Una utopia urbanistica del '500* (Rome, 1973); A. Chastel (ed.), *Le Palais Farnèse*, 2 vols. (Rome, 1980–82), particularly the contributions of Lotz on the building history and Spezzaferro and Tuttle on urbanism; C.L. Frommel, "Antonio da Sangallo and the Practice of Architecture in the Renaissance," in Frommel and Adams, *The Architectural Drawings of Antonio da Sangallo the Younger and his Circle*, vol. 2 (New York and Cambridge MA, 2000).

For other palaces: Frommel, *Der Römische Palastbau*; Jones and Penny, ; Frommel et al., *Raffaello architetto*; H. Wurm, *Der Palazzo Massimo alle Colonne* (Berlin, 1965).

CHAPTER 6   For Architectural Practice: J.S. Ackerman, "Architectural Practice in the Italian Renaissance," *Journal of the Society of Architectural Historians*, 13: 1954, 3– 11; M.G. Lewine, "Roman Architectural Practice during Michelangelo's Maturity;" *Stil und Überlieferung in der Kunst des Abendlandes*, Acts of the 21st International Congress for Art History, Bonn, 1964 (Berlin, 1967), vol. 2, 20– ; C. Wilkinson, "The New Professionalism in the Renaissance," in S. Kostof (ed.), *The Architect: Chapters in the History of the Profession* (New York, 1977); A. Morrogh, *Disegni di architetti fiorentini 1540–1640* (Florence, 1985), for much new information on later Medicean projects; H. A. Millon, "Models in Renaissance Architecture," in H.A. Millon and V.M. Lampugnani (eds.), *The Renaissance from Brunelleschi to Michelangelo: The Representation of Architecture*, as well as the wealth of information on drawings contained in the catalog entries; C.L. Frommel, "Antonio da Sangallo and the Practice of Architecture in the Renaissance," in Frommel and Adams, *The Architectural Drawings of Antonio da Sangallo the Younger and his Circle*, vol. 2.

For Antonio da Sangallo the Younger: G. Giovannoni, *Antonio da Sangallo il Giovane*, 2 vols. (Rome, 1959), now largely superceded by Frommel and Adams, *The Architectural Drawings of Antonio da Sangallo the Younger and his Circle*, vols. 1 and 2 (New York and Cambridge MA, 1994–2000).

For Baldassare Peruzzi: C.L. Frommel, *Die Farnesina und Peruzzis architektonisches Frühwerk* (Berlin, 1961); H. Wurm, *Baldassare Peruzzi: Architekturzeichnungen* (Tübingen, 1984), illustrations only; S. Pepper and N. Adams, *Firearms and Fortifications: Military Architecture and Siege Warfare in Sixteenth-Century Siena* (Chicago, 1986), as well as numerous articles by Adams listed in the bibliography; M. Fagiolo and M.L. Madonna, *Baldassare Peruzzi: pittura, scena, e architettura nel Cinquecento* (Rome, 1987); H. Burns, "Baldassare Peruzzi and Sixteenth-Century Architectural Theory," in J. Guillaume (ed.), *Les traités d'architecture* (Paris, 1988); C. Tessari, *Baldassare Peruzzi: il progetto dell'antico* (Milan, 1995).

For the Treatises of Sebastiano Serlio: the fundamental study is still W.B. Dinsmoor, "The Literary Remains of Sebastiano Serlio," *Art Bulletin*, 24: 1942, 55–91 and 115–54. Of the numerous versions and modern reprints of Serlio's treatises, as well as the unpublished manuscripts, the most useful are Serlio, *Architettura e Prospettiva* (Ridgewood NJ, 1964) reprint of books 1–5 and 7, and the *Libro strordinario* as book 6; M. Rosci and A.M. Brizio, *Il trattato di architettura di Sebastiano Serlio*, 2 vols. (Milan, 1966) with vol. 2 as a facsimile of the Munich edition of the Sixth Book; M.N. Rosenfeld, *Sebastiano Serlio: On Domestic Architecture* (Cambridge MA and New York, 1978, reissued with a new introduction, Mineola, 1998), a facsimile of the Avery Library version of Sixth Book; Serlio (F.P. Fiore ed.), *Architettura civile* (Milan, 1994), facsimile manuscripts of books six to eight in Munich and Vienna; Serlio (trans. V. Hart and Peter Hicks), *Sebastiano Serlio On Architecture*, 2 vols. (London and New Haven, 1996–2001), critical introduction and translation of published and unpublished books.

For Sebastiano Serlio in general: M.N. Rosenfeld, "Sebastiano Serlio's Late Style in the Avery Library Version of the Sixth Book on Domestic Architecture, *Journal of the Society of Architectural Historians*, 28: 1969, 155–72; C. Thoenes (ed.), *Sebastiano Serlio* (Milan, 1989), especially Tuttle on Serlio's early career; S. Frommel, *Sebastiano Serlio architetto* (Milan, 1998), with emphasis on his career in France.

CHAPTER 7   For Venetian environment and its influence on the arts: S.J. Freedberg, *Painting in Italy 1500–1600* (Harmondsworth and Baltimore, 1971) especially 76–77; N. Huse and W. Wolters, *The Art of Renaissance Venice: Architecture, Sculpture, Painting 1460–1590* (Chicago and London, 1990); P. Humfrey, *Painting in Renaissance Venice* (New Haven and London, 1995); P. Fortini Brown, *Art and Life in Renaissance Venice* (New York, 1997); D. Howard, *Venice and the East* (New Haven and London, 2000).

For theatricality and Venice: E.J. Johnson, "Jacopo Sansovinio, Giacomo Torelli, and the Theatricality of the Piazzetta in Venice, *Journal of the Society of Architectural Historians*, 59: 2000, 436–53.

CHAPTER 8

For general studies of Venetian architecture: D. Howard, *The Architectural History of Venice* (London, 1980); R. Lieberman, *Renaissance Architecture in Venice 1450–1540* (New York, 1982); M. Tafuri, *Venice and the Renaissance* (Cambridge MA and London, 1995); R. Goy, *Venice: the City and its Architecture* (London, 1997); E. Concina, *A History of Venetian Architecture* (Cambridge UK, 1998).

For individual architects: M. Tafuri, *Jacopo Sansovino e l'architettura del '500 a Venezia* (Venice, 1969); L. Puppi, *Michele Sanmicheli, architetto di Verona* (Padua, 1971); D. Howard, *Jacopo Sansovino: Architecture and Patronage in Renaissance Venice* (New Haven and London, 1975); L. Puppi, *Michele Sanmicheli architetto: opera completa* (Rome, 1986); H. Burns et al., *Michele Sanmicheli: architettura, linguaggio, ed cultura artistica nel cinquecento* (Milan and Vicenza, 1995), especially essays by Frommel, Burns, and Davies; M. Morresi, *Jacopo Sansovino* (Milan, 2000).

For quotes by Carleton and della Cueva, see D. Chambers and B. Pullan (eds.), *Venice: a Documentary History, 1450–1630* (Oxford and Cambridge, MA, 1992), 26–35.

CHAPTER 9

For Vignola in general: J. Coolidge, "Vignola's Character and Achievement," *Journal of the Society of Architectural Historians*, 4: 1950, 10–14; M. Walcher Casottti, *Il Vignola*, 2 vols. (Trieste, 1960); R.J. Tuttle, entry in *Dictionary of Art*; C. Thoenes, "La Regola delli cinque ordini del Vignola," and "Architettura e società nell'opera del Vignola," in Thoenes, *Sostegno e adornamento*; R.J. Tuttle, "On Vignola's Rules of the Five Orders of Architecture," in V. Hart and P. Hicks (eds.), *Paper Palaces* (New Haven and London, 1998).

For specific projects: M. Lewine, "Vignola's Church of S. Anna dei Palafrenieri in Rome," *Art Bulletin*, 47: 1965, 199–229; T. Falk, "Studien zur Topographie und Geschichte der Villa Giulia in Rome," *Römisches Jahrbuch für Kunstgeschichte*, 13: 1971, 101–78; D. Coffin, *The Villa in the Life of Renaissance Rome* (for Villa Giulia); E. Kieven, "Eine Vignola-Zeichnung für S. Maria in Traspontina in Rome," *Römisches Jahrbuch für Kunstgeschichte*, 19: 1981, 245–47; P. Dreyer, "Vignolas Planungen für eine befestige Villa Cervini;" *Römisches Jahrbuch für Kunstgeschichte*, 21: 1984, 365–96; R.J. Tuttle, "Vignola's Facciata dei Banchi in Bologna, *Journal of the Society of Architectural Historians*, 52: 1993, 68–87.

For Pius IV and Ligorio: L. Pastor, *History of the Popes* (St. Louis, 1928), 16: 404–57; G. Smith, *The Casino of Pius IV* (Princeton, 1977); D.R. Coffin, *The Villa in the Life of Renaisance Rome* (Princeton, 1979), 267–79.

CHAPTER 10

For general studies of courts and courtly life: K.W. Forster, "Metaphors of Rule: Political Ideology and History in the Portraits of Cosimo I de'Medici," *Mitteilungen des Kunsthistoriches Institutes in Florenz*, 15: 1971, 65–104; M. Levey, *Painting at Court* (New York, 1971); G. Spini, *Architettura e politica da Cosimo I a Ferdinando I* (Florence, 1976); H. Trevor-Roper, *Princes and Artists: Patronage and Ideology at Four Hapsburg Courts, 1517–1633*, (London, 1976); N. Elias, *Power and Civility* (New York, 1982); C. Robertson, *'Il Gran Cardinale'. Alessandro Farnese: Patron of the Arts* (New Haven and

London, 1992); R. Starn and L. Partridge, *Arts of Power: Three Halls of State In Italy, 1300–1600* (Berkeley, 1992); M. Warnke, *The Court Artist: On the Ancestry of the Modern Artist* (Cambridge UK, 1993).

For individual architects and gardens: C. Lazzaro, *The Italian Renaissance Garden: From the Conventions of Planting Design, and Ornament to the Grand Gardens of Sixteenth-Century Italy* (New Haven and London, 1990); L. Satkowski, *Giorgio Vasari: Architect and Courtier* (Princeton, 1993); C. Conforti, *Giorgio Vasari architetto* (Milan, 1994); M. Kiene, *Bartolomeo Ammannati architetto* (Milan, 1995)

CHAPTER 11   For Ferrara: B. Zevi, *Biagio Rossetti architetto ferrarese* (Turin, 1960); C. Rosenberg, *The Este Monuments and Urban Development in Renaissance Ferrara* (Cambridge, 1997).

For Fortifications: J.R. Hale, "The Early Development of the Bastion: An Italian Chronology 1450–c.1534," in J.R. Hale, et al., *Europe in the Late Middle Ages* (London, 1965); H. De La Croix, *Military Considerations in City Planning: Fortifications* (New York, 1972); S. Pepper, "Planning vs. Fortification: Sangallo's Project for the Defense of Rome, *Architectural Review*, 159: 1976, 162–69; J.R. Hale, *Renaissance Fortification: Art of Engineering* (London, 1977); R.J. Tuttle, "Against Fortifications: The Defense of Renaissance Bologna," *Journal of the Society of Architectural Historians*, 41: 1982, 189–201; Pepper and Adams, *Firearms and Fortifications: Military Architecture and Siege Warfare in Sixteenth-Century Siena*.

For the Street: T. Magnuson, *Studies in Roman Quattrocento Architecture* (Stockholm, 1958); E. Poleggi, *Strada Nuova: una lottizazione del Cinquecento a Genova* (Genoa, 1968); L. Vagnetti, *Genoa, Strada Nuova* (Genoa, 1970); C.W. Westfall, *In This Most Perfect Paradise: Alberti, Nicholas V, and the Invention of Conscious Urban Planning In Rome, 1447–55* (University Park and London, 1974); S. Anderson (ed.), *On Streets* (Cambridge MA and London, 1978); A. Ceen, *The Quartiere dei Banchi: Urban Planning in Rome in the first half of the Cinquecento* (New York and London, 1986); C. Burroughs, *From Signs to Design: Environmental Process and Reform in Early Renaissance Rome* (Cambridge MA and London, 1990); C.L. Frommel, "Papal Policy in the Planning of Rome during the Renaissance," in Rabb and Brown, *Art and History: Images and their Meaning*; Z. Celik et al., *Streets: Critical Perspectives on Public Space* (Berkeley, 1994); G.L. Gorse, "A Classical Stage for the Old Nobility: The Strada Nuova and Sixteenth-Century Genoa," *Art Bulletin*, 79: 1997, 301–327.

For Piazza San Marco: W. Lotz, "Sixteenth-Century Italian Squares," in *Studies in Italian Renaissance Architecture*; N. Adams and L. Nussdorfer, "The Italian City, 1400–1600," in Millon and Lampugnani (eds.), *The Renaissance from Brunelleschi to Michelangelo: The Representation of Architecture*; M. Morresi, *Piazza San Marco: istituzioni, poteri e architettura a Venezia nel primo cinquecento* (Milan, 1999).

For Gonzaga towns: P. Carpeggiani, *Sabbioneta* (Mantua, 1972); K.W. Forster, "Stagecraft and Statecraft: the Architectural Integration of Public Life and Spectacle in Sabbioneta," *Oppositions*, 9: 1977, 63–89; H.W. Kruft, "Una nuova Roma-Sabbioneta," in *Le città utopiche* (Bari, 1990); M. Gallarati, *Architettura a scala urbana* (Florence, 1994), for centers other than Sabbioneta.

For Sixtus V: S. Giedion, *Space, Time, and Architecture* (Cambridge, MA, 1966, 5th ed.); T. Marder, "Sixtus V and the Quirinal," *Journal of the Society of Architectural Historians*, 37: 1978, 283–294, also for earlier bibliography; T. Magnuson, *Rome in the Age of Bernini*, vol. 1 (Stockholm, 1982), ch.1.

For the Ghetto: M. Luzzati, *Il ghetto ebraico* (Florence, n.d.); E. Concina et al., *La città degli ebrei. Il ghetto di Venezia: architettura e urbanistica* (Venice, 1991); C. Benocci and E. Guidoni, *Il Ghetto. Atlante storico della città italiane. Roma, 2* (Rome, 1993).

323

Nicholas Adams 165, 167.
Alinari-Art Resource, New York
2, 6, 21, 22, 32, 36, 45, 75, 84, 120, 148.
Art Resource, New York 14.
Artists Rights Society © 2002 Artists Rights Society
(ARS), New York/ADAGP, Paris/FLC 47.
Avery Architectural and Fine Arts Library,
Columbia University in the City of New York
89, 90.
Biblioteca Marucelliana, Florence 139.
Bibliotheca Hertziana, Rome
16, 28, 29, 33, 46, 48, 59, 126, 161, 163, 164, 182.
© Copyright The British Museum, London 9.
Reprinted with the permision of Cambridge
University Press 92, 93.
Deutsches Archäologisches Institut Rome 76.
Fine Arts Museums of San Francisco
(Gift of The de Young Museum Society, pur-
chased from funds donated by the Charles E.
Merrill Trust, 66.14) 154.
Fototeca Unione, American Academy in Rome 146.
Gabinetto Fotografico degli Uffizi, Florence
23, 24, 27, 34, 41, 60, 69, 70, 71, 77, 78, 172, 185.
Gemäldegalerie, Berlin 8.
George Gorse 174, 175.
Harvard University Press 181.
Istituto Centrale per il Catalogo e la Documentazione,
Rome
5, 11, 12, 30, 31, 35, 37, 38, 40, 42, 43, 66, 73, 79,
81, 82, 83, 103, 134.
Eugene J. Johnson 142.
Kunstbibliothek, Berlin 122, 144.
Ralph Lieberman
1, 18, 19, 20, 26, 44, 51, 53, 65, 94, 97, 101, 102,
104, 105, 107, 108, 109, 110, 124, 125, 132, 149,
151, 153, 156, 157, 158, 159, 160, 186.
Museum Kunst Palast, Dusseldorf.
Sammlung der Kunstakadamie (NRW), inv. KA
(FP) 109020-22, 49.
Museo Correr, Venice 106.
The Pierpont Morgan Library, New York. 1978.44 f.
71v-72. 39.
Oliver Radford 68, 130.
Réunion des Musées-Art Resource, New York 135.
Leon Satkowski
3, 4, 10, 13, 15, 17, 50, 52, 54, 55, 57, 58, 61, 62,
63, 64, 72, 74, 87, 88, 91, 95, 96, 100, 111, 112,
113, 114, 115, 117, 118, 119, 123, 129, 131, 133,
136, 138, 140, 143, 145, 150, 152, 155, 162, 168,
169, 176, 177, 179, 180, 183.
Statens Konstmuseer, Stockholm 56.
The Walters Art Museum, Baltimore 7.
Yale University Press 98, 99, 127, 137.